Praise for *Beyond Policing*

"A sweeping overview of the movement to create a police-free future and a vision of how to get there."
— Alex S. Vitale, author of *The End of Policing*

"*Beyond Policing* encourages us to think critically about the past and boldly about our futures. This work weaves together McHarris's personal story, rigorous research, and visionary thinking in a powerful way so that everyday people can connect and be agitated into meaningful collective action."
— Charlene A. Carruthers, author of *Unapologetic:
A Black, Queer, and Feminist Mandate for Radical Movements*

"In *Beyond Policing*, Philip V. McHarris traces the origins and history of policing from its early roots to the expansion of mass policing in the US in the mid-1900s. In doing so, he draws a direct line to the epidemic of police violence today. In this deftly researched yet accessible book, McHarris argues that popular reforms such as body cameras, de-escalation training, procedural justice, and diversity among police will never stop police violence. Instead, he proposes decriminalization, decarceration, and defunding punitive institutions that have created the current police and carceral systems all while calling us to courageously imagine a world beyond the police.

"*Beyond Policing* connects data and personal accounts, including incisive stories from the author's life, to bring context to the weight and toll of policing on communities—putting at the center the people the system insists it is designed to serve. With a rise of authoritarianism globally, it's incumbent on us all to imagine a world free from the systems of coercion and control that animate fascism and limit democracy and freedom. *Beyond Policing* is a bold step in that direction."
— Maurice Mitchell, national director of the Working Families Party

"In *Beyond Policing*, McHarris proves that police abolition has the power to unite us all around achieving true public safety without sacrificing anyone as collateral damage. McHarris opens with a history of policing in America, its exponential expansion, and the danger in recent reforms that depend on data and surveillance. Then, through vignettes and introductions to existing community-led solutions, we get glimpses into the world that would actually keep us safe: one full of relationships, prevention, and strategic interventions. [The] book tears down the myth of policing and prisons as necessary and replaces it with a vision of safety that leaves none of us behind. [This] book makes the best case for what abolition could look like in practice. If we dare to try."

—Brea Baker, author of *Rooted*

"At a time when so many feel rightfully disillusioned by the state of our nation's criminal justice system, *Beyond Policing* offers a rare beacon of hope. Philip V. McHarris shares accessible insights to help us both understand and reimagine a world focused on reducing harm and centering on community care. While the path forward will be a difficult one, McHarris's words will no doubt help us get there."

—Franchesca Ramsey, creator-host of *MTV Decoded* and author of *Well, That Escalated Quickly*

"This book is not only a primer for how we got here, detailing the birth and maturation of the carceral state, but also a visioning forward of what we could do to build and resource safe, healthy, and equitable communities. Let's make it so. It is a must read and a must share for all who wish to understand the world we have for the sake of building the world that should be."

—Ash-Lee Woodard Henderson, co–executive director of the Highlander Research and Education Center

"McHarris reminds us that abolition isn't the absence of safety; it is the presence of care. When we courageously move 'beyond policing,' we distance ourselves from the chaos and destruction it creates, moving towards the justice and freedom we deserve."

—Zellie Imani, cofounder of the Black Liberation Collective

WHAT BETTER WAY TO MAKE THE CASE FOR
A POLICE-FREE WORLD THAN TO SHOW
A WORLD WHERE IT'S POSSIBLE

BEYOND
POLICING

PHILIP V. MCHARRIS

LEGACY
LIT

NEW YORK BOSTON

To those who have borne, and bear, the weight

Legacy Lit
Hachette Book Group
1290 Avenue of the Americas
New York, NY 10104
LegacyLitBooks.com
Twitter.com/LegacyLitBooks
Instagram.com/LegacyLitBooks

First edition: July 2024

Legacy Lit is an imprint of Grand Central Publishing. The Legacy Lit name and logo are registered trademarks of Hachette Book Group, Inc.

The publisher is not responsible for websites (or their content) that are not owned by the publisher.

The Hachette Speakers Bureau provides a wide range of authors for speaking events. To find out more, go to hachettespeakersbureau.com or email HachetteSpeakers@hbgusa.com.

Legacy Lit books may be purchased in bulk for business, educational, or promotional use. For information, please contact your local bookseller or the Hachette Book Group Special Markets Department at special.markets@hbgusa.com.

Print book interior design by Bart Dawson

Library of Congress Cataloging-in-Publication Data

Names: McHarris, Philip V., 1992– author.
Title: Beyond policing / Philip V. McHarris.
Description: First edition. | New York, NY : Legacy Lit, [2024] | Includes bibliographical references.
Identifiers: LCCN 2023051831 | ISBN 9781538725665 (hardcover) | ISBN 9781538725689 (ebook)
Subjects: LCSH: Police—United States. | Police administration—United States—Finance. | Police-community relations—United States.
Classification: LCC HV8139 .M42 2024 | DDC 363.2/30973—dc23/eng/20240131
LC record available at https://lccn.loc.gov/2023051831

ISBNs: 9781538725665 (hardcover), 9781538725689 (ebook)

Printed in the United States of America

LSC-C

Printing 1, 2024

CONTENTS

There is nothing new under the sun, but there are new suns.

—Octavia Butler

INTRODUCTION

Now, what I have said about Harlem is true of Chicago, Detroit, Washington, Boston, Philadelphia, Los Angeles and San Francisco—is true of every Northern city with a large Negro population. And the police are simply the hired enemies of this population. They are present to keep the Negro in his place and to protect white business interests, and they have no other function. They are, moreover—even in a country which makes the very grave error of equating ignorance with simplicity—quite stunningly ignorant; and, since they know that they are hated, they are always afraid. One cannot possibly arrive at a more surefire formula for cruelty. . . .

I am writing a report, which is also a plea for the recognition of our common humanity. Without this recognition, our common humanity will be proved in unutterable ways. My report is also based on what I myself know, for I was born in Harlem and raised there. Neither I, nor my family, can be said ever really to have left; we are—*perhaps*—no longer as totally at the mercy of the cops and the landlords as once we were. In any case, our roots, our friends, our deepest associations are there, and "there" is only about fifteen blocks away.

—James Baldwin, "A Report from Occupied Territory"[1]

In 1966, James Baldwin published "A Report from Occupied Territory" in the *Nation* magazine. In the report, he described the realities of police violence within the context of poverty and systemic racism in Black communities. Importantly, Baldwin charged: "These things happen, in all our Harlems, every single day. If we ignore this fact, and our common responsibility to change this fact, we are sealing our doom."

These words have never rung more true. Decades later, we are still trapped in cycles of violence from the state and within communities. This book presents my notes from occupied territory, from a society that polices crisis to preserve power. I share these thoughts not only to describe the conditions of Black communities and beyond as they relate to police but to chart a way out, for us to dream about what could be in a fresh, new society.

My questions around policing stem from my own experiences and those of people I've been close to, since I was young. My first memory of the police is from outside my Bronx home. That day is still cloudy — but I must have been around five or six years old. The red-blue lights were flashing. They pierced right through the window and curtains. I remember my dad standing by the door, defensive of himself and us. He told them not to come in. There was yelling and shouting. Whatever was going on, I knew then that there was no reason for people who had the ability to take his life — and ours — to be that close to us. The feeling of those lights — and their power — cycles through my body till today. Looking back, I see that there could have been so many other responses. The day left a lasting, traumatic impression on me not because it was inevitable but because there were no other options available to manage concerns that the police couldn't address.

Throughout life, I've had to navigate conflict and violence. In those moments, I've never called the police. If I did call anyone, they were people I knew and trusted. I focused instead on building relationships with others and developing my own capacity to protect myself and people I cared for.

I've been trying to avoid the police for as long as I remember. As a kid, I knew they were trouble. I heard stories about the police being violent, saw them harass and arrest people, and saw how they enforced unjust laws. And at around thirteen, I started to experience it myself. It happened in a town in New Jersey, not far from where I lived. School had let out early that day, and my friends and I were just hanging out. It was a rare, carefree afternoon for us. No tests to take, no classes to attend, no gym to sweat in — just us laughing, talking about whatever young teenagers talk about — our latest crush, a teacher that frustrated us, a pair of sneakers we wanted, but couldn't quite afford.

But our sense of freedom quickly evaporated when the police showed up. They thought we were skipping school. We weren't skipping, just trying to have some fun and enjoy the day. But that didn't matter to them.

The officer zeroed in on me. I remember how he spoke to me. His tone and questions implying that I was doing something wrong as he searched for deference. Implying that I was some kind of danger to him, not seeing that I was a boy with his friends, draping his jacket over his body for warmth. There was no weapon, no threat—I was just a kid. But that wasn't enough for him.

Frustrated by how I was being treated, I wasn't deferential in my responses, because I knew I hadn't done anything wrong. Then, suddenly, he grabbed me. For a brief moment, I thought about resisting, about trying to stop him. But I realized quickly that any resistance on my part might escalate things and cost me my life.

In a single moment, memories of my father and that basement apartment, the flashing lights outside our window. The fear in his eyes and now the fear in my own. So I didn't resist. I let my body go limp as he violently threw me to the ground. He held me there for a while, then put me into the back of his police car. I sat in a daze, feeling powerless. He walked back and forth outside the car, threatening to send me to Jamesburg, a juvenile detention facility. I had no idea why. I was just sitting there, confused and afraid.

Eventually, he let me go. The incident wasn't just a personal trauma; it made concrete what I already felt: the police were there to harm, not protect me. To him, it was just another day of work. For me, it left a lasting scar. And it wouldn't be the last.

Whatever the police did, they weren't there to protect me. It felt like they were there to stop me, harass me, assault me, and maybe kill me. But definitely not to protect me or people who looked like me. So I tried to build a world where I would have to see, interact, and be around them as little as possible. I still do. Unfortunately, in a society that has one of the largest police forces in the world, that isn't easy.

––––––––––

Across the United States, police are everywhere. In a way, America has made it impossible to avoid policing. Police have flooded Black and marginalized communities. Police violence has continued to spark national outrage. And people throughout the world know about the violence of policing in the United States. While it can seem as if the injustice of policing is new, it is anything but. Policing was built on controlling race-class-oppressed communities. And while the specific functions and administration have changed vastly since early forms of policing sprang up in the New World in the early 1700s, policing has continued to control dispossessed communities and reinforce societal inequality.

I don't remember the first time I heard of police abolition, but I know I was drawn toward the concept from the start. The idea that society can exist with no police took me some time to wrap my head around. It required me to put myself into a world that doesn't exist yet; to imagine the different ways we would respond to crises and to harm and ultimately respond to the needs that people have. It was hard for me at times to think about all the terrible things people are capable of and ask myself: If there are no police but there's a shooting or home invasion or domestic violence, how do folks get help? What other resources are available for people to rely upon in dangerous situations? How can we prevent these moments from happening altogether? How do we create a fundamentally less violent society? As we explore these questions together, you will learn that I am certain that policing is not the answer to societal problems. In the first part of the book, I will address the reasons why. In the final chapters, I will share a vision of a world without police and take us on a journey where we will learn about how people around the world are helping prove that a world without policing is possible.

Throughout this book, I will also be exploring the theory and practice of abolition. Those who identify as police abolitionists want an end to policing, a world where policing does not exist. When people hear this, it often sparks questions and fear. If there are no police, then whom will we call when we're in danger? Who will stop people from hurting others? Won't society fall apart? The questions make sense. From a young age, we're told that police are here to keep us safe. We also live in a world that can be hurtful and violent. So without police, who will protect those in need of protection?

But the notion that police are here to protect and serve us is contradicted by the fact that countless numbers of people continue to experience violent and unjust interactions with police. These include the murders of Michael Brown, Breonna Taylor, Aiyana Stanley-Jones, George Floyd, and countless others. Even more, what we're told police do and what police actually do are two very different things, even outside of tragic cases of police violence. The truth is that police do very little to actually generate safety. And there's a reason why: policing was not created to cultivate safety for all. Rather, policing was created to control oppressed people and preserve power for those who have it while offering a semblance of protection to those deemed worthy of it. These functions often coincide, as those with power rely on police for protection from those considered dangerous, which is often shaped by race, class, and gender.

Police abolition is centered on creating societies that have safety and accountability without the coercive violence of policing. Many abolitionists have experienced harm themselves, which makes safety and accountability an utmost priority for them. It is the desire for safety that brought me to police abolition and continues to be the driving force behind my work.

Many people still believe that policing can be reformed into a system that will bring about safety for everyone and in which police violence isn't a recurring issue. And some, especially those who live in more financially well-off locations,[2] may feel that there aren't any pressing problems around policing that need to be addressed. But the recurring cycle of police violence, protest in response, and the promise and illusion of reform have us stuck in a pattern where we re-create history over and over again. And it will take radical change to end this cycle. It turns out that the same solution to ending police violence also will address the reason that many people do not feel safe every day, even as the United States maintains one of the largest police forces in the world.

This book answers questions about what we would do if there were no police. It may sound jarring, unrealistic, and impossible. It may bring up fears, experiences, and questions. But through taking this journey, I'm positive that you'll understand why a growing number of people see police abolition as a clear answer to a persistent problem. And for those who may already believe in the promises of abolition, *Beyond Policing* will offer visions and bridges forward.

Policing is centered on monitoring, surveillance, and control. Thus, policing can be—and is—carried out by a range of actors and entities, including social service agencies; vigilantes; corrections, parole, and probation officers; and the military. Police power in particular is drawn from the use or threat of violence to coerce and control. While I focus on police directly, I also discuss the broader ecosystem of policing that reaches beyond cops, particularly toward Black, Latinx, Indigenous, poor, and other oppressed communities.

My vision of a police-free world does not mean one in which there is an absence of safety and help. During my early years in the Bronx and Newark, New Jersey, I learned that the police did not address my concerns of safety; they added to them. The police were present when it felt unnecessary and nowhere when they seemed to be needed, and my communities needed interventions to feel safe. The fact that I experienced situations that felt hostile and unsafe growing up is a large reason why I became so deeply invested in police abolition. To this day, I exert much of my energy trying to manage concerns around safety for myself and others. And it's the search for safety entirely outside of (and from) policing that continues to animate my work.

In order to imagine worlds without police, we first have to address the reasons they exist. If people have their basic needs met and have the resources to thrive, the situations in which police seem to offer a semblance of a solution would be dramatically reduced. We've long known that poverty and precarity are among the largest predictors of actions that lead to conflict and harm. In addition, we must invest in community-based approaches to safety and accountability, approaches that address the underlying causes of harm, violence, and conflict.

We need to imagine a different kind of existence and different ways of relating to one another. Ones where we can eat and feed our families, where the work we do is meaningful and contributes to a more livable and sustainable world for everyone. Ones where we live in safe and accountable communities. Ones where, when something does happen, we have resources and people to call who can help without causing more harm. Ones where we can be in relation to one another in ways that affirm our humanity. Where we feel free.

We must have the courage to imagine new worlds and develop the power to create that which we imagine. Not because it is easy or guaranteed but simply because it is our only option. Ideas that may have seemed impossible at the outset have changed the world. There was a time when the abolition of slavery seemed impossible to many. So, too, did the advances made by decolonialization movements across the global South. Police abolition is no exception.

In *Beyond Policing*, I explore what it means to endure harm or the threat of it while remaining committed to advocating for abolition. My journey has been marked by encounters with violence and personal losses. Yet, in those challenging circumstances, I never turned to the police. My stance largely comes from being a part of a community that has been systematically targeted by various facets of policing.

This book confronts a harsh reality often faced by Black communities: our experiences as victims and survivors of violence are frequently overlooked, except when they serve to perpetuate damaging narratives such as the notion of "Black on Black crime." This dismissal by the broader society and the criminal-legal system[3] only reinforces the importance of understanding how we, as a community, navigate harm and violence. It emphasizes the need to find solutions outside of policing, solutions that don't rely on a system that was designed to harm, not protect us.

Beyond Policing is a deeply personal and scholarly journey, tracing my evolving understanding of policing and community safety. This exploration is rooted in my experiences growing up young and Black in the Bronx and later in New Jersey and being heavily skeptical of the police. That skepticism led me to a number of questions that I began to explore in my academic studies at Boston College as an undergraduate and Yale as a PhD student in sociology and African American studies. Those studies helped me understand the histories and contemporary realities of policing in the present moment.

My experience in activist spaces from 2014 onward, through organizations such as BYP100 and protests in Ferguson, Baltimore, New York City, and elsewhere during the height of unrest against police violence, provided more insight into police power, as well as the movement to build community safety. It was in those spaces that envisioned new futures that I learned of police abolition and became committed to the need to build community safety approaches.

Throughout *Beyond Policing*, my personal journey—from being young and Black in the Bronx to the academic halls of Yale, to the front lines of protests—serves as a continuous narrative thread. This journey is not just a critique of the present but an exploration and advocacy for a world where safety and justice are redefined and upheld by the community itself. From early understandings of police in my youth to a more nuanced political understanding over time, my journey into these issues began as skepticism and evolved into a commitment to abolition. As I explored the history of policing, engaged in activism, and saw the range of popular reforms in academic and political spaces, I became increasingly committed to the idea of abolition as the way forward.

The book unfolds across three interconnected parts offering unique perspectives on the evolution, impact, and transformation of policing. In the first part, "Histories," I delve into the first chapter, "The Origins of Policing," exploring how policing systems were initially formed not to keep everyone safe but as a mechanism of social control. This foundational understanding of how policing evolved into its current form is crucial for grasping contemporary realities and potential futures. The subsequent chapter, "The Police Boom," builds on this foundation, examining the significant growth of policing in America during the twentieth century and its profound impact on Black, Indigenous, Latinx, and other marginalized communities. It was a time when politicians on all sides became invested in expanding police capacity and involvement in all aspects of social life, most notably during the 1960s amid nationwide protests and rebellions.

In "Currents," the second part of the book, I shift to examining contemporary policing. My initial understanding of police power came from several sources: direct personal experiences with policing over time, my activism against police violence starting in 2014, and extensive study into the history of policing to comprehend its evolution to the present day. In the chapter "The Tide," I present a critical examination of contemporary policing, the recurring patterns of police reform, and the resistance movements against police violence. This is followed by a chapter titled "Solutions for a New World." In this chapter, I explore various community-led safety initiatives. These initiatives are presented as models that can guide us toward a new paradigm in which police no longer monopolize our approach to ensuring safety.

The final part, "Futures," culminates with my vision of a transformative future. "The Transformation of Justice" explores viable approaches to accountability and justice, such as restorative and transformative justice models. In "An Abolitionist Future," I present an imaginative and hopeful perspective on a society free from policing, emphasizing community care and mutual support.

In the interludes of the book, I share personal accounts. From facing threats of gun violence in my community to encountering police abuse and violence, these experiences have been pivotal in shaping my perspective. These stories, integral to the narrative, illustrate the stark realities that led me to question the existing structures of policing and justice.

Through this journey, I've realized the need for a cultural change to truly move beyond policing and toward meaningful safety—a change from a culture of punishment shaped by greed, profiteering, and capitalism. The transformation of justice, as I've learned, means changing how we understand it and how we relate to one another altogether. Imagination is critical to abolition, and in *Beyond Policing*, I share what I dream of when I think of a new world shaped by commitments to community safety and accountability. This book is an invitation to imagine and create together a world beyond policing.

PART I

HISTORIES

CHAPTER 1

THE ORIGINS OF POLICING

Police violence is a part of the DNA of the United States....
There has been no golden age of policing in which violence and
racism were not central to the job.

— Keeanga-Yamahtta Taylor,
From #BlackLivesMatter to Black Liberation[1]

At every gate through which we were to pass, we saw a
watchman—at every ferry a guard—on every bridge a
sentinel—and in every wood a patrol. We were hemmed in
upon every side. Here were the difficulties, real or imagined—
the good to be sought, and the evil to be shunned.

— Frederick Douglass, *Narrative of the Life of
Frederick Douglass, an American Slave*[2]

ONCE I BEGAN LEARNING MORE ABOUT POLICING IN COLLEGE, SO MANY
questions began to trouble me: Why do the police exist? Where did they
come from? What does actual public safety[3] look like? If so many people
believe that police don't keep them safe, why do we still advocate for them?
What would it take to stop police violence and put an end to policing altogether? How do we create safe, accountable communities?

In graduate school, I wanted to learn more about the history of policing.
But in 2014, when I started my PhD in sociology and African American

studies at Yale, this proved to be a challenge. The historical accounts that I found often gave simplified overviews of the police that largely focused on their professionalization over time. I found more histories of prisons and prison abolition, such as *The New Jim Crow: Mass Incarceration in the Age of Colorblindness* by Michelle Alexander, *Golden Gulag: Prisons, Surplus, Crisis, and Opposition in Globalizing California* by Ruth Wilson Gilmore, and *Are Prisons Obsolete?* by Angela Y. Davis. These accounts revealed how race, class, and gender produced the prison-industrial complex, the web of interrelated systems that make up mass imprisonment.

But it was more difficult to find overviews and examinations of policing. Beyond that, much of the mainstream dialogue at the time centered on training, data, restrictive policies, diversity, and an emphasis on the "community" as solutions to police violence. I sought out books and articles that provided a more critical history. As I stitched together different histories and studies of policing, it became apparent to me that policing hadn't been designed for public safety.

The history of policing is long and storied. In reality, there's no one linear tale of policing in the United States. Rather, the history is fragmented and developed differently in different areas. But what became especially apparent to me was that the history of US policing is international in scope. It involves the inflow and outflow of information and strategies related to managing and maintaining colonization. Policing wasn't constructed out of a desire for public safety but out of a desire to preserve power and the status quo.[4] Policing has existed since colonialism and slavery appeared in the United States and began as a colonial project. Previously, Indigenous populations had navigated concerns in ways that were autonomous, context specific, and aligned with Indigenous customs and values.[5] Early colonial formations of policing in the United States included slave patrols in the South and watchmen policing groups in the North. Specific features of policing have changed over time, but it has remained a key force in managing inequality and preserving power.

Police entities over time have varied widely from the models we see today. Their size, scope, and functions have changed as history has developed. These shifts and changes have created different forms of police from the slave patrols and strikebreakers that were common in the past. But an understanding of history reveals that despite these differences in policing, what has remained constant is the use of policing to control and punish Black, Indigenous, Latinx, immigrant, poor, and other dispossessed communities. The rampant racial disparities in the policing of race-class-subjugated communities[6]—a term developed by Joe Soss and Vesla Weaver to describe the interconnectedness between race and class, especially as it relates to governing institutions and policing—that we see today are part and parcel of a long legacy of policing colonized and oppressed people throughout the world.

Resistance to police violence and crises over the legitimacy of policing within society have played important roles in shaping the history of policing. Major transformations related to policing have often been propelled by communities resisting the power and authority of policing in society. Historically, the response to dissent against policing has been to make policing stronger and more deeply tied into the social fabric of everyday life. In order to understand the fragmented histories of policing in the United States, we have to examine its international roots and its focus on race-class control.

The government, media, and mainstream social institutions have socialized us to believe that police are the only organizations that can effectively provide public safety—which justifies the idea that police need to maintain a monopoly on the legitimate use of violence. For most of modern history, though, police weren't seen this way. Rather, they were seen as a violent occupying force that largely served the interests of those in power. For communities targeted by police violence, the idea that police weren't created in the interest of safety isn't a surprise. Police are said to be the stewards of public safety, but up and down the country, policing emerged in the seventeenth century as a tool of racial and class domination and control. Policing is centered on maintaining the status quo, which has been shaped by white supremacy, patriarchy, and capitalism—systems that create unjust conditions for those oppressed by them. The status quo is reliant on the subjugation of Black people and marginalized communities because freedom, justice, and liberation for these communities would require the transformation of society as we know it. The police violence we see today is not a fluke or aberration. The criminal-legal system today is not broken; it is operating exactly as it was designed to: as a violent tool of race and class control that protects very few.

THE FOUNDATIONS OF POLICING, 1630–1800

Where does policing in the United States stem from? The earliest policing models in the United States included watchmen and constable systems in the North and slave patrols in the South. Those early forms of policing and surveillance relied largely on volunteers, were loosely organized, and were hyperlocal. They focused on maintaining the moral codes, social order, and criminal law structured by those with power. Watchmen were widespread in cities and early on were largely focused on enforcing vice codes and labor control, while patrols were principally responsible for preserving slavery.[7]

The first night watch in Boston was organized in 1631 and was a precursor to later, more formal policing. Another early night watch system included the "rattlewatch" formed in 1651 to discourage crime and disorder in the Dutch colony of New Amsterdam and investigate those suspected of causing them.[8] In the latter part of 1658, its funding expanded as the eight-man rattlewatch group began "drawing pay, making them the first municipally funded police organization."[9] They would also use wooden rattles to alert nearby people of smoke or fires.

The first known constable in the United States was Joshua Pratt in 1634, responsible for Plymouth Colony. At the time, nonuniformed constables came into their positions through appointment or were elected for a specific duration and weren't compensated with a traditional salary, receiving pay from serving writs and executing warrants. The positions were developed in early colonial America and based on the parish constable system in the United Kingdom. Constables were responsible for doling out punishments, making arrests, and handling land surveys. Soon after the takeover of New Amsterdam by the British in 1664, the area would become New York City. The English installed a constable (whose name has not been well documented) whose "job was to keep the peace, suppress excessive drinking, gambling, prostitution, and prevent disturbances when church services were in progress."[10]

Night watches, such as those formed in Boston, New York City, and Philadelphia (in 1700), were commonplace during this period and were precursors of later policing forces.[11] Those largely decentralized entities were not particularly well organized or connected to other law enforcement formations in different regions. They were also highly context specific and formed with the purpose of addressing a region's particular concerns, largely driven by the desires of those in power, which involved controlling workers, preventing rebellion, and expanding the US empire. Private citizens were also able to enforce laws and arrest people who allegedly engaged in crime or committed offenses. Those early, decentralized models emerged from European models of watch groups that had existed for many centuries prior, including in the Roman Empire as Vigiles[12] and the Praetorian Guard.[13]

Watch groups such as those formed the early embers of what would become the policing we now see today. Policing in those early watch groups, as well as in more modern policing agencies, was modeled after systems in Europe and England, which were made up primarily of volunteers, including civilians, watch groups, sheriffs, constables, and patrols. Additionally, they employed a compulsory system called *posse comitatus*, which allowed sheriffs or other law enforcement officers to conscript people for law enforcement assistance. Empires and nation-states have long relied on policing and military use, or violence work, as Micol Seigel has poignantly put it in *Violence Work: State Power and the Limits of Police*, to expand power and manage inequality. As Seigel wrote:

> That is the distinction between work that must be done by police and work that police could pass on to others: work that relies upon violence or the threat thereof. Violence work....
>
> Police realize—they *make real*—the core of the power of the state. That is what I mean to convey by calling police "violence workers."...
>
> "Violence workers" is a more disturbing term than euphemisms such as "law enforcement" or "security workers," and we should be disturbed. It is more accurately broad than the misleadingly governmental "police." It effectively conveys the full panoply of people whose work rests on a promise of violence, thereby displacing some of the weight of the assumption that policing is only or even primarily a state project or that the state is a watertight container or boundary for "the police," or even that police in the United States operate solely in US territory.[14]

SLAVE PATROLS

In the South, the first organized policing entities began as slave patrols.[15] Slave owners and local civilian officials paid patrollers to prevent slave revolts and preserve the institution of slavery.[16] Slave patrollers would patrol private property and public spaces to ensure that enslaved people weren't carrying any weapons or concealing fugitives, conducting any meetings, or gaining literacy. Members of slave patrols also patrolled the roads to catch any enslaved people who attempted to escape to the North. A majority of the slave patrols dominated rural areas and were loosely organized. With the rise of industrialization, enslaved African Americans sometimes had to work far from their owners' property, so there were large numbers of unaccompanied enslaved people within cities. Officers were thus viewed as even more necessary for supervising, monitoring, and inspecting enslaved people who worked in urban areas.[17] Slave patrols emerged during the transatlantic slave trade across the Americas, including the United States, the Caribbean, and Latin America, with strategies and tactics being transported across colonial contexts.[18]

In the United States, slave patrols originated in the Carolinas as early as 1704 and were organized to deter rebellion and prevent enslaved people from freeing themselves. The Charleston Guard and Watch emerged out of the patrols in 1785 and was one of the first modern policing entities in the United States. As the theological scholar Andy Alexis-Baker wrote:

> In 1785 the first modern police force arose out of slave patrols in Charleston, South Carolina called the Charleston Guard and Watch. This department had a distinct chain of command, uniforms, sole responsibility for policing, salary, authorized use of force, and a focus on preventing "crime." According to one member, the unit's main responsibility was "keeping down the niggers," which it did with terrifying precision; "crime" and "black" were synonymous. Over time, similar departments emerged in other cities.[19]

In 1793, Congress enacted the Fugitive Slave Act, which outlined laws regarding the detention and return of enslaved people, further solidifying the power and centrality of oppressive entities such as slave patrols in American society.[20] In places such as Virginia and South Carolina, slave patrols were organized from members of state militias. As a result of fears of revolt following events such as the planned rebellion led by Denmark Vesey, a community leader and formerly enslaved man who orchestrated one of the most well-known planned slave uprisings in the United States, white enslavers built arsenals and further developed their slave patrols. The Citadel and the Virginia Military Institute were created to help oversee the arsenals built to stamp out revolts of enslaved people and serve as recruiting sites for state militias to form slave patrols.[21] These colleges were also created to provide structure and efficiency for slave patrols in stamping out slave rebellion and revolt. These links point to policing and military formation as two sides of the same coin: violence in service of preserving and expanding the power of those who have it.

Patrollers weren't the only ones engaged in the policing of Black people during periods of legal enslavement. After the Fugitive Slave Act of 1850, private citizens were enlisted in returning enslaved people suspected of running away to their plantations.[22] There were penalties for refusing to return enslaved people who liberated themselves, and the act required the compliance of private citizens even in states that had abolished slavery. The enlisting of white citizens in the policing of enslaved people shows that organized law enforcement isn't the only purveyor of policing. While formal organizations handle the main policing duties for the state, a wider range of individuals and groups have played, and can play, key roles in policing and punishment.

W. E. B. Du Bois, in *The Souls of Black Folk*, incisively commented on policing and the court system in the South during and after formal emancipation:

> Its police system was arranged to deal with blacks alone, and tacitly assumed that every white man was *ipso facto* a member of that police. Thus grew up a double system of justice, which erred on the white side by undue leniency and the practical immunity of red-handed criminals, and erred on the black side by undue severity, injustice, and lack of discrimination. For, as I have said, the police system of the South was originally designed to keep track of all Negroes, not simply of criminals; and when the Negroes were freed and the whole South was convinced of the impossibility of free Negro labor, the first and almost universal device was to use the courts as a means of reënslaving the blacks. It was not then a question of crime,

but rather one of color, that settled a man's conviction on almost any charge. Thus Negroes came to look upon courts as instruments of injustice and oppression, and upon those convicted in them as martyrs and victims.[23]

Du Bois pointed to important truths: that policing was not designed for safety and that reality was evident in how police and the court system engaged with white and Black populations. Importantly, policing of Black people as a form of racial control did not end after the fall of slavery; it transformed. Police and the court system became the main tools of the convict leasing system, where prisons leased incarcerated people out to private businesses and individuals. After the abolition of slavery, convict leasing became a tool to coerce Black people back into forced labor. Policing was also used as a tool to keep track of and control Black communities. Coercive patterns of policing centered in securing the interests of property owners and business elites structured much of the history of policing in the South from slavery onward.

In Celeste Winston's insightful work, *How to Lose the Hounds: Maroon Geographies and a World beyond Policing*,[24] she reimagined the concept of marronage as a pivotal framework for understanding and advancing the movement for police abolition. She drew from the history of Maroon communities, where enslaved Black individuals claimed their freedom by escaping slave patrols and those seeking to reenslave them. Those communities were largely established outside the predatory confines of plantation systems and colonial governments.[25]

Winston's examination focused on the history of Black Maroon communities in the Maryland suburbs. She highlighted how these spaces, formed in resistance to the oppressive forces of slavery, have continually faced the onslaught of anti-Black police violence. Her exploration of these "maroon geographies" within the discipline of Black Geographies[26] uncovered not only a lineage of Black resistance and placemaking but also presented a transformative vision of public safety and community well-being. This vision is rooted in life-affirming traditions of Black autonomy and resilience. As she noted, Black communities developed their systems of justice and lived their daily lives outside the realms of policing, plantation control, empires, and nation-states in those Maroon communities.

Winston's book is a crucial contribution, contextualizing historical practices of resisting oppressive conditions and police power among Black communities.

POLICING THE NEW WORLD

American colonies date back to the early seventeenth century. European empires, particularly England, Spain, the Netherlands, and France, developed colonies in what is now known as North America. Those various colonies contributed directly and indirectly to the development of the United States of America. The first successful English colony was Jamestown, established in 1607 in what is now Virginia. It was followed by the founding of Plymouth in 1620 in present-day Massachusetts and then the Massachusetts Bay Colony in 1630. The settlements were founded by Europeans who were seeking economic opportunities and religious freedom and forming new societies—and who were willing to do so through violent means. Throughout the 1600s and 1700s, English colonies continued to emerge along the Eastern Seaboard. That colonial expansion was founded through violence, dispossession, and the decimation of Indigenous populations who'd long stewarded the land.[27]

The settler colonies were governed by charters, grants, and proprietary arrangements, but the British Crown continued to maintain overarching control over colonial life and affairs. As a result of rising tensions between the American colonies and the British government due to taxation, representation, and a range of other issues, the American Revolutionary War began in 1775. In 1776, the thirteen colonies declared independence, and the war ended in 1783 with the Treaty of Paris and recognition of the United States as an independent nation. The Constitution was written in 1787, followed by the acquisition of more territories through the Louisiana Purchase of 1803, the Oregon Treaty of 1846, and the Mexican Cession of 1848. The United States grew due to the acquisition of those territories and continued its westward colonization.[28]

Policing in the United States unfolded as an overlapping and interlocking story that develops differently across geographies. Despite regional differences, policing in the United States maintained central features: it was developed as a tool for social control, specifically of racial- ethnic- and class-oppressed populations; it shape-shifts as communities and reformers point out the violence and injustice of the institution; crime is framed as a justification for the necessity of police; and police leaders rely on strategies and tactics that were developed through imperialism and colonialism.

The United States also employed colonial policing through the Texas Rangers.[29] In 1823, during the initial stages of the Anglo-American colonization of Texas, then under Mexican control, Stephen F. Austin established the Texas Rangers, originally known by names that included "ranging companies, mounted gunmen, mounted volunteers, minutemen, spies, scouts and mounted rifle companies."[30] Their main role was to manage any concerns or resistance while colonizers encroached on Native American tribal land. During the Texas Revolution from 1835 to 1836, the Rangers aided in battles against Mexican forces to serve Texas's desire to seize the land and become an independent nation, which occurred in 1836. As Texas claimed statehood and began expanding westward, the role of the Rangers became more intertwined with the state's colonization endeavors. They served as the primary law enforcement forces in emerging communities and repressed conflict and dissent by Native tribes, as well as cattle theft and whatever else was seen as lawlessness.

One of the most significant impacts of the Rangers was on Native American tribes, which resisted the encroachment onto their lands. The Rangers played a central role in providing defenses against Native American tribes and promoting further colonization while protecting colonizing populations—those who were deemed worthy in the context—from Native American resistance. The Texas Rangers tracked down and violently suppressed Native American resistance, helping to establish a sense of security among colonizers that would encourage more colonization. The Texas Rangers were employed to protect the interests of newly arriving white colonists under the Mexican government and later under the independent Republic of Texas.[31] The Texas Rangers hunted down Native populations that were accused of attacking white settlers. Rangers also facilitated white colonial expansion by pushing out Indigenous Mexicans through violence, intimidation, and political interference. Mexicans and Native Americans who resisted were subjected to beatings, killings, intimidation, and arrests.[32]

Over time, the Texas Rangers transformed into a contemporary law enforcement body. At present, the Texas Rangers investigate major criminalized activity, public corruption, cold cases and officer-involved shootings and oversee the Texas Department of Public Safety's border security and tactical and crisis negotiation programs. Their historical role in facilitating westward colonial expansion while displacing and facilitating the decimation of Indigenous populations remains a critical aspect of their legacy. Here we see that when they originated, the police served two functions: to protect those deemed worthy and to engage in race-class control to the benefit of those with privilege and power.

ANTI-ASIAN POLICING

In the late nineteenth century, Chinese immigrants living on the West Coast of the United States faced an escalating wave of racial discrimination and violence.[33] Editorials with anti-Asian animus were published, alleging that Chinese people were, for example, "barbarians taking jobs away from whites."[34] A particularly tragic episode occurred in 1871 in Los Angeles, known as the Chinese Massacre. Amid a conflict over an arranged marriage that escalated into a shooting between two Chinese factions, police and a local resident arrived, firing at the people involved. They fired back, and the local resident, Robert Thompson, was killed. The cop, Jesus Bilderrain, was injured. News spread, and a mob of around five hundred white and Latino residents stormed Chinatown, attacking, robbing, and murdering its Chinese residents largely on Calle de los Negros, also known as "Negro Alley." Nineteen Chinese immigrants were brutally killed. Despite the chaos, the Los Angeles police and other local authorities largely refrained from intervening. This points to the nature of police forces: they are structured to protect those deemed worthy of protection and to practice race-class control.

Racial animus in that period paved the way for the Chinese Exclusion Act of 1882.[35] The legislation suspended Chinese immigration and remained in effect until 1943. Local police departments, particularly in areas with significant Chinese populations, such as San Francisco's Chinatown, were foundational in the enforcement of the act. Chinese residents routinely experienced racial profiling and harassment, with law enforcement officers often demanding immediate proof of legal residency. It became commonplace for Chinese people to be arrested based solely on mere suspicion of illegal residency or to experience police raids of their homes or businesses. That resulted in many Chinese people constantly carrying their certificates of residence. After the 1906 San Francisco earthquake destroyed many public records, some Chinese residents claimed US citizenship, alleging they had been born in the United States and at times sponsoring others immigrating from China as their children. Those "paper sons" and "paper daughters" often found themselves being harassed, detained, and subjected to intense interrogations at sites such as the Angel Island Immigration Station.[36]

The anti-Chinese fervor eventually led to discrimination against other Asian communities. By the turn of the twentieth century, as the enforcement of the Chinese Exclusion Act intensified, the United States began to see a rise in Japanese immigrants, especially in California. Like the Chinese residents who had arrived before, they encountered prejudice.[37] The California Alien Land Law of 1913 specifically targeted them, prohibiting "aliens ineligible for citizenship" from owning agricultural land or acquiring long-term leases.[38] The racist laws were enforced largely by police.

In the early twentieth century, Filipino immigrants also started arriving in significant numbers, primarily to work on farms in California. They were also met with hostility and discrimination. In 1930, the tension led to the Watsonville riots, in which Filipino agricultural workers were the targets of white mob violence.[39] Police largely allowed the violence to occur and at times participated in it.

The anti-Asian animus worsened for Japanese Americans during World War II. Following the attack on Pearl Harbor and Executive Order 9066, signed by President Franklin D. Roosevelt on February 19, 1942, the US government ordered the forcible relocation and internment of approximately 120,000 Japanese Americans—two-thirds of whom were US citizens.[40] California was home to the nation's largest Japanese American population at the time. Local police and military officials actively conducted the forced relocations, reinforcing the gratuitous discrimination Asian communities had endured during the nineteenth and twentieth centuries. This legacy has not ended. Though police violence against Asian communities does not receive widespread attention, patterns of police abuse have continued for various Asian American and Pacific Islander (AAPI) communities, with rates higher for some communities than previous data had led some to believe.[41]

THE EMERGENCE OF MODERN POLICING, 1800–1900

The origin of modern policing in the United States is closely tied to British colonial oppression and police development. Prior to the nineteenth century,

British colonists used brute force in the form of military occupation and watch groups to preserve oppressive agricultural regimes. Irish workers and farmers resisted those deplorable conditions, and oppressive regimes and the British government tried various approaches to control and quell the resistance. Many of the colonial strategies and tactics the British brought to the New World were first developed in Ireland to control Irish populations, including various strategies of policing and colonial occupation. The London Metropolitan Police, a broader and more professionalized force than traditional colonial policing formations, is often considered the foundation of modern city policing. A significant focus of its policing was Irish populations. The policing of Irish populations was often done through wanton violence, intense surveillance, and a focus on their being the *other*. Inevitably, the development of policing in London largely shaped the development and structure of early policing models throughout Europe as well as cities in the United States, such as Boston.[42]

The London Metropolitan Police emerged in the early, pre-Victorian 1800s, due largely to a politician who would eventually become prime minister, Sir Robert Peel.[43] Peel served as home secretary first from 1822 to 1827 and then from 1828 to 1830. During that time and throughout his extended political career—he later served as prime minister and a member of the House of Commons—he introduced a number of laws and policies that would change policing. Prior to 1829, a constellation of night watchmen, soldiers who wore red coats, peacekeepers, and constables were responsible for dealing with perceived conflict and disorder. Peel, the namesake and founder of the "bobbies" or "peelers," sought to create a more professionalized and consistent force that was expansive in size and scope. Bobbies carried short clubs as well as whistles while walking their beats and called for backup with their whistles when they saw fit.

Peel successfully argued for the state to create a police force by zeroing in on what he saw as inefficiencies in the system of the time, despite pushback and fears that police would be an abusive entity. Peel's Metropolitan Police Act 1829, passed during Arthur Wellesley's, the first Duke of Wellington's, government, launched the expansion of policing in various metropolitan areas of London.[44] Police were charged with preventing crime, quelling disorder, and establishing social control in authorized regions. Police initially took on other roles, such as lighting lamps, keeping watch for fires, and announcing the time. But the police were not widely accepted and were seen as obstructive to everyday life and unfair to the poor. As a result, policing expanded only slowly to other towns, boroughs, and rural areas. All police were under the authority of the home secretary and headquartered at Scotland Yard. After the passage of the Metropolitan Police Act 1829, a thousand additional men were recruited to join the four hundred police officers who had first been recruited.[45] Training was carried out by the commissioners who led police forces, and the funds for salaries and policing expenses came from a special parish rate—or local tax—sourced by the "overseers of the poor." Police were to focus on detecting and preventing crime, and what was considered crime was also determined by the state.

The Metropolitan Police Act 1829, which modernized policing in England, laid the foundation of urban policing, including in the United States. It was established that uniformed police officers would use paramilitary structures to coerce control. The first police commissioners were Lieutenant Colonel Charles Rowan and Sir Richard Mayne, a barrister. Along with Peel, early police leaders sought to establish a seemingly professional police force that would use quasi-military structures to prevent crime.[46] Under the Municipal Corporations Act 1835, all boroughs were ordered to set up a police force controlled by a watch committee. In 1839, the Rural Constabularies Act was passed, providing further pressure for police forces to be established in areas that were still slow to create them and setting guidelines for their organization.[47] The central features of the London model were uniforms, expanded presence, and emboldened state powers and protection.

The Metropolitan Police of London received a detective department in 1842; by the mid-1850s there were approximately twelve thousand police throughout England and Wales.[48] In 1856, Parliament established that provinces needed to maintain their own police forces, and the Police Act 1856 mandated policing across territories. That was when policing began to expand into areas that were hesitant to rely upon police forces.[49] After 1880, the detective division was also expanded to address fears of attacks from Irish colonial dissidents, which was deemed terrorism.[50]

Commonly attributed to Peel, the following nine principles were outlined for policing in this early period:

PRINCIPLE 1 "The basic mission for which the police exist is to prevent crime and disorder."

PRINCIPLE 2 "The ability of the police to perform their duties is dependent upon public approval of police actions."

PRINCIPLE 3 "Police must secure the willing cooperation of the public in voluntary observance of the law to be able to secure and maintain the respect of the public."

PRINCIPLE 4 "The degree of cooperation of the public that can be secured diminishes proportionately to the necessity of the use of physical force."

PRINCIPLE 5 "Police seek and preserve public favor not by catering to the public opinion but by constantly demonstrating absolute impartial service to the law."

PRINCIPLE 6 "Police use physical force to the extent necessary to secure observance of the law or to restore order only when the exercise of persuasion, advice and warning is found to be insufficient."

PRINCIPLE 7 "Police, at all times, should maintain a relationship with the public that gives reality to the historic tradition that the police are the public and the public are the police; the police being only members of the public who are paid to give full-time attention to duties which are incumbent on every citizen in the interests of community welfare and existence."

PRINCIPLE 8 "Police should always direct their action strictly towards their functions and never appear to usurp the powers of the judiciary."

PRINCIPLE 9 "The test of police efficiency is the absence of crime and disorder, not the visible evidence of police action in dealing with it."[51]

Peel laid a foundation for developing police forces that, on its face, seems legitimate. In his marketing and lobbying for the formation of police entities, he focused on public appeals to sway the public to being open to police development and expansion. The history of police origination in London reveals that modern policing was constructed less than three hundred years ago. It took a number of efforts and strategies for modern policing to expand, as many people were skeptical of it. A primary function of those police forces was to control colonial Irish populations and enforce moral codes that discriminated against poor and working-class communities.[52] But Peel also made sure to appeal to people's concerns about safety. Here we see that while police emerged as a tool of race-class control, they were also framed by politicians such as Peel as those who would keep those deemed worthy of protection safe. A number of punitive and mandatory strategies from the state required boroughs and towns to establish police forces. The history of policing in London also reveals how militarism in structure and leadership, as well as strategies from colonial occupation, have been central to the development of policing. Finally, the legitimacy of policing was never taken for granted but was always in question, and police leaders such as Peel, Rowan, and Mayne had to craft strategies to convince the public that the police were legitimate and capable of being professional.[53] Importantly, those leaders used the fear of crime as a central strategy to justify the expansion of policing, rather than other solutions that addressed structural inequality and injustice. Four months after the act passed, the Duke of Wellington wrote to Peele, congratulating him, to which Peel replied:

> I am very glad indeed to hear that you think well of the Police. It has given me from first to last more trouble than anything I ever undertook. But the men are gaining a knowledge of their duties so rapidly that I am very sanguine of the ultimate result.
>
> I want to teach people that liberty does not consist in having your house robbed by organised gangs of thieves, and in leaving the principal streets of London in the nightly possession of drunken women and vagabonds.
>
> The chief danger of the failure of the new system will be, if it is made a job, if gentlemen's servants and so forth are placed in the higher offices. I must frame regulations to guard against this as effectually as I can.[54]

FROM LONDON TO THE UNITED STATES

The London model largely shaped models of urban policing in the United States, which had previously taken the forms of night watches and day police.[55] The first modern urban policing entity was in Boston, where city leaders began to appoint police officers starting in 1838 and a formal police department was created in 1854. In Boston, there were sustained efforts by workers and unions, who struck and rioted in response to unjust labor conditions. To control those populations, in a shift from the private police forces employed by the political-economic elite, the city established a public police force to repress and surveil unions as well as immigrant populations perceived as disorderly. Police were also responsible for enforcing laws related to social disorder and emerging criminal codes. Importantly, throughout industrialization in the 1800s, modernized policing emerged as a way to control the interests of capitalists looking to secure their financial interests through repressing labor organizing, preventing theft, and disrupting any activities or forms of resistance that would result in a loss of profits.

Boston created one of the first publicly funded city police entities, but on May 7, 1844, New York State passed the Municipal Police Act, which authorized the formation of a police force and led to the abolition of the night watch system.[56] In 1845 in New York City, the Municipal Police replaced the night watches formed by groups of men authorized to deter crime, engage in law enforcement capacities, and perform other services deemed necessary.[57] The replacement process was ushered in by Mayor William Havemeyer. The Metropolitan Police replaced the Municipal Police in 1857.[58] Throughout that period, immigration from Europe was growing, as was immigration from China, and elites relied on police to enforce laws and dominant norms that some migrants were believed to disrupt. Policing was also heavily drawn on as a tool of labor control, with police attempting to quell and suppress labor organizing sparked by unjust work conditions on docks.

Broader civil society at the time also saw professionalized police forces as a solution to racial-ethnic unrest and violence. After the police departments were formed in Boston and New York City, Cincinnati followed in 1853 and Philadelphia in 1855. Policing entities were then formed in Newark, New Jersey, and Baltimore in 1857.[59] By the late 1800s, policing entities were taking the place of watchmen and constable systems in cities across the United States.

Those shifts also occurred within the larger context of a push toward international coordination among police, seen most notably in the activities of the International Association of Chiefs of Police, founded in 1893.[60] Since its founding, the organization has hosted annual meetings with the aim of aligning administrative, technical, and operational practices while facilitating the recruitment of police forces internationally. International efforts to coordinate policing philosophies, strategies, and practices shed light on parallels in violent and coercive police tactics around the globe that have existed for decades.

POLICING IN THE EARLY TWENTIETH CENTURY, 1900–1950

In the late nineteenth and early twentieth centuries, public perception of the police was shaped by widely shared incidents of corruption, police violence, and relationships between the police and political entities. Upton Sinclair's 1906 novel *The Jungle* is known for its criticism of conditions in the US meatpacking industry during the late nineteenth and early twentieth centuries. But the novel also delved into police corruption in Chicago, including political partnerships and bribery as well as police corruption. *The Jungle* illustrated the close entanglements among politicians, businessmen, and police and the brutalization of working-class immigrants. As Sinclair wrote:

> The law forbade Sunday drinking; and this had delivered the saloon-keepers into the hands of the police, and made an alliance between them necessary. The law forbade prostitution; and this had brought the "madames" into the combination. It was the same with the gambling-house keeper and the pool-room man, and the same with any other man or woman who had a means of getting "graft," and was willing to pay over a share of it: the green-goods man and the highwayman, the pickpocket and the sneak-thief, and the receiver of stolen goods, the seller of adulterated milk, of stale fruit and diseased meat, the proprietor of unsanitary tenements, the fake-doctor and the usurer, the beggar and the "push-cart man," the prize-fighter and the professional slugger, the race-track "tout," the procurer, the white-slave agent, and the expert seducer of young girls. All of these agencies of corruption were banded together, and leagued in blood brotherhood with the politician and the police; more often than not they were one and the same person—the

police captain would own the brothel he pretended to raid, and the politician would open his headquarters in his saloon.[61]

Despite being a novel, this illustration showcases the deep nexus among politics, business, and policing that was commonplace.

Evidence of and commentary on corruption and abuse were even evident in government reports. The Lexow Committee of 1894–1895 uncovered the entanglement of the New York Police Department with Tammany Hall, the city's dominant political machine.[62] That connection was further revealed by satirical political cartoons mocking the NYPD's association with Tammany Hall and its widespread corruption.[63] In the 1900s, police abuse and corruption continued. The Wickersham Commission of 1931 painted a clear picture of police practices, stating "The third degree — that is, the use of physical brutality, or other forms of cruelty, to obtain involuntary confessions or admissions — is widespread."[64] These varied sources, from popular media to official reports, provide a window into widespread understandings of police illegitimacy and abuse. As James Baldwin wrote in *No Name in the Street*:

> It means nothing, therefore, to say to so thoroughly insulated a people that the forces of crime and the forces of law and order work hand in hand in the ghetto, bleeding it day and night. It means nothing to say that, in the eyes of the black and the poor certainly, the principal distinction between a policeman and a criminal is to be found in their attire.[65]

Policing experienced a number of developments around the turn of the twentieth century. Through the late 1800s and early 1900s, policing in cities was known to be widely corrupt, violent, and seen as illegitimate. This is on par with the perception of police in many cities during that era as policing entities became increasingly present in urban areas: police were not widely accepted as necessary, legitimate guarantees of safety but carried out the political and economic bidding of elites and worked on behalf of themselves. While politicians and economic elites may have had more favorable attitudes toward police given that they benefited most from them, skepticism toward police was widespread. Police would often carry out the wishes of local politicians, acting as enforcers of local political machines, which included intimidating political opponents and attempting to affect elections.[66] This culminated in the professionalization era of policing, which began in the early 1900s. During that era, key police reformers sought to professionalize policing through training, codes of conduct, hiring decisions, and organizational structure.

One of the most important developments emerging from the period was the development of a federal policing entity.[67] The Federal Bureau of Investigation, or FBI, was created in 1908 under President Theodore Roosevelt. The FBI was initially founded to address interstate criminalized activity that outpaced the capacities of local law enforcement. The FBI would also target the organized crime networks that had flourished during the Prohibition era. In 1924, J. Edgar Hoover was appointed director of the FBI and greatly expanded it, which propelled it into a new era. Under Hoover, the bureau introduced tools such as the fingerprint file, the crime lab, and the FBI Academy. Hoover used the bureau as a tool to shadow and intimidate those he deemed threatening to national security or social harmony. Civil rights activists, suspected Communists, and others fell under his watchful eye, sparking controversy and igniting accusations of infringing on civil liberties. That repression with heightened power and scope set a legacy for the FBI that would continue throughout the coming decades.

Policing at the turn of the twentieth century also saw the emergence of attention toward diversity in policing. In New York City, Samuel J. Battle was appointed as the first Black police officer in 1911, and Mary A. Sullivan also joined the force as the first female police officer in the same year. Rather than curtailing the power of the police, these professionalization and reform efforts, including the turn toward diversity, created better organized and stronger policing entities that were more professionalized and diverse in certain ways but also had an expanded capacity for violence. Even more, the veneer of professionalism masked, at times, the illegitimate violence work that police were doing in society. As the political scientist Dr. Naomi Murakawa has argued:

> Reformers try to enhance people's procedural rights as if arming individuals with legal protections might slow the churn of criminalization. But consider the crowning glory of the procedural

rights revolution, the 1966 *Miranda v. Arizona* Supreme Court decision requiring cops to recite the speech that contains some version of "You have the right to remain silent." Outraged conservatives griped about liberal courts handcuffing the cops. But police simply learned a new protocol. After Miranda rights are read during an arrest, most people waive their rights, and police secure incriminating statements in more than half of all interrogations—rates comparable to those pre-*Miranda*. Police routinely use lies, intimidation, and confinement in interrogation, but simply saying the magic words became proof of professionalism. In short, *Miranda* offers good protection—for police, not the people they interrogate....

We pursue reform on the premise that the system is broken. But as [the abolitionist and antiviolence organizer] Mariame Kaba tells us, "The system isn't broken but highly functioning just as the powers that be intended." I agree and will add this: Police reform does not fail. It works—for the police.[68]

After the abolition of slavery, slave patrols no longer existed, but policing—and prisons—as tools of race-class control continued.[69] Systems of formal policing expanded in small towns and rural areas and were used to suppress, intimidate, and control newly freed Black populations and force them into convict leasing and sharecropping.[70] In the South, sharecropping was a widespread agricultural system after the Civil War. Newly freed Black populations, as well as poor white laborers, worked as tenant farmers on land often owned by well-off white elites.[71] Instead of paying rent in cash form, sharecroppers gave portions of their crops to the landowner. Sharecropping often led to a cycle of debt and dependency, as sharecroppers would frequently end up owing more to the landowner for the tools and supplies they used than they could repay by sharing their crops. Sharecropping became a means of maintaining a labor force in economically oppressive conditions after the abolition of slavery. No longer prioritizing the prevention of slave rebellions, the police enforced laws that outlawed vagrancy in order to criminalize Black people and force them into convict leasing through the sharecropping system—which maintained exploitative labor conditions consistent with those under slavery.[72] Officers also routinely enforced poll taxes and checked proof of employment of any Black person on the road. Those early forms of policing across the nation served to maintain the interests of the dominant class of white elites. By criminalizing newly freed Black Americans[73] as well as the working class and certain groups of immigrants as deviant, morally inferior, and uneducated, municipal, county, and state police forces used brute force to ensure that they remained in oppressive conditions. Black spaces and sites of socializing were also criminalized and targeted by police, especially in regard to policing Black masculinity, which the scholar Rashad Shabazz showcased throughout Chicago in his book *Spatializing Blackness: Architectures of Confinement and Black Masculinity in Chicago*.[74] The towering scholar and intellectual W. E. B. Du Bois, in *Black Reconstruction in America, 1860–1880*, revealed the earliest ways in which policing served as a mechanism of social control and domination. He stated:

> The system of slavery demanded a special police force and such a force was made possible and unusually effective by the presence of the poor whites....Considering the economic rivalry of the black and white worker in the North, it would have seemed natural that the poor white would have refused to police the slaves. But two considerations led him in the opposite direction. First of all, it gave him work and some authority as overseer, slave driver, and member of the patrol system. But above and beyond this, it fed his vanity because it associated him with the masters....The result was that the system was held stable and intact by the poor white.... Gradually the whole white South became an armed and commissioned camp to keep Negroes in slavery and to kill the black rebel.[75]

As Du Bois made clear, the widespread policing of Black enslaved people by white citizens and later armed forces was essential to maintaining the institution of slavery.

In 1900, the antilynching journalist Ida B. Wells-Barnett described a racist lynch mob that had terrorized New Orleans. "During the entire time the mob held the city in its hands," she wrote, "...the police and the legally-constituted authorities showed plainly where their sympathies were....The ring-leaders of the mob were at no time disguised....Not only were they exempt from prosecution by the police while the town was in the hands of the mob, but even now that law and order is supposed to resume control, these men, well known, are not now, nor ever will be, called to account for the unspeakable brutalities of that terrible week."[76] Over a hundred years later, Wells-Barnett's words, highlighting that the police did not exist to protect Black people, continue to ring true.

During the Jim Crow era, police often enabled and worked with white supremacist vigilantes such as the Ku Klux Klan to maintain social, political, and economic racial hierarchies. Meanwhile, northern political leaders feared an influx of newly freed rural Black populations, which were viewed as inferior in every aspect. As a result, northern cities established segregated areas and used police officers to enforce racial boundaries through violence, discrimination, and harassment. In both the North and the South, the police employed brute force to impose geographical, social, and political limitations on Black communities.[77] The use of alcohol and drugs became a central justification for the expansion of policing, police power, and police technology during the early 1900s.

As Dr. Carl L. Hart has discussed,[78] cultural myths about Black men who used cocaine, which began to rise in the late 1800s and early 1900s, seemingly led some police forces to begin using higher-caliber weapons because of stereotypes of the strength of the mythical "Black cocaine fiend."[79] The myths surrounding Black cocaine use paved the way for the 1914 Harrison Narcotics Tax Act, the first federal law passed by Congress that mandated regulations on and taxing of the production, importation, and distribution of opiates and cocaine.[80] The Harrison Act paved the way for the Eighteenth Amendment, which established the prohibition of the manufacture, sale, and transportation of alcohol and other draconian drug and alcohol policies. This highlights the way police often step in to regulate drugs, particularly when they become popular in marginalized communities, as cocaine was being used across the United States by many different populations. The policing of drugs, as well as anything labeled a vice crime, has long been used to justify expanding policing and police power. As stated by David F. Musto in *The American Disease: Origins of Narcotic Control*:

Fear of cocaine might have contributed to the dread that the black would rise above "his place," as well as reflecting the extent to which cocaine may have released defiance and retribution. So far, evidence does not suggest that cocaine caused a crime wave but rather that anticipation of black rebellion inspired white alarm. Anecdotes often told of superhuman strength, cunning, and efficiency resulting from cocaine. One of the most terrifying beliefs about cocaine was that it actually improved pistol marksmanship. Another myth, that cocaine made blacks almost unaffected by mere .32 caliber bullets, is said to have caused southern police departments to switch to .38 caliber revolvers. These fantasies characterized white fear, not the reality of cocaine's effects, and gave one more reason for the repression of blacks.[81]

Sarah A. Seo showcased in *Policing the Open Road: How Cars Transformed American Freedom* that the advent of automobiles in the early 1900s dramatically shifted the size and scope of policing. When cars were introduced into American society on a large scale, the state responded by expanding laws and the capacity of police to regulate driving. Partly as a response to fears of crime being carried out with vehicles and police being unable to respond, partly out of the state's belief that it needed to regulate driving, police became the primary regulators of traffic. Access to and resources for marked police vehicles took off after the 1930s, and the expanding power police had to stop, question, and penalize drivers became central to policing. That expanded police power and interactions with the public.

As a result of driving-related policing, it was not just oppressed communities coming into constant interaction with police: people from all backgrounds were now being stopped for traffic violations. The expanding use of cars and the evolution of laws surrounding the policing of traffic and vehicles played a central role in police professionalization, as police were now interacting widely not just with immigrant, poor, working-class, Black, and other dispossessed communities but with drivers from all backgrounds, including more elite ones. To be sure, the policing of drivers affected Black drivers and others from oppressed backgrounds at disproportionate rates from early on.[82] As automobiles created new forms of mobility, police began policing Black drivers in ways that created new forms of control in terms of race and space.

INTERNATIONAL INTERPLAY AND THE ORIGINS OF POLICING

> The colonized world is a world divided in two. The dividing line, the border, is represented by the barracks and the police stations. In the colonies, the official, legitimate agent, the spokesperson for the colonizer and the regime of oppression, is the police officer or the soldier.
>
> —Frantz Fanon[83]

As mentioned earlier, the history of policing in the United States is a transnational one. In the early centuries of settler colonialism, colonial elites relied on policing strategies to control populations such as Irish colonial subjects, Philippine resisters of colonialism, and enslaved people in the Caribbean. Those models were then imported and adapted for the geographic context of the United States. The people involved in developing US colonial policing in its early phases had their own histories and places of origin, which they drew on when creating models of policing. There was innovation, of course. In the United States, due to unique aspects of its colonial history and growing capitalist economy, political leaders crafted flexible systems of policing and military control. Those systems were designed to maintain existing power structures and to further empower those already in control. This approach was applied not just within the mainland United States but also in territories including Guam, Hawaii, the Philippines, and Puerto Rico.[84]

Sociologist Julian Go argues, police militarization—in which police adopt military strategies, tactics, and tools in routine policing—began to increase in intensity in the early twentieth century as a result of what he calls "imperial feedback," whereby police expand their power and strength by drawing on military-style strategies, methods, and models from the United States' imperial history of establishing dominance and rule over other territories.[85] Police adopted strategies and tactics used by the imperial military to control colonial subjects abroad to control racial and class minorities in the United States, including African Americans and Indigenous communities.

As Alex S. Vitale noted in *The End of Policing*, some policing agencies were formed explicitly to deal with labor organizing and to suppress workers' rights. The Pennsylvania State Police was founded in 1905 as a result of the Anthracite Coal Strike of 1902.[86] Coal workers and miners staged a powerful protest against their working conditions. At the time, mill and mine owners employed private police forces to suppress worker strikes and disobedience. Local police and sheriffs either did not have the capacity to quell rebellion or chose not to. Senate Bill 278, signed by Governor Samuel Pennypacker, established the Pennsylvania State Police, which was ultimately praised by President Theodore Roosevelt.[87] The troopers engaged in labor repression and suppression tactics, many of which were drawn from imperial strategies of the Philippine Constabulary, which had been created to manage the US occupation of the Philippines, where officials engaged in counterinsurgency strategies to suppress dissent and maintain the broader imperial order.[88] A central strategy was for constabularies to build closer relationships with colonized populations in order to gain legitimacy and intelligence about potential anticolonial efforts. As later seen in the development of communication systems in US policing, radios, telephones, and other telecommunication modes were central to police attempts to quell and prevent labor, antiracism, and anticolonial efforts in real time. On this connection between imperial conquest and US policing, Vitale stated that Jesse Garwood, "a major figure in the US occupation forces in the Philippines, brought the methods of militarized espionage and political suppression to bear on Pennsylvania miners and factory workers."[89]

As Christopher J. Coyne and Abigail R. Hall noted in their book *Tyranny Comes Home: The Domestic Fate of U.S. Militarism*:

> ... these veterans significantly influenced the evolution of America's police forces. August Vollmer, for example, incorporated military structure, technology, and techniques into the police departments of Berkeley and Los Angeles, California; worked as the head of national police organizations; and served as a consultant to a number of other police groups. Others like Jesse Garwood, known for their brutal tactics in the Philippines, returned to the United States and established constabularies modeled after the one created in the islands. Lieutenant Colonel Harry Bandholtz employed the psychological techniques he learned in the war against miners in West

Virginia. Major General Smedley Butler used his wartime training in the battle against alcohol during national Prohibition, leading his team on an estimated five thousand raids.[90]

The relationship between policing and militarism has long been a tightly woven one. The history of policing reveals that imperialism and colonialism have been central to its development.[91] This is true in terms of US colonialism and the dispossession and decimation of Indigenous people as well as in terms of policing strategies developed abroad and used to police race-class-oppressed communities at home. As a strategy of expressed reform, police leaders and politicians also embrace militarism as a way to professionalize police forces.

POLICE PROFESSIONALIZATION

Early police forces were known to be corrupt and politically tied to power structures, as evidenced by commission reports, politicians, and the onset of what is commonly referred to as police professionalization.[92] The prohibition of alcohol between 1919 and 1933 intensified policing. There were thousands of speakeasies across the United States, and organized crime networks met the demand for prohibited liquor. Police enforced vice and prohibition laws at their own discretion. Police throughout the United States were corrupt and colluded in criminal syndicate endeavors, gambling, prostitution, and other vice activity. That vast corruption and involvement in crime syndicates included the forming of prostitution, alcohol, and gambling syndicates, as well as assassinations, bribery, and intimidation.[93] Police corruption also included political policing, whereby particular political leaders commanded police to harass their opponents, influence elections, and heckle the supporters of opposing politicians. This is all corroborated by a number of commissions and grand jury investigations.[94]

Throughout the history of New York City, commissions investigated police corruption, revealing how widespread it was. One of the earliest of these commissions was the Lexow Committee of 1894–1895, initiated due to growing public concerns about police misconduct and management. The committee's investigation unearthed the fact that officers were regularly involved in extorting money from illegal businesses such as gambling establishments, promising them protection from legal actions and raids. Its findings revealed that this corruption spanned all levels of the police department. In 1912, the Curran Committee, chaired by alderman Henry H. Curran, conducted an investigation into police corruption. Its findings were similar to those of the Lexow Committee: officers were involved in a variety of illicit activities, including receiving bribes and protecting vice operations. The probe underscored the deeply rooted culture of corruption that had largely become synonymous with the department.

Two decades later, in 1932, the Hofstadter Committee, spearheaded by lawyer and judge Samuel Seabury, took on the daunting task of investigating not just the police department but also the judicial system and other public offices. While the committee's scope was broad, its findings related to the police were consistent with those of earlier investigations. The revelations also implicated the magistrate's courts, where corruption was widespread, with judges involved in accepting bribes and mishandling justice. The far-reaching findings of the Seabury Committee's work led to the resignation of Mayor Jimmy Walker. Collectively, these committees paint a portrait of a city that has maintained a police force with systematic corruption.

The 1949 grand jury investigation into the New York Police Department was another showcase of widespread corruption. The jury was convened as a result of continued allegations of widespread corruption within the NYPD, particularly related to gambling and other forms of vice. The allegations weren't just about patrol officers; they also went up into the higher levels of the department. The investigation resulted in a series of indictments against police officers and exposed a network of payoffs and corruption deeply embedded within the department. In coming decades, the Knapp Commission of 1970 and the Mollen Commission of 1992 would reveal drug sale and use, as well as corruption, theft, and wanton violence, by police. Such commissions and investigations were widespread, involving Los Angeles, Philadelphia, New Orleans, Atlanta, San Francisco, and more.[95] The recurring accounts of police corruption, even during that period of alleged reform, reveal that professionalizing the police had not addressed the problems and violence of policing endemic to police power.[96]

They also show that the police were not the widespread keepers of safety they are often portrayed as today.

Just as the state used the police force to maintain the inferior position of enslaved people and later of freed African Americans, policing in the North began as informal, privately funded night watch patrols to control working-class immigrants and growing unrest among the industrial working class. Northern cities experienced an influx of immigrants and rapid industrialization during the late 1800s and early 1900s, which instilled fear and resentment into white elites. They often viewed Irish and other working-class immigrants as uneducated, disorderly, and politically militant. Labor strikes and riots broke out, inducing fear, anxiety and, demands for the preservation of law and order. Although the informal night watch system was intended to prevent looting and labor organizing, it failed at that, which resulted in the emergence and expansion of formalized public policing to protect the interests of property and business owners. The creation of the police enabled the enforcement of morality laws, such as restrictions on drinking. However, the early urban police were openly corrupt, as they were often chosen based on political connections and bribery. Qualifications to become a police officer didn't entail formal training or the passing of civil service exams. Political parties also used police to suppress opposition voting and to spy on and suppress workers' organizations, meetings, and strikes.[97]

Because of the high degree of police corruption, journalists often reported on it, which brought it widespread attention. The 1894–1895 Lexow Committee, for example, was preceded by investigative journalism about police corruption. The outcry that came from a range of people, in addition to the resistance by marginalized communities, put pressure on politicians and police leaders, and police reform became a central issue that continues today. In response to public pressure, policing became increasingly professionalized through civil service exams and centralized hiring processes, training, and new technology. Management sciences were also introduced.[98] Reformers such as August Vollmer, who drew his ideas from his experiences in the US occupation forces in the Philippines, also implemented police science courses, which introduced new transportation and communication technologies, as well as fingerprinting and police labs. Police reformers of the twentieth century paved the way for the increasingly intertwined relationships among standardized technology, policing, and surveillance. But professionalization did not solve the problems of policing and in the end served to further exacerbate them by expanding police power. What police professionalization did accomplish was providing a veneer for policing that would communicate to the public that police were becoming more legitimate and less problematic.

At the turn of the twentieth century, political leaders of the United States radically changed the organization and responsibilities of the police department. For much of history, the general public had perceived the police as illegitimate and riddled with corruption.[99] Reformers in the 1920s and '30s attempted to rid departments of organizational corruption and sever their close ties with political elites. They emphasized that the role of police departments was in crime control and arrest. Changing expectations of police led to organizational changes in which police departments took on a more centralized, bureaucratic, paramilitary organizational structure.[100]

As Naomi Murakawa revealed in *The First Civil Right: How Liberals Built Prison America*, in the 1940s liberals concerned with racial violence began thinking that modernized policing and carceral machinery could address white mob violence and vigilantism. While their intention was to develop policing and carceral systems to combat white mob and vigilante violence, this approach inadvertently expanded carceral power. That expanded authority was later used against marginalized groups, particularly in the 1960s. Inevitably, that reform era led to police professionalization that further cemented the power of the police and allowed them to do more unchecked harm. The shifts led to changes in how a police department's success was measured, putting the focus increasingly on higher arrest rates and "efficiency," as determined by rapid responses to emergency calls. By the 1950s, those priorities were having devastating impacts on marginalized communities of color, beginning with Black communities.[101] Scholars have long shown that poverty and disadvantage, shaped by centuries of structural racism, increase the likelihood of violence and harm within neighborhoods. The expansion of police power from the onset of policing into the mid–twentieth century did not address those structural realities: it inflamed them.

INTERLUDE I

(PART A) NOTES FROM FERGUSON

I'm still searching for language to describe my experiences in Ferguson during the 2014 uprisings.

There's something about the tear gas, the militarized police, the military—and at times these days it's hard to tell the difference between the two—the batons, the shields, the guns...the deaths, and the way that they can affect the body, and the spirit, that make them incredibly difficult to capture.

I remember one night in particular. It was dark, cold. The air was thick. I have yet to shake its grasp loose, and I may never do so.

It was the weekend that a grand jury decided not to indict Darren Wilson.

Protesters gathered near and across from where a line of police and military stood in front of the Ferguson Police Department building, protecting the building that housed a police department that had taken on the responsibility of generating a revenue stream for the city off of the backs of Black bodies.

A group of protestors entered the street. There were clear orders to stay on the opposite end, though, as is done in rebellions, folks were challenging state power.

There was an announcement that if the protestors did not return to the sidewalk, they might be arrested, and when their orders were not met, the police and military organized themselves as if they were preparing for combat and within seconds rushed the line of protesters in the street.

They confronted the group violently, and when they began to push, body slam, and arrest people, everyone who had mobilized, even those not in the street, ran. There was an instinct to run because folks knew the extent of the state's arbitrary and wanton violence.

At the time I was with my older sister Nesha. We immediately began running with the crowd, and as I started to turn to make sure my sister was still with me, I realized we had gotten separated in the chaos of the crowd running.

During that time, police and military descended from every single direction where there was a way out.

By the time I was almost fully turned around, I heard my name: "Philip!" I turned to where the voice had come from and saw my sister walking up a hill where the police were descending, their tactical lights flashing to disorient and their guns leveled to the protestors in front of them, including my sister. The guns appeared to be shotguns filled with beanbags.

I yelled her name back, she turned, and we rejoined each other.

That moment made clear to me the power of the state and what the courage of love looks like in the face of state violence. And it's that type of love that has allowed Black folks to imagine the impossible in the face of terror.

I later asked my sister what she'd planned to do, and she said she didn't know. She'd moved because her love had overridden her fear of the state.

So I've learned a great deal over the years about state violence, resistance, and the courage to love and imagine.

Those nights under clouds of tear gas, surrounded by militarized police—and the military itself—have given me the language to describe exactly what a just democracy isn't more clearly than I can tell you what one looks like. Because for Black people in this country there have never been such things as lives free of state violence—whether it be by the police, the public assistance office, schools, local hospitals, or the continued political decisions that prioritize profit and punishment over Black lives. But this book represents my analyses of the roots of police violence, the complexity—and persistence—of it today, and its range in all its social and political implications—and ways to move forward. Principally I put forth a vision, my vision, of a world—a safer world—without policing or cages.

When I think back to that night in Ferguson with my sister, who was willing to walk into anything out of love, what surfaces is this idea of courage.

To create a new world requires the courage to imagine. And the courage to do what seems impossible to actualize dreams of freedom.

(PART B) THE TYRANNY OF TEAR GAS

As April 12, 2015, began in Baltimore, it revealed a city in the midst of unrest. Graffiti, murals, and memorials about Freddie Gray emerged throughout the city, visible markers of a community's grief, anger, and demands for justice. The art and memorials were emblematic of the city's struggle with systemic problems, providing a platform for voices that often felt unheard. I and my two older twin sisters, Nesha and Tammy, found food and drove around the city. It was the quiet before the storm.

The confrontation between youths and police at Mondawmin Mall earlier that day—the day of Freddie Gray's funeral—served as a precursor of the night's tension. High school students, cornered and without their usual transport home, faced off against riot gear–clad officers. What began as a standoff quickly escalated, setting the tone for the days to follow. But amid the chaos, the community activated. Members of the local church group, arms linked, formed human barriers between protesters and police, aiming to prevent violence. Volunteer cleanup crews, armed with brooms and trash bags, worked diligently each morning to repair the physical scars of the previous night's events.

However, the city's wounds ran much deeper than shattered glass and burned buildings. Years of neglect, systemic racism, and socioeconomic challenges had created a powder keg. The conditions for an uprising had long been set. Freddie Gray's tragic death was the spark that ignited it.

As the day progressed, the streets, usually alive with the hum of everyday life, felt tense. I hurriedly wrote a paper for my political science graduate class while stopped at red lights. The city braced itself. It was clear to everyone that things would intensify by night. With the imposition of a police curfew, the looming threat of more confrontations hung heavily in the air.

On North Avenue, local businesses had started boarding up, anticipating the unrest, while some community leaders implored young activists to protest but not rebel. But the issue was evident: How do you remain calm when police murder your friend or someone you see so much of yourself in?

I remember one protest during the day. A police helicopter hovered above, its speaker blaring messages so loudly it felt as if someone were right beside me with a bullhorn. It was a sonic representation of police presence and technology — inescapable and overwhelming.

That day my twin sisters and I navigated the charged landscape. My 2006 Honda Civic wasn't just a vehicle; it became an impromptu ambulance. The violence had escalated to such a point that even the street medics, often the first responders during protests, were absent. But we were committed to helping where we could.

One poignant memory remains. The police were trying to disperse a protest as the curfew approached. It was still light outside, and people were just protesting. But as the police pressed on, tension began to brew. Then the police started to let off tear gas into the crowd. A panic ensued. Throughout the protests, the scorch of tear gas and the sting of pepper spray had become agonizingly familiar. Tear gas infiltrated our car. My sisters and I were in the car, and through the rearview mirror I saw a teenager on the ground, his friends around him. Seemingly having respiratory problems, he lay unconscious, and his friends tried to pick him up. People were running and there was chaotic panic, and it was hard for his friends to carry him while running. They hastily placed the teenager in the back of our car. I drove away from the front line, and my sisters attended to him. As we drove away, he eventually came to, confused but having a sudden jolt back to consciousness. In a surreal moment, he asked, "Y'all wanna buy some socks?" It was a bit of comedic relief amid the chaos. The moment captured the essence of Baltimore's unrest — a blend of stark brutality with fragments of everyday life.

One particularly heart-stopping moment occurred when I heard the rumbling of a police Humvee — they look like tanks — nearby. Alone in the car, with my sisters treating injured people outside, I sank into my seat, praying I was invisible to the police. The fear wasn't just about arrest; it was the tangible threat of violence that hung in the air, more toxic than the tear gas. Once the coast was clear, I hurried and found my sisters helping to treat people feeling the sting of the tear gas. I told them there was a tank circling the area, because that was what it looked like. They got back into the car. Once we got a bit away, we saw an older man, obviously struggling after being hit by the chemical agent. We hastened to help another older man, who had just been in the area near a bus station trying to get home and had been caught by the tear gas. We finally departed from the epicenter of the uprising, my sisters aiding the man, whom we took to his home.

The recurring cycle was almost ritualistic in its predictability: a flare-up of police violence in response to genuine cries for justice, followed by a smattering of superficial reforms. Yet the bedrock issues persisted. The murder of Freddie Gray was not an isolated incident but a symptom of a deep-rooted malaise. The heart of the issue was that many in Baltimore lacked the basic resources to live, let alone thrive. They were trapped in a cycle of poverty and neglect, their aspirations smothered by systemic problems.

CHAPTER 2

THE POLICE BOOM

What white Americans have never fully understood—but what the Negro can never forget—is that white society is deeply implicated in the ghetto. White institutions created it, white institutions maintain it, and white society condones it. . . .

"Prior" incidents, which increased tensions and ultimately led to violence, were police actions in almost half the cases; police actions were "final" incidents before the outbreak of violence in 12 of the 24 surveyed disorders.

—Kerner Commission report, 1968

SINCE I STARTED TO STUDY POLICING, ONE QUESTION HAS LINGERED: How did policing become so massive in such a short period? The readings and research kept pointing me to the mid-1900s. The tumult of political resistance, politics, and racism produced a climate so charged that it would lay the foundation for mass policing and mass incarceration for decades to come. Policing had already begun to expand, but the investments and efforts by politicians and police leaders during the mid-1900s set history on a course where policing would swell in ways that few could have predicted at the time. Still, there were organizers and activists who named policing and incarceration as tools to manage oppression.

The violence of policing was widespread throughout the 1950s, as it had been in previous decades and would be in decades to come. Police used violence and force to enforce Jim Crow laws and the subjugation of marginalized communities. They engaged in racial profiling, wanton violence, and the suppression of political resistance. During the civil rights movement, which spanned the mid-1950s through the 1960s, especially in southern US cities such as Birmingham and Selma, Alabama, police employed brutal tactics to suppress protests and activism. Cops used attack dogs to intimidate and harm protestors. High-pressure water cannons were unleashed on crowds, causing injury and chaos. Tear gas was frequently used to disperse marches and demonstrations, causing respiratory distress and panic among protestors. Those violent tactics were part of a larger strategy by police to repress activism and maintain racial segregation and discrimination. The images of those violent confrontations, broadcast on national television and printed in newspapers, shocked the conscience of the nation and galvanized support for the civil rights cause. Police also enforced racial boundaries at parks, at schools, on modes of transportation, at pools, and in entire communities. As agencies attempted to suppress activists and protests, more attention was brought to the violence of policing that was integral to the foundations of policing itself. The violent tactics led to outrage and calls for change. Policing has long focused on reinforcing power structures. These power structures center largely on capital and profit accrual, which have a history of organizing themselves along racial lines. The mid-1900s saw the development of mass policing, which would balloon in decades to come.

Police corruption was widespread during the mid–twentieth century, as it had been in previous decades. Officers engaged in individual acts and rings of corruption, which included bribery, graft, and participation in organized crime syndicates. The growing strength of the syndicates in the early and mid-1900s provided them with power and influence in various regions, and police developed relationships with them. The corruption was widely known and contributed to calls for change.

The Kefauver Committee hearings, officially known as the Senate's Special Committee on Organized Crime in Interstate Commerce, were launched in 1950 to investigate the sprawling network of organized crime across the United States. Chaired by Senator Estes Kefauver, the hearings were notable for being among the first major congressional inquiries to be televised, reaching a wide audience and dramatically revealing the scale and depth of mob activities in the United States. It was estimated that nearly thirty million Americans watched the televised hearings in 1951.[1] Throughout the hearings, which took place in several major cities, the committee uncovered extensive evidence of systemic corruption within various police departments and law enforcement agencies.[2] This corruption often involved police officers accepting bribes, colluding with organized crime syndicates, and facilitating criminalized activities like gambling and drug trafficking. The public exposure of such widespread corruption and criminal infiltration into law enforcement put police illegitimacy into sharp focus and spurred subsequent calls to curtail police corruption.

Police also engaged in intense surveillance and political repression of Communists and labor organizers during the mid–twentieth century. The government orchestrated a series of raids in 1919 and 1920 — known as the Palmer Raids, as they were spearheaded by Attorney General A. Mitchell Palmer — to arrest and deport suspected radicals, mainly anarchists and Communists. That set the stage for the policing and surveillance of leftist activists and anyone seen as a Communist in the 1940s and 1950s. There was an increased focus on monitoring individuals and groups deemed to be potential threats to the status quo. The Red Scare of the early 1900s and the subsequent McCarthy era, or Second Red Scare, in the 1940s and 1950s, created an environment of fear and discrimination against anyone suspected of being a Communist, anarchist, or leftist. A social and political climate arose that ushered in the intense surveillance and harassment of such people. As Charisse Burden-Stelly discussed in *Black Scare/Red Scare*, anti-Black racism also compounded with anti-Communism during this period to create a hostile and repressive environment for Black communities seeking transformation.[3] During the Red Scares, many people were ostracized from employment and civil society because of actual or perceived Communist affiliations or beliefs. Those actions often violated their civil liberties, reflecting the intense anti-Communist sentiment of the time. Local police departments collaborated with federal agencies to surveil and disrupt civil rights, labor, and political activism using unjust and violent practices.

In the 1950s, there was also growing transnational radicalism. US activists were in solidarity with others around the globe seeking to end various forms of oppression. Decolonialization movements were also under way. Radical activists and decolonialization movements in the United States, Africa, Latin America, and the Caribbean engaged in dialogue with one another and followed various migration pathways that brought thinkers into conversation with one another across the Americas and globally.[4]

Many policing strategies had been imported to the United States prior to the 1900s, but toward the middle of the twentieth century, with the Cold War and the expanding US empire, the United States became an exporter of policing and approaches to colonial occupation. As Stuart Schrader discussed in *Badges without Borders: How Global Counterinsurgency Transformed American Policing*, the precursor of the Office of Public Safety (OPS) was established in 1954, initially as part of the International Police Academy under the International Cooperation Administration. It later evolved into the OPS in 1962, directed by CIA operative and police reformer Byron Engle, serving as the US government's instrument for the exportation of police training and counterinsurgency techniques globally until 1974. It was designed to assist pro-US governments in professionalizing their police forces to manage their populations, suppress rebellion, and curb Communist aspirations. During this period, techniques such as community policing, in which police embed themselves in communities to build relationships that can be mobilized for enforcement efforts, were developed and employed as tools of counterinsurgency.[5]

In post-1940s America, Black communities across the nation began to experience a transformation in their relationship to safety. With the rise of police power, long-standing practices of self-defense and community protection came under scrutiny. Popular narratives promoted the idea that the police were there to safeguard everyone, irrespective of race. Such narratives appealed to those who yearned for a more integrated society. Still, it's worth noting that even staunch advocates of nonviolence, such as Dr. Martin Luther King Jr., recognized the importance of self-defense. Charles E. Cobb Jr. in his book *This Nonviolent Stuff'll Get You Killed: How Guns Made the Civil Rights Movement Possible*, noted, "Most black people took whatever measures necessary to ensure their own safety and that of their loved ones, and this often included firearms."[6] As Cobb remarked, Glenn Smiley, one of King's advisers, once observed that King's home had so many guns that he called it an "arsenal."

By the 1960s, the expansion of policing in the United States was influenced by a confluence of factors, and racial repression and tensions were central. That growth also undermined many community-led safety initiatives. The Black Panther Party, for example, was known for its survival programs and copwatch initiatives—where communities monitor the police to document and prevent abuse—but those faced resistance and suppression.

As policing became more dominant, there was a push against the idea of Black communities arming themselves. The underlying message was that only the police could guarantee safety. Subsequently, there were efforts to restrict Black communities' access to firearms. The implication was clear: the state and its policing institutions were the primary arbiters of safety. With the introduction of systems such as the nationwide 911 emergency number in 1968, communities were socialized to rely on the police instead of turning to each other.

This isn't to suggest that firearms are the ultimate solution to safety concerns or that all Black communities have given up their ties to self-defense. However, this evolution in the perception of safety and the regulation of weapons highlights the challenges Black communities faced in their quest for safety. While they sought protection from various forms of violence, the emerging police-centric model wasn't the answer. Instead of eroding community-driven safety initiatives, it would've been more beneficial to empower Black communities with the resources to enhance their own safety structures. Black communities needed safety from white supremacist, state, and interpersonal violence, but the police did not solve those problems. Strengthening, rather than weakening, a community's ability to manage its concerns about safety and conflict is key to building safe, accountable communities.

THE POLICE BOOM

The evolution of policing during the 1960s and its effects on society have been pivotal aspects of US history, greatly influencing the fabric of civil life.

During the decade, widespread antiwar demonstrations, feminist rallies, labor organization, student movements, and various forms of political resistance united radical political organizers from different backgrounds and causes. Concurrently, the ongoing Cold War was inspiring a new generation of anticapitalists. Protests, including civil disobedience, mass mobilizations, and direct actions, disrupted the societal order, fueling the expansion of policing. That expansion was already under way, but the 1960s were a turning point. During that era, police used a variety of tactics to control oppressed populations in the United States and implemented counterinsurgency methods—inspired by military tactics—to manage protest movements.[7] Internationally, US policing methods were exported to assist in Cold War efforts and sustain favored governments abroad.[8]

As opposition to the Vietnam War continued to grow throughout the 1960s, antiwar protests became increasingly widespread. Police agencies often responded to the protests with a militaristic approach, using tear gas, batons, and arrests to suppress dissent. The clashes between police and antiwar protestors, most notably at the Democratic National Convention in Chicago in 1968, demonstrated the repressive nature of policing that stifled dissenting voices.[9]

By the 1960s, Black political repression was on the rise, with local and state police joining the FBI and other agencies in repressing Black political leaders and organizations such as Malcolm X, Fred Hampton, the Black Panther Party, the Congress of Racial Equality (CORE), the Student Nonviolent Coordinating Committee (SNCC), and Martin Luther King Jr. Protests and uprisings, particularly in the wake of King's assassination, placed significant political pressure on elected officials at all levels. This climate was influential in the passage of the Voting Rights Act, among other significant legislative changes. But as the political scientist Vesla M. Weaver argued in the formidable article "Frontlash: Race and the Development of Punitive Crime Policy," the advances made by racial justice organizers in the 1960s triggered a political "frontlash," which Weaver described as:

> the process by which formerly defeated groups may become dominant issue entrepreneurs in light of the development of a new issue campaign. In the case of criminal justice, several stinging defeats for opponents of civil rights galvanized a

powerful elite countermovement. Aided by two prominent focusing events—crime and riots—issue entrepreneurs articulated a problem in a new, ostensibly unrelated domain—the problem of crime. The same actors who had fought vociferously against civil rights legislation, defeated, shifted the "locus of attack" by injecting crime onto the agenda.[10]

This reactionary frontlash played a significant role in the large-scale expansion of policing and incarceration that would be felt in the years to come.

Despite some liberal shifts in policy during the period, the inception of the war on crime in 1965 by President Lyndon B. Johnson created new avenues for police expansion and a wider presence of the criminal-legal system, as the historian Elizabeth Hinton asserted in *From the War on Poverty to the War on Crime: The Making of Mass Incarceration in America*.[11] Policing became more widespread and more institutionalized than ever before, evolving into an area that politicians would rely on for campaigning. Moreover, beginning in 1965, tough-on-crime initiatives have served as banners under which political actors have lobbied for expanding the US criminal-legal system into a larger and more punitive system centered on punishment and control. Passed in 1965, the Law Enforcement Assistance Act (LEAA) provided a federal funding stream that would take various forms in the coming decades.

At the height of the professionalization occurring in US police departments, President Johnson declared a war on crime. Soon after that declaration, Congress passed the LEAA, which created the first federal funding stream enabling local law enforcement to acquire military-grade gear and hire more officers. The act was made permanent in 1968 with the passage of the Omnibus Crime Control and Safe Streets Act, in part due to the riots of the 1960s in response to structural inequality, systemic racism, and police violence.[12] Over the years, billions of dollars went to local law enforcement agencies so they could acquire more and more forms of technology and equipment for race-class-biased crime control, as well as to protest and riot suppression efforts.[13]

As Hinton found, President Johnson saw local law enforcement officers as the frontline soldiers in the newly declared war on crime and the LEAA as an avenue of new ideas for the future of US policing. Over the years, the professionalization of police and the fortification of police departments through grants from the federal government expanded both the capacity of police to arrest people and their incentives to do so and led to the militarization of US policing.[14] Indeed, consistent with the history of police enforcing racial boundaries and maintaining the racial order, the expanded capacity of police departments enabled the mass arrest and incarceration of Black people and increasingly Latinx people,[15] a legacy that continues today.[16]

Hinton's findings provide invaluable insights into the relationship between policing and social welfare institutions. Her analysis of the war on crime and the war on poverty provides a crucial context for understanding the evolution of policing within the social welfare framework. Hinton's research reveals how, under Lyndon Johnson's administration, the lines between policing and social welfare began to blur. Her findings indicate that Johnson's policies did not just expand the policing system; they also embedded policing within the social welfare state. This intersection is pivotal to understanding how initiatives designed for public welfare have, over time, incorporated elements of surveillance and control, characteristic of policing practices.

The historical intertwining of the war on crime with the war on poverty, as Hinton noted, led to a crucial realization: that efforts to strengthen the social welfare state must be cautious of its potential carceral aspects. This understanding challenges the notion that an enhanced welfare state, in its current form, can be an effective solution to societal issues without addressing its entanglement with carceral systems. Hinton's work also shed light on the broader implications of this entanglement. The integration of policing into social welfare under Johnson's policies demonstrates how the state can co-opt welfare programs, leading to a more carceral approach to social issues. This historical context is crucial for any contemporary discussion on reforming or enhancing social welfare and public services.

To place the changes in policing into further context, one can look to the work of scholars who have examined the origins of the contemporary large-scale criminal-legal system. As mentioned, Vesla M. Weaver argued that the punitive turn in the criminal-legal system can be traced back to 1965, the first year in which Americans considered crime the number one issue of public concern. As Weaver contended, the newfound focus on crime control in legislation was a direct response to the gains of the civil rights movement: politicians, displeased with the gains of Black Americans, took to crime policy to express anti-Black resentment. And as a result of federal and state agendas and newly enacted laws, the US prison population grew exponentially.[17] Police played a critical role in the ballooning of the incarcerated population by heavily enforcing laws about drug crimes and other offenses in predominantly poor, Black, and Latinx communities.

During the 1960s, US police experienced a large-scale increase in their ability to engage in surveillance and policing. Police forces were able to mirror the military through often military-grade equipment and the expansion of police budgets and personnel through federal funding, profit-driven punishment,[18] and reductions to social services spending.[19] In California, police militarization included the onset of special weapons and tactics (SWAT), which began after the Watts riots in 1965. The first significant deployment of SWAT was a raid to look for weapons kept by the Black Panther Party at its headquarters in Los Angeles on December 9, 1969.[20] The incident led to thousands of rounds of ammunition being fired, as the Panthers resisted the authority of the forty-man SWAT team before they stood down. The assault on the BPP headquarters revealed the role of activism and Black resistance to structural inequality in driving police expansion and militarization.

Throughout the 1960s and '70s, local and state elites also relied on the Texas Rangers for political suppression of Mexican Americans' suffrage rights and worked to subvert farmworker movements through similar tactics. Using intimidation, they prevented voter rallies and threatened opposing candidates and their supporters. After organizing resistance, communities pushed back against the Texas Rangers, which ultimately led to greater civil rights for Mexican Americans.[21]

RISING UP AGAINST POLICE VIOLENCE

One of the most intense uprisings in US history began in Newark, New Jersey, on July 12, 1967, after the arrest and brutalization of John William Smith, a Black cabdriver.[22] Smith was pulled over by two white police officers for an alleged traffic violation near the Hayes Homes public housing development. The officers took Smith into custody, assaulted him, and took him to the Fourth Precinct station, where he was further beaten. As news of the arrest and beating spread, a crowd began to form outside the precinct on Seventeenth Avenue in the Central Ward of Newark. False rumors that Smith had been killed in custody fueled the anger of the growing crowd. Some local leaders attempted to calm the situation and were permitted to see Smith to assess his condition. They reported that Smith was alive, but the visible signs of his abuse and the prevailing belief that police were violent and unjust only intensified the community's outrage. The assault of John Smith was the spark to an existing powder keg of frustrations related to racial discrimination, economic inequalities, and police abuse that led to a rebellion.

The response to the rebellion was violence from a combination of local police, state troopers, and the National Guard. That revealed a militarized approach that moved beyond local police in military gear to actually include the military. Their tactics, which included the use of rifles and tanks, further inflamed tensions. By the time the uprising ended, twenty-six people had been killed and more than seven hundred injured. Most of the dead and injured were Black civilians killed or wounded by police officers, state troopers, or national guardsmen. Although in the aftermath, politicians and police leaders promised to foster stronger relations between the police and the community, highly militarized strategies had been established and had set the stage for heightened tensions between police and the Newark community for decades to come. Over the next six days, the city was plunged into a state of rebellion as anger boiled over.

In 1959, the NYPD created the Tactical Patrol Force (TPF), which played a prominent role in suppressing dissent during the Stonewall riots in 1969. After the Stonewall Inn, a gay bar in Greenwich Village, was raided on June 28, 1969, protests and demonstrations broke out in response to the police's brutal raid of the venue. On the second night, the TPF was brought in to help suppress the riots. The TPF was characterized by its use of military-inspired equipment, such as riot control helmets and long, menacing batons, as well as its particularly assertive methods of crowd management. Those aggressive tactics inflamed the protestors, leading to more days of dissent. The militarized response to the Stonewall riots showcased the intense militarized turn in New York City.[23]

President Johnson's war on crime and the passage of the 1965 Law

Enforcement Assistance Act expanded the push to empower local law enforcement by legitimating the police as stewards of public safety. The 1965 Law Enforcement Assistance Act (LEAA) authorized the US attorney general to make grants for the training and expansion of state and local law enforcement personnel.[24] As the president told Congress in 1966, "The front-line soldier in the war on crime is the local law enforcement officer." The LEAA subsequently created the first federal funding stream for local policing efforts.[25] At the height of an era that professionalized policing, Johnson's financial support and valorization of local police reinforced a paradigmatic shift toward the public perception that local law enforcement was the only legitimate guardian of public safety.

The coming decades would set the stage for the mass incarceration and policing of today. The emergence of police strategies out of Johnson's war on crime that were specifically aimed at violently policing and punishing Black people, poor people, and marginalized communities had widespread consequences.[26] Those criminal-legal efforts included the war on drugs, the war on gangs, and the increasingly draconian punishment of poverty, homelessness, and occupations such as sex work. During the 1960s, a large number of the urban rebellions that rocked the nation were directly prompted by incidents of police brutality.[27]

The Counterintelligence Program, or COINTELPRO, was a covert initiative begun and led by the Federal Bureau of Investigation (FBI). The program officially existed from 1956 until 1971. Its aim was to monitor, infiltrate, disparage, and disrupt domestic political groups that the FBI identified as subversive. The program was launched by FBI director J. Edgar Hoover. A range of organizations and individuals fell under its purview, from members of the Communist Party USA, who sought to challenge capitalism, to eminent civil rights leaders such as Martin Luther King Jr.; the Black Panther Party, which sought freedom and liberation; protestors against the Vietnam War; and other political activists considered disruptive to the status quo.

COINTELPRO used strategies such as surveillance, the planting of agents and informers within targeted groups, harassment, defamation campaigns, and, in some instances, the inciting of violence.[28] The FBI often coordinated its activities with local law enforcement agencies across the country. A group of activists broke into an FBI office in Media, Pennsylvania, in 1971 and exposed COINTELPRO through documents they seized, which were later given to the press. That sparked widespread anger and led to an investigation by a US Senate group overseen by Senator Frank Church, known as the Church Committee.[29] The committee further exposed COINTELPRO's brutal activities and abuse of political activists and organizations. COINTELPRO was officially ended in 1971, but its legacy would be carried on through the activities of law enforcement agencies in the years to come. The memory of COINTELPRO serves as a stark illuminator of the extent to which domestic surveillance, counterintelligence, and warfare tactics can repress generations of activists and activist organizations.

One notable case of COINTELPRO's violent suppression of Black activists was the case of Fred Hampton, who was murdered in his home during a raid conducted by the Chicago Police Department and the FBI.[30] Hampton was a prominent activist and deputy chairman of the Illinois chapter of the Black Panther Party. He had been born in Summit, Illinois, and quickly rose to leadership positions in the BPP due to his charisma, organizing skills, and commitment to Black communities. Hampton, who was a socialist, was especially skilled in building multiracial alliances, notably the Rainbow Coalition, which included groups such as the Young Patriots Organization, whose members were white activists, and the Young Lords, composed of Latinx activists. Hampton's ability to unite various groups with a commitment to social transformation was perceived as a significant threat by law enforcement and led to his being targeted and murdered along with another BPP member, Mark Clark. Fred Hampton's fiancée, Deborah Johnson, now known as Akua Njeri, was in the apartment when the raid and assassination occurred. At the time, she was eight and a half months pregnant with their son, Fred Hampton Jr. Njeri was in the bed next to Hampton when the shooting took place and has recounted the traumatic experience of that night, including the fact that officers forced her out of the bedroom after Hampton had been shot.[31]

During that period, COINTELPRO also set its aims on dismantling the American Indian Movement (AIM) through coercive violence.[32] The American Indian Movement, which emerged in the late 1960s, sought to address issues of sovereignty, treaty rights, and police brutality against Native Americans. As AIM gained momentum, drawing national attention to the plight of Indigenous peoples in the United States, it also attracted the scrutiny of COINTELPRO. The FBI, viewing the movement as a threat to the existing social order, employed a range of covert operations to undermine AIM's efforts.

Those operations included disinformation campaigns, infiltration of the movement to sow discord and suspicion, and overt acts of coercion and violence.[33] Notable among them was the FBI's involvement in the 1973 siege at Wounded Knee when AIM members occupied the town of Wounded Knee, South Dakota, in protest against both the US government and tribal leadership. The standoff, which lasted for several months, resulted in numerous casualties and arrests and highlighted the extent of state-sponsored aggression toward Indigenous activists.

The targeting of AIM by COINTELPRO exemplifies the program's broader strategy of suppressing movements advocating for social change and civil rights, particularly those representing marginalized communities. By disrupting and discrediting AIM, COINTELPRO not only sought to dismantle the movement but also aimed to silence a critical voice in the struggle for Native American rights.

During that period, many other activists were jailed, injured, and killed by local, state, and federal law enforcement. COINTELPRO and related initiatives during the time, such as the Prison Activists Surveillance Program (PRISACTS),[34] reveal that the focus and function of policing and the carceral system throughout the period were to depoliticize and suppress anyone who posed a threat to the status quo.

The confluence of police repression, systemic injustice, and widespread political dissent created a number of watershed moments. During the 1960s, a number of uprisings and rebellions were sparked by police violence in addition to the uprisings previously mentioned, leading to increased attention to the issues. These included:

1. The Harlem riot of 1964: This riot erupted in New York City in July 1964 following the fatal shooting of James Powell, a Black teenager, by a white police officer. The incident sparked protests against police violence and racial inequality.

2. The 1964 Columbia Avenue riot: This uprising erupted in Philadelphia in August 1964 following the violent arrest of Odessa Bradford, a Black woman, amid escalating tensions over police

violence. Subsequent false rumors that police had beaten a pregnant Black woman to death further fueled unrest.

3. The Hough riots: The Hough neighborhood of Cleveland witnessed a series of uprisings in July 1966 following incidents of police brutality against Black residents. The riots exposed deep-seated racial tensions and socioeconomic subjugation in Cleveland.

4. The Detroit riot: Also known as the Twelfth Street riot, this erupted in July 1967 following a police raid at an unlicensed bar. The uprising lasted five days and led to the deployment of the National Guard.

The uprisings were significant moments of social unrest and resistance against police violence and systemic racism during the 1960s.[35] Mainstream media framed the events as irrational and violent, with limited scrutiny of the structural realities that had given rise to what were actually uprisings and rebellions. While the uprisings brought widespread attention to the immediate incidents that had caused them, such as accounts of police brutality or killing, the attention did not stop police violence. As they occurred, police, at times alongside the military, responded with heightened violence.

Beyond that, in the aftermath of uprisings, rather than addressing the underlying issues, governments used them to justify the expansion of police capacity and technology. The 1968 Kerner Commission report, officially titled *Report of the National Advisory Commission on Civil Disorders*, was a significant study conducted in response to the widespread racial unrest and riots that occurred across the United States during the 1960s. President Johnson established the commission in 1967, directing it to investigate the root causes of the unrest and propose solutions to racial tensions and inequality.

The best-selling report concluded that the riots were primarily a result of deep-rooted racial discrimination and social inequality in US society. It highlighted critical issues such as police brutality, poverty, limited economic opportunities, segregated housing, and inadequate education as central factors. The Kerner Commission report put forth several noteworthy recommendations, calling for investment in job creation, training programs, and efforts to improve housing opportunities. It emphasized the importance of enhancing educational opportunities and advocated for community-based policing. Those proposals addressed the underlying systemic problem and promoted opportunity structures for Black communities. But policing continued to expand, while structural problems were not addressed. This points to the state prioritization of social control over meaningful social transformation. Police focus on race-class control, and as a result, underlying problems can be deprioritized and go unaddressed. But the rebellions continued. As Martin Luther King Jr. stated:

> A riot is the language of the unheard. And what is it that America has failed to hear? It has failed to hear that the promises of freedom and justice have not been met. And it has failed to hear that large segments of white society are more concerned about tranquility and the status quo than about justice, equality, and humanity . . . as long as America postpones justice, we stand in the position of having these recurrences of violence and riots over and over again.[36]

Although the Kerner Commission report was initially well received, the implementation of its recommendations faced significant challenges. The report also recommended increasing police capacity in the form of militarization to prevent and quell future uprisings, as well as surveillance tools and counterinsurgency-inspired police technology. Governments were not invested in ending patterns of systemic inequality and racial oppression that had existed since the advent of the American colonies. At a watershed moment in history, governments had the opportunity to invest in communities as a pathway forward but chose to expand policing and police technology, further cementing systemic inequality and the inherent problems of policing, especially in race-class-subjugated communities. The large-scale expansion of policing also paved the way for expanding police industry markets, where private companies would come to benefit from making profit by supplying police with technology, equipment, and services. This is true especially in times of protest over police violence.[37]

A key factor in the ongoing public acceptance of policing lies in its adaptive response following societal upheaval. Postrevolt, police systems often undergo transformations, giving the impression that they are becoming more inclusive. This perceived inclusivity aims to extend the perception of being "worthy of protection" to a broader segment of society. However, for marginalized groups, this extended status is often conditional and precarious. The reality is that the state, and by extension its policing institutions, has proven that it does not genuinely prioritize the well-being of the most marginalized people, despite claims to the contrary.

The functions and structures of policing are not inherently designed to ensure safety for all members of society. Rather, these reforms are often symbolic gestures. The core of police reform is predominantly about maintaining appearances. It projects the illusion that the scope of those considered worthy of protection is widening. In reality, this expansion either is symbolic or serves as a form of placation. True safety, which encompasses the needs and concerns of all societal members, particularly the most vulnerable, remains unachieved.

Supreme Court rulings have also granted protection for and expanded power to the police, specifically during their interactions with the public. Qualified immunity—a legal doctrine in US law that shields law enforcement and other government officials from being held personally liable for actions conducted within their official capacity unless the actions violate "clearly established" state and federal laws or constitutional rights—first emerged during the trial *Pierson v. Ray* (1967). The Supreme Court established it with the rationale of protecting law enforcement officials from lawsuits and financial liability in cases where they had acted in supposed good faith. In 1968, the Supreme Court ruled in *Terry v. Ohio* that police could perform a "limited search" on a person for weapons if they had reasonable suspicion that the person might be involved in criminal activity and pose a threat to the officer. That ruling would pave the way for millions of violating, racially discriminatory searches across the country in the decades to come,[38] which very rarely led to police finding weapons. Subjugated communities started to organize against police violence through copwatch initiatives, policy battles, protests, and neighborhood patrols, all while the same communities had few resources to carry them out.

The formation of the Black Panther Party and its armed copwatch patrols, which started in 1966 with BPP members monitoring the behavior of officers of the Oakland Police Department, marked a turn toward a different form of organizing for safety from police violence.[39] The BPP decided to combat police violence through patrolling neighborhoods, monitoring police-community interactions, and disrupting police brutality and injustice. As the party declared in its Ten-Point Program, a policy platform and set of guidelines, "7. We Want an Immediate End to Police Brutality and Murder of Black People. We believe we can end police brutality in our Black community by organizing Black self-defense groups that are dedicated to defending our Black community from racist police oppression and brutality."

At the same time, they were organizing survival programs to ensure that the communities they'd emerged from had resources and institutions to decrease precarity and increase stability.[40] Those programs included free breakfast programs for children and community pantries; free health clinics and ambulance initiatives; free clothes, furniture, and transportation programs; and Liberation Schools—free, alternative schools for Black youths that aimed to address educational disparities and promote empowerment in Black communities.[41]

Collectively, those initiatives—along with the broader revolutionary aims of the Party—were meant to transform social and material conditions for Black people across the country. Importantly, in its Ten-Point Program, the BPP declared, "We want an immediate end to police brutality and murder of Black people." Along with that, the BPP demanded full employment, an end to capitalist exploitation, dignified housing, education that includes the true history of the United States, just housing, and an end to wars of aggression, among other things. The BPP also stated, "8. We Want Freedom for All Black Men Held in Federal, State, County, and City Prisons and Jails," as well as "9. We Want All Black People When Brought to Trial to Be Tried in Court by a Jury of Their Peer Group or People from Their Black Communities, as Defined by the Constitution of the United States." The power of this approach made the BPP a target of COINTELPRO and violent police repression.

On the subject of police suppression and the Black Panther Party, one can also look to the violent repression of the BPP and to the gun control laws that spread after the Black Panthers staged a protest at the California state capitol in 1967. The protest was in response to a proposed bill to outlaw open carry, sparked by fears of armed Black Panther patrols in Oakland, which had been organized to prevent police violence.[42] Later in 1967, Governor Ronald Reagan signed the Mulford Act, which had been passed by the legislature, banning open carry and therefore armed Black Panther patrols and protests.[43] In the years to come, the police would violently raid the homes and meeting places of Panthers—including in LA, where the first significant SWAT raid in the United States was used to search a BPP headquarters for weapons. SWAT raids have been targeting Black communities ever since.[44]

THE CREATION OF 911

The national emergency response number—911—didn't always exist. It's actually a fairly recent development. The now-widespread emergency response number was created in 1968. The idea for a centralized dispatch for fire emergencies was advanced in 1957 by the International Association of Fire Chiefs. In 1966, the National Academy of Sciences suggested that a single emergency number could lead to quicker responses to injuries and prevent accidental and unnecessary deaths. A few years later, police officials began advocating for a centralized dispatch number. In 1967, the Kerner Commission report, in its "Supplement on the Control of Disorder," recommended a single number for all emergency situations to prevent future riots. By 1968, the chosen number was 911, and AT&T began rolling it out across the United States. The focus on riot control and disorder became the force which drove the ultimate creation of 911.[45] The "Supplement on Control of Disorder" from the Kerner report, which was not usually included in public versions, emphasized the aggressive militarization of policing, undercover operations within Black communities, and strategies to repress dissent.

Up until 1987, only 50 percent of the US population had access to the 911 emergency number.[46] The widespread use of 911 as we know it today has existed for only the past twenty years, but it fundamentally shapes how we understand and relate to emergency response. In many Black neighborhoods, the problem of policing extends to 911, as it is the primary line of communication to law enforcement and is deeply associated with the police. People who need emergency assistance but fear involving the police may not call the number.

The 911 emergency number has roots in racism. As Katrina Feldkamp and S. Rebecca Neusteter wrote:

> The crucible of the 911 system itself was the racist white response against Black Americans' demands for equality during the Johnson

administration, inflamed by President Richard Nixon's successful 1968 law-and-order election campaign.…

White America rejected the recommendations of the Kerner Report and decades-old demands from countless community leaders to confront the racism and poverty at the roots of American society. Instead, they chose to expand law enforcement's capacity to suppress Black communities' demands for dignity and equality. Our 911 system is a direct result of that choice.[47]

In addition to its general findings about racism in America, the Kerner Commission report declared that the police, rather than private citizens, often escalated and incited reactions. In their article on 911, Feldkamp and Neusteter noted that the commission's internal conflicts were clear. The commission's executive director, David Ginsburg, fired 120 staffers who found that the riots were a logical response to racism.[48] While some of its recommendations focused on change as a mechanism of addressing the underlying problems, other recommendations focused on increasing police capacity and resources to prevent and repress unrest.

Arnold Sagalyn, who had an extensive background in policing and studied police and military strategies globally, was the commission's associate director for public safety.[49] Sagalyn advanced the idea of a universal emergency services number similar to one initiated by the US government in Venezuela in 1963 for counterinsurgency efforts and to suppress dissent. That led to discussions among Sagalyn, the Federal Communications Commission (FCC), and AT&T, which culminated in the current 911 system.[50]

There had been prior initiatives to establish a universal number, but the concept gained significant traction after the Kerner Commission endorsed it. In 1968, President Johnson also advanced the 911 system as a remedy for slow emergency response times and as a tool for alleged crime fighting. He steamrollered ahead, advocating for expanding police capacity through the 911 system. That culminated in the ceremonial debut of 911 on February 16, 1968, in the small town of Haleyville, Alabama, when the Alabama speaker of the house Rankin Fite made the first call to 911. The call was received by US representative Tom Bevill on a distinctive red phone at the Haleyville police station. Eugene "Bull" Connor, the Alabama Public Service Commission president, who had violently suppressed civil rights and was explicitly racist, took part in the launch ceremony and is featured in a photo from the ceremonial call, sitting next to Bevill.[51] As Feldkamp and Neusteter noted, "Five years prior and 65 miles southeast during a protest by the Birmingham Children's Crusade against segregation, Connor conducted mass arrests of Black children and unleashed police dogs, fire hoses and officers with clubs."

New York City was the first major city to adopt the system of the nationwide 911 number, and after its adoption, calls spiked—most of them unrelated to emergencies. Still, police deployment increased by nearly 7.5 percent in New York City.[52] Interestingly, while it was adopted more readily in smaller towns and suburbs, many large cities resisted the emergency response number, as police and fire officials claimed that they wanted a direct line to callers.[53] As reported by the *New York Times*, "During the first nine months of 1969, the public dialed the emergency number 4,884,750 times, an average of 17,000 times per day. This is a 17% increase over the previous period in 1968."[54] The NYPD received more calls than it could handle and requested that people keep calls "brief, explicit and calm" and call the precinct's "local administrative numbers" for nonemergencies.[55] This points to the fact that while people may have needed someone to call, police were presented as the primary option for a range of issues, which police and politicians would then use as a justification for police expansion.

The Kerner Commission's mention of racism as a motivator of unrest and the need for systemic change led to a backlash. President Johnson, yielding to political pressure, distanced himself from the report and its more critical findings. The unrest following the assassination of Martin Luther King Jr. in 1968 led to a wave of uprisings and rebellions,[56] contributing to the frontlash described by Vesla M. Weaver. Establishing 911 and expanding police power, not making systemic changes, were the priorities. That reality was consistent with the prioritization of the war on crime rather than the war on poverty, which Elizabeth Hinton detailed in *From the War on Poverty to the War on Crime*.[57]

RICHARD NIXON, THE WAR ON DRUGS, AND REAGANOMICS, 1970S–1980S

The 1970s ushered in a new era with the presidency of Richard Nixon. The conservative leader amplified the rhetoric against drugs and crime, often using coded and explicit language to disproportionately target Black communities, most notably references to "law and order" as a way to refer to controlling Black communities. The war on drugs, despite some of Nixon's more liberal policies, led to unprecedented militarization, focusing on drug use and sale among disadvantaged populations while largely ignoring drug use among the wealthy and white populations. The war on drugs not only increased police power in terms of resources and ideological justification but also fueled condemnation of Black communities. As a result, the growth of punishment and policing accelerated when President Nixon declared the war on drugs.[58] As anti-Black hysteria regarding crack peaked in the mid-1980s, the perceived need to police Black communities with military-grade equipment was further justified. That period also marked a peak in documented violence and harm across the United States, making violence — and by association, drugs — central issues.

Anti-Black sentiments fundamentally framed policing and punishment as solutions to homelessness, poverty, drug use, housing insecurity, mental health problems, and interpersonal/communal violence; consequently, the expansion of and increased funding for policing tore at the social fabric of Black communities and in many cases worsened social conditions.[59] Nixon's administration continued to channel hundreds of millions of dollars to local law enforcement in the name of curbing drug use and distribution.

While Nixon launched the war on drugs officially in June 1971, the United States has used drug laws to selectively target specific communities for more than a century.[60] In the 1870s, Chinese immigrants were targeted by antiopium laws, despite the fact that opium was being used by whites as well.[61] Throughout the 1910s and 1920s, Mexican Americans and migrants were targeted by anticannabis laws in the Midwest and Southwest.[62] John Ehrlichman, a top Nixon aide, stated the racist nature of the war on drugs plainly in a 1994 interview:

The Nixon campaign in 1968, and the Nixon White House after that, had two enemies: the antiwar left and black people. You understand what I'm saying? We knew we couldn't make it illegal to be either against the war or black, but by getting the public to associate the hippies with marijuana and blacks with heroin, and then criminalizing both heavily, we could disrupt those communities.

We could arrest their leaders, raid their homes, break up their meetings, and vilify them night after night on the evening news. Did we
know we were lying about the drugs? Of course we did.[63]

In *The New Jim Crow: Mass Incarceration in the Age of Colorblindness*, Michelle Alexander explores the profound racial disparities in the
criminal-legal system, which spiked during the war on drugs, highlighting
that although Black and Latinx Americans were arrested for drug offenses at
significantly higher rates than their white counterparts, there is no evidence
to suggest they engaged in drug use or sales more frequently than other
racial or ethnic groups. In fact, Alexander highlighted the fact that white
Americans were more likely to use and sell drugs than Black Americans.[64]
This points to clear racial discrimination, whereby Black and Latinx populations are targeted by police and the criminal-legal system. The war on
drugs both reinforced the criminalization of Black people and, in practice,
disproportionately targeted Black and other racially marginalized and poor
communities, facilitating the mass incarceration of large numbers of Black
and Latinx people.[65]

During the 1970s and onward, police developed and expanded tools
such as hot-spot and problem-oriented policing (which rely on data that is
perceived to be unbiased to direct heightened police presence and attention), stop-question-frisk (which allow police to make discretionary
decisions—often shaped by discriminatory logics—about stopping, ques-
tioning, and frisking individuals), investigatory traffic stops, surveillance
devices such as wiretaps, and police tactics driven by the use of data analytics as
new standards. The 1970s marked shifts in policing strategies influenced by
changing social conditions and widespread political resistance. During that
period, politicians also continued the widespread police expansion that had
begun in the 1960s. Resistance to police violence also continued, including
the Camden riot of 1971, which erupted in August 1971, sparked by the
death of Rafael Rodriguez Gonzalez during a traffic stop in Camden, New
Jersey.[66] The police killing of Gonzalez fueled tensions in Camden's Puerto
Rican community, especially after the mayor took no action against the
officers. Days of rebellion ensued. The uprising underscored deeper issues of
unemployment, discrimination, and police abuse in the city.

The war on drugs had large-scale effects on policing practices and communities across the United States. The implementation of aggressive tactics, such as explicit racial profiling, no-knock raids, and asset forfeiture—where police seize control of funds associated with criminal activity to reuse in other ways—resulted in heightened tensions within Black and Latinx communities. The war on drugs, like the preceding war on crime, ushered in widespread police expansion and draconian strategies.

Some scholars of policing argue that beginning in the late 1970s, in large part due to the social upheavals of the 1960s and 1970s and the limits of existing policing strategies, there was a transition to the community-policing, problem-solving era in which police sought to engage populations in ways that enhance legitimacy and solve problems.[67] Despite the continuing commitment of many police departments, there is little evidence that these police practices have reduced crime or improved community-police relations.[68] In fact, while some scholars still remain relatively optimistic about the future of community policing for subjugated communities,[69] police stops and arrests occurred more and more as the years went on, and instances of police misconduct and excessive uses of force continue to this day. The new equipment and technology provided by the federal government in the 1960s and '70s allowed police to surveil and arrest people at much greater rates as they served as "front-line soldiers" in the war on crime, according to former President Johnson, and played a pivotal role in the creation of the modern police and carceral state. Commitments to community policing are a symbolic public relations strategy by politicians and police leaders and forces to manage questions of legitimacy while police continue to engage in various forms of violence.

During the 1970s, policing took two notable pathways. On the one hand, traditional draconian policing practices continued. But as a result of protests and uprisings, reformers sought to introduce a softer face of policing in the form of community policing and diversity efforts. The aim of those efforts was to make police appear not as violence workers of the United States but as nicer, more procedurally just cops who reflected and respected the communities they policed. The interplay of those two faces of policing—draconian, heavy-handed law enforcement and purportedly community-driven, nice cops—set the future of policing and police expansion for the decades to come. Importantly, the focus on community, representation, and trust created a veneer for the heavy-handed violence of policing and the actual functions of policing overall. Those efforts were supported by massive public relations and marketing efforts by politicians, police leaders, and police societies that helped law enforcement rebrand itself and conceal its core functions as reform efforts had done in previous periods, such as the initial reform era. The history of reform showcases that politicians and police leaders offer promises of change in moments of unbridled dissent as a strategy to quell anger. In the end, these promises have led to reforms that often expand police power, albeit in more subtle and concealed ways.

In the 1970s, there were further investigations into policing practices, which led to revelations of deep-seated corruption within police departments. One notable case was the Knapp Commission. Established in response to widespread allegations, this commission exposed the extent of corruption in the New York City Police Department (NYPD). Its findings, released in 1972, disclosed a culture of corruption that had permeated the police force. Officers were found to be accepting bribes to overlook criminalized activities, providing protection for illegal operations such as gambling and drug trafficking, colluding with organized crime networks, and even partaking in police-led robbery and extortion. The exposure of such corruption by the Knapp Commission in the 1970s was a watershed moment, shedding light on the systemic nature of police misconduct. However, discussions on reform often ignore the systemic roots of such corruption, focusing instead on individual accountability and procedural changes.

The policing of children has also intensified globally since the 1930s, particularly for working-class youths.[70] In the mid-1900s, US police further immersed themselves in the lives of children through police athletic leagues, criminal laws, traffic safety, curfew laws, and other initiatives and approaches.[71] The Officer Friendly program was a notable public relations initiative in the United States from the 1960s to the 1980s, designed to develop relationships between children and law enforcement.[72] A police officer, usually in full uniform, would visit classrooms and give presentations about safety and the role of the police. This officer, referred to as "Officer Friendly," was supposed to represent a protective, service-oriented aspect of policing. The officer would often engage with the children and sometimes gave them coloring books, stickers, or other interactive materials. Research has shown that the intervention had no impact on how Black children perceived or interacted with police but did have some impact on developing more favorable atti-tudes toward police for white children.[73]

The Officer Friendly program spread nationwide. It was one of the first and largest public relations police campaigns. Since then, a continued flow of community-oriented public relations campaigns and strategies has been employed by police to shape public perceptions of law enforcement. In 1974, the Sears-Roebuck Foundation partnered with John H. Coleman Jr. who worked at the Hampton, Virginia, police department, and Hampton City Schools to revise the program. They developed new classroom kits that included coloring books, videos, board games, and teaching guides.[74] The coloring books were filled with illustrations of officers assisting people, managing traffic, and engaging in community service. As children colored the pages in the books, they were socialized to the presented roles of police. The kits also contained short educational videos. The clips portrayed a tai-lored view of a day in the life of a cop, highlighted the tools they used, and showed scenarios of police helping communities. The board games revolved around the theme of collaboration between the police and a com-munity. In the games, children could assume roles such as cop, firefighter, or community member. The games focused on having the youths work to address concerns within communities that centered around police involve-ment. Last, the teaching guides helped teachers and educators design their own pro-police lessons. They focused on safety within communities, the portrayed role of police, and promoting police-inspired forms of teamwork. Educators were equipped with lesson plans, discussion questions, and activ-ities, all tailored to create conversations that would create a positive view of police.[75] The newly revised classroom kits were given to at least forty school districts in the United States. Similar initiatives during the period and in the coming decades included police athletic leagues and Drug Abuse Resis-tance Education (D.A.R.E.). Those initiatives revealed the intense focus of police on brand identity management and public relations efforts, per-formed within the framework of community-oriented policing.

RONALD REAGAN'S AMERICA

The 1980s were a tumultuous period in US history. They included tumult caused by policing. The war on drugs, begun by Richard Nixon, was expanded throughout the 1980s with grave impacts. The emergence of crack cocaine and the related anti-Black hysteria also fanned the flames and contributed to police expansion.[76] The disintegration of any semblance of a safety net was also under way during Ronald Reagan's presidency. Reagan ushered in a range of market-based policies that would further chip away at social welfare programs, lessen economic opportunity structures for low-income workers, and create a powder keg that could blow at any time into rebellion within many communities. Even more, communities were reeling from the violence and destruction committed by local, state, and federal law enforcement toward political organizations. COINTELPRO left a number of Black communities dealing with the aftermath and trauma of targeted warfare by the state.

In the 1980s, the war on drugs reached its peak under President Reagan because of the anti-Black hysteria about the use of crack cocaine, fueled by the platforms of both the Democratic and Republican parties. The hysteria drove even more government funds to local police, who were pressured to expand arrests to demonstrate success and justify these new budgets.[77] Under the guise of the war on drugs, police militarization and expansion hurt Black and Latinx communities, with no-knock raids—when police would break in and raid a house without knocking or making any announcement—drug sweeps, and an increased police presence replacing much-needed resources and support. Those aggressive tactics fractured the social fabric and deeply affected individuals, families, and entire communities.

The continued expansion of prisons and punitive criminal laws along with the large-scale growth in policing led to the start of mass incarceration. The United States has the highest incarceration rates of any country in the entire world, and there is a reason why: during the latter half of the twentieth century, all levels of government invested intensely in policing, prisons, and the criminal-legal system. That expansion enabled the policing, imprisonment, and correctional control of millions of people living in America.

It bears highlighting that regardless of the reasons for police expansion at various periods, it was not confined to whatever the original justification had been. As policing expanded, law enforcement was given a large degree of latitude. For this reason, expansions in policing in response to any particular issue led to a larger capacity by police to engage in all other forms of policing. As Reagan's policies deepened economic disparities and inequality, policing increasingly served as a tool for managing social fallout, with law enforcement extending into areas that required community resources and investment. During this era and the decades to come, qualified immunity doctrines were strengthened, providing broad leeway for police actions under the guise of legal protection, continuing to empower and embolden police forces nationally.

Reagan, with his widespread conservative, market-driven policies—often referred to as Reaganomics—continued Nixon's slashing of social welfare programs. In part due to the weakening of social safety nets, dispossessed communities experienced high rates of poverty and diminishing economic opportunities. Structural racial inequality had already led to limited opportunities, and as industrial jobs were globalized, Black and other disadvantaged communities had even fewer possibilities. Even more, as drugs were imported into the United States at high rates, people had the ability to make a living at or otherwise engage in harmful practices within their community. If those communities had been provided with resources and opportunities, outcomes might have been different. But unbridled expansion of policing and incarceration at a time when communities were experiencing the aftermath of political warfare and high rates of poverty contributed to the sparks of violence within communities.

As in previous eras, the 1980s saw a range of political activism that police also sought to suppress. Those movements included the tail end of the Black Arts and Black Power movements, LGBTQ+ justice organizing, including the Stonewall Riots that led to the annual Pride parades, and the push for nuclear disarmament. With their expanded capacity, numbers, and technologies, police continued to respond with surveillance, infiltration, and repression of those movements. As discussed by the anthropologist Orisanmi Burton in his book *Tip of the Spear: Black Radicalism, Prison Repression, and the Long Attica Revolt,* one result of the mass repression and incarceration of organizers and radical activists was the politicizing of many people incarcerated in prisons.[78] Those people would politicize other incarcerated people, which led to efforts to repress growing political beliefs and dissent.

Forms of violence such as shootings and assaults peaked within race-class-subjugated communities throughout the 1970s and 1980s. Although those problems were attributed by governments and politicians to drugs, underlying the tumultuous period were legacies of racial inequality, state violence, and heightened precarity. In response, governments used police to address social issues, which often made the issues worse. Mass policing and incarceration didn't stop the various forms of harm and violence within communities; rather, they displaced the problems to prisons or temporarily held them off. But they surely did not lead to sustainable solutions.

As a result, some communities began to mobilize. The House of Umoja in Philadelphia provided a powerful violence interruption approach that was community based, seemingly lowered violence drastically, and provided communal spaces across the city. Politicians largely defunded, deprioritized, and delegitimized initiatives such as the House of Umoja, which I discuss in further detail in chapter 3.[79] This privileging of policing and the criminal-legal system over Black communities' efforts to address harm directly without prisons or police became a feature of historical recurrence. The prison abolition movement was already under way.[80] Thus, as in other periods, it was not that the growing police state went unchecked; it just bulldozed through dissenting voices.

The interplay between punitive housing policies and the criminal-legal system became clear in the tragic murder of Eleanor Bumpurs on October 29, 1984.[81] Bumpurs was a sixty-six-year-old Black grandmother who lived in public housing in the Bronx. She had been withholding rent due to repair requests that had not been addressed. A psychiatrist said that Bumpurs was "psychotic," and a social services supervisor claimed that the best way to help her would be to evict her and then hospitalize her. When the New York City Housing Authority attempted to evict her, workers told the police that she was mentally ill and requested assistance. Police came and drilled a hole through Bumpurs's lock, saw that she was naked, and broke into her home to evict her. They later alleged that she had been brandishing a knife. One of the officers shot her twice with a shotgun, killing her. The case led to outrage, which was furthered when the officer was acquitted of the murder. The housing authority, social service providers, and health workers all failed Bumpurs. They should have helped her with the nonpunitive resources and support she needed rather than deciding that taking her home away was the best choice, leading to the police murdering her.

The confluence of Reaganomics, the war on drugs, the policing of those threatening the status quo, and notable cases of police violence marked the 1980s. Alongside the growing prison-industrial complex, the ability of the state to engage in violence work and containment skyrocketed. During the 1988 presidential campaign, an independent ad campaign supporting George H. W. Bush used racial fears to generate political support and diminish his Democratic opponent, Massachusetts governor Michael Dukakis. Specifically, the ads featured images of Willie Horton, who was serving a life sentence for murder in Massachusetts. Horton had been released on furlough from prison and had engaged in acts of violence in Maryland. The Willie Horton ads prompted racially coded fears and were used to portray Dukakis, who had been in office at the time Horton was furloughed, as soft on crime. The image drove white voters' anxiety and fear about safety and perpetuated stereotypes about the Black community.[82] The strategy also created a political context that would make the broader public more supportive of punitive laws and policies targeting Black and marginalized communities.

The militarization of local police has facilitated the use of surveillance technologies, such as night vision and stingray military technology, which enable police to capture large swaths of data from a wide net of people. Sponsored by the Department of Homeland Security, Department of Defense, and Department of Justice, these tools have been given to police through programs such as the 1033 Program, which was created in 1989 and provides excess Department of Defense equipment to police agencies across the United States. This has augmented the capacity of police to surveil without much oversight, which has large implications for their ability to violate civil liberties.[83]

Throughout the 1980s and 1990s, the cultural war against social services, particularly those that were seen as disproportionately used by Black people, led to the decline of public housing funding, which led to worsening conditions. Alongside difficult financial times for race-class-subjugated communities that saw a disappearing opportunity structure, violence spread in many cities. The drug war structured policing efforts. As a result, police flooded Black communities in places such as public housing. Federal policies paved the way for draconian enforcement and one-strike rules in public housing. The increasing criminalization of public housing allowed for individuals and their families to be evicted if they committed an expanding list of evictable offenses. It also restricted access to a range of individuals and families that were barred access to public housing by the onset of punitive local, state, and federal housing policies.[84] The divestment of resources from public housing was met with investments in policing and surveillance of public housing, which has led to widespread incarceration and punitive evictions of a range of people who once called public housing their home.[85]

FILLING THE PRISONS: CRIMINALIZATION AND THE INCARCERATION NATION, 1990S

If mass incarceration and policing began to expand in the mid-1900s, they came of age in the 1990s. Incarceration rates peaked in the 1990s, devastating communities and creating a carceral state. As prisons grew, so did policing. Policing, prisons, and the broader criminal-legal system are all linked. Importantly, the criminalization of people and spaces is a key way in which police and politicians justify the policing and imprisonment of communities.[86] The 1990s were a period of intense criminalization and police and prison expansion that targeted Black, Latinx, poor, and other oppressed communities. While the foundation had been laid in the decades before, policing experienced one of the largest periods of emboldening during the punitive tumult of the 1990s.

There were a number of high-profile incidents of police violence during this period. The assault of Rodney King was one moment that highlighted police violence and inequality within Black communities. On March 3, 1991, King, an African American, was brutally assaulted by four Los Angeles Police Department (LAPD) officers following a high-speed car chase. The officers struck him more than fifty times with their batons, kicked him, and shot him with stun guns. A bystander, George Holliday, captured most of the assault on videotape from his balcony. The footage was subsequently broadcast widely on television, triggering international outrage. The officers involved were tried for use of excessive force, but on April 29, 1992, they were acquitted. The acquittal led to what is commonly referred to as the 1992 Los Angeles riots. Over six days, sixty-three people were killed, thousands were injured, and LA residents engaged in a rebellion against policing and systemic inequality. The assault of Rodney King, along with growing police militarization[87] and presence within Black communities, combined with increasing poverty and deprivation, created a powder keg that blew up.

One system that facilitated mass criminalization was zero-tolerance policing, of which "broken windows" policing is the most notable example. The broken windows theory, proposed by James Q. Wilson and George L. Kelling in 1982, encouraged the intense policing of Black and Latinx communities.[88] Kelling and Wilson posited that visible signs of disorder and social decay, such as broken windows, lead to an increase in serious crime.[89] Thus, aggressive order-maintenance policing would signal to potential criminals that the community residents cared about the area and would not tolerate crime, which in Kelling and Wilson's argument would reduce more serious crime in the long run. The strategy was taken up ardently in New York City by Police Commissioner William Bratton in the 1990s and spread to other cities, despite the lack of evidence of its effectiveness, as the scholar Bench Ansfield pointed out in an essay entitled "The Broken Windows of the Bronx: Putting the Theory in Its Place."[90]

The broken windows theory is deeply connected to concepts that were foundations of urban sociology, particularly those related to the idea of "moral zones" as advocated by certain Chicago School sociologists. However, the theory has deeper roots in urban sociology, reflecting narratives about the breakdown of social cohesion and community norms. The theory aligns with the Chicago School's focus on urban environments and social disorganization, particularly the work of sociologists such as Clifford R. Shaw and Henry D. McKay, who developed the social disorganization theory.[91] It extends beyond crime prevention, encompassing broader sociological concerns about maintaining public order and moral standards in communities.

George Kelling was a proponent of police-community initiatives, advocating strategies that involve closer interaction between police and communities as a method of maintaining order.[92] This aspect of Kelling's work reveals the relationship between the velvet glove and iron fist of appeals to the "community" and the emergence of legitimacy policing, which focuses on attempting to appear legitimate through communication strategies and traditionally heavy-handed enforcement.[93] Balancing the two allows for the stabilization of policing, particularly in periods when there is widespread skepticism about the legitimacy of police.

This connection underscores the influence of mainstream urban sociology and the broken windows theory on contemporary policing strategies, offering a comprehensive critique of police-community initiatives and the broader implications of policing models that focus on minor infractions and the enforcement of norms. Such analysis highlights the necessity of a careful reevaluation of these theories, particularly in terms of their impact on shaping policing practices that often prioritize maintaining order over addressing more profound societal challenges. A critical examination of these theories is pivotal for advancing community safety in ways that move beyond policing.

Popular debates around policing often serve as commentaries on the cohesion, norms, and structure of Black communities. These commentaries have long been a part of public discourse in the United States. A critical example of this is *The Moynihan Report* (officially titled *The Negro Family: The Case For National Action*), authored by Daniel Patrick Moynihan in 1965.[94] While this report was ostensibly a study of the Black family, it simultaneously became a commentary on what Moynihan perceived as the breakdown of the Black family, attributing this to antisocial behaviors and poor cultural values being transmitted intergenerationally.

Moynihan's report also delved into issues of "crime" and "deviance" within Black communities, positing that the family structure's disintegration had contributed to these societal problems. This perspective, controversial and widely debated, reflects a broader narrative that links family and social structures within Black communities to broader issues of crime and disorder.

The logic underpinning *The Moynihan Report* finds echoes in the broken windows theory developed by Kelling and Wilson. The theory aligns with Moynihan's views on the Black family and community structures. Both perspectives suggest that visible signs of social disarray, whether in physical environments or in family structures, are precursors of more significant societal issues, including crime.

Incorporating these perspectives into the discussion about policing provides a broader context for understanding how societal narratives about Black communities have influenced policing practices. They highlight a historical trend where aspects of Black community life are scrutinized and often problematized in discussions about crime and policing.

This intersection of sociology, family studies, and criminology in the context of Black communities is crucial for a comprehensive understanding of the complex dynamics at play in debates about policing. It underscores the importance of critically examining these narratives and their role in shaping public and policy perspectives on crime, policing, and societal order within Black communities. The intersection of these areas also reveals why the policing of families and children by child protective services has taken on the form it has, which I discuss in the following chapter.

Challenging the broken windows theory, the sociologists Robert J. Sampson and Stephen W. Raudenbush conducted a study in Chicago. They discovered that the observable signs associated with that conception of disorder were not significant predictors of crime rates, nor were they closely aligned with residents' perceptions of social disorder in their communities. Instead, their research highlighted that the economic and racial context of a neighborhood played a more substantial role in shaping residents' perceptions of disorder. Sampson argued in *Great American City: Chicago and the Enduring Neighborhood Effect* that because of a legacy of stereotypes about Black Americans, there is an almost immediate association between Blackness and disorder, crime, and violence in popular discourse and the public imagination. [95] The conflation of disorder and Blacks as the broken windows theory gained traction explains, in part, the selective overenforcement of Black communities—and the acquisition of military-grade equipment facilitated the process of increasing enforcement. Broken windows policing, in the context of the war on crime and the war on drugs, led to heightened, violent interactions between police and residents, particularly Black, Latinx, and other racially marginalized communities.

As Sampson argued, "Few ideas are more influential than broken windows in the urban policy world, with police crackdowns in numerous cities on elements of social and physical disorder. New York City is the most well-known example of aggressive police tactics to control public incivilities."[96] Thus, while police departments were purportedly committing to community-oriented policing, a theory emerged that advocated the aggressive enforcement of quality-of-life/order-maintenance offenses.[97] Community policing has proven ineffective at lowering measurements of crime,[98] and there is little evidence to suggest that it improves relationships with communities. Rather, it serves as a strategy for local law enforcement to appear more legitimate. In fact, aggressive order maintenance was a key factor in the development of community-oriented policing.[99] Community policing ultimately brought more and more people into contact with police through routine stop-and-frisks and created more extreme instances of wanton police violence.

In 1992, a cluster of structural realities came to a head in the Dominican uprising in Washington Heights in New York City. As historian Pedro A. Regalado noted, the uprising was spurred by the police shooting of twenty-two-year-old José "Kiko" Garcia.[100] Garcia's murder mobilized the Dominican community in Washington Heights. US Attorney for the Southern District of New York Rudolph Giuliani demonized the uprising, which earned him support in his campaign for mayor in 1993. As Regalado made clear, Giuliani's rise to mayor through the criminalizing narratives of the rebellion in response to police violence was consequential for the criminalization of Latinx communities in New York City. Giuliani relied on a law-and-order, tough-on-crime approach while portraying his opponent, Mayor David Dinkins, as being soft on crime and antipolice.[101] The recurring pro-police campaigns by politicians at all levels illustrate the power of the police and the strategies that politicians use to appeal to residents' concerns of safety through a lens of law, order, and pro-police rhetoric. Giuliani would make good on his pro-police platform through facilitating police expansion and discriminatory police strategies in the years to come.

CompStat—short for Compare Stats—was introduced in 1994 by the NYPD as a performance management system.[102] The department held frequent CompStat meetings during which police reviewed crime statistics in various areas to identify patterns and direct resources. CompStat would quickly become used in cities across the country to map out where and when crimes occur. But crime—which can be harmful but is not always so—is largely shaped by what those in power deem as such and what areas are targeted for police attention.[103] It becomes a reinforcing loop, as disadvantaged groups are typically surveilled and policed the most. The data illustrate increased criminalized behaviors wherever the police concentrate their focus, which in turn justify police presence and expansion in those communities.

While there are continued tragic accounts of police violence, particular instances spark outrage and resistance. The tragic murder of Amadou

Diallo on February 4, 1999, was widely reported and prompted protest and outrage. Diallo was a twenty-three-year-old Guinean immigrant who was on his way home from a meal. Four officers, a part of the Street Crime Unit, which would later be disbanded, approached Diallo, stating that they thought he was a suspect in a rape. The officers claimed they thought that Diallo was reaching for a gun and fired forty-one shots, nineteen of which hit Diallo. No gun was found. Diallo had been reaching for his wallet.

The murder prompted widespread protest and activism. Importantly, such moments of protest are not isolated from past or future incidents; they shape and contribute to movement formation. The information shared and the momentum gained often determine the character and nature of future events, especially as the world becomes more linked through news, television, phones, and the internet. The murder of Diallo and the subsequent protests were shaped by past cases of police violence and community protest. They would also serve as a catalyst for protest and rebellion in the years to come.

FIRE FROM ABOVE: THE ROLE OF FEDERAL POLITICS

By the 1990s, the rhetoric around policing was centered on addressing crime and violence. The early 1990s saw high rates of community violence and harm as measured by metrics such as shootings and murders. But toward the middle of the 1990s, the rates of reported violence began to drop. Despite that, the federal government, already fully invested in the process of building up penal and police capacity due to reactionary political work and fearmongering, continued increasing incarceration capacity rates and mass policing. While this took place at all levels of government, the most notable policy to increase policing and punitive incarceration since the Law Enforcement Assistance Act of 1965 was the Violent Crime Control and Law Enforcement Act of 1994.

In response to concerns about Democrats' image of being soft on crime, President Bill Clinton advocated a tough-on-crime platform as a way to build political capital. His adoption of a harsh approach to combating crime is exemplified by his signing of the 1994 crime act—the largest act to expand the criminal-legal system since the LEAA. Clinton touted the number of additional police officers that the legislation put onto the streets through the Community Oriented Policing Services (COPS) program. COPS was a seemingly liberal attempt to better police-community relations and reduce crime, but it flooded Black and other racially marginalized communities with police officers, fueling mass incarceration rather than reducing violence and harm within communities.[104]

Today, police and prison spending takes up hundreds of billions of dollars that could be spent elsewhere, such as in developing the infrastructures of communities and developing nonpunitive alternatives to prisons and policing. The COPS office plays a key role in channeling funds from the federal level down to local and state agencies. President Joe Biden, who was a principal architect of the bill as a senator, has remained committed to the COPS office, citing its success in improving community relations and reducing crime, despite evidence showing that the office has not definitively led to safer communities, has flooded schools and communities with police, and has expanded racist and militaristic policing.[105] The COPS office has channeled over $20 billion since 1994 to efforts they define as advancing community policing.[106]

The influx of federal funds in the mid-to-late twentieth century also created a cascading effect that led city- and state-level governments to join the cry to expand the police. This has all occurred at the expense of public safety, and the 1994 crime act has played an enduring role in the expansion of the carceral state. The bill contributed to a culture of punishment that has devastated Black communities across the country. In 1993, while sponsoring the 1994 crime bill, then senator Biden stated, "We have predators on our streets that society has in fact, in part because of its neglect, created. They are beyond the pale, many of those people, beyond the pale."[107] He continued, "We have no choice but to take them out of society." At least four people are currently on death row and may be executed solely because they committed crimes that were made eligible for the death penalty by Biden's 1994 bill.[108]

Local law enforcement would also experience expanded power to engage in immigration enforcement, especially following the Illegal Immigration Reform and Immigrant Responsibility Act of 1996 (IIRIRA). Police increasingly became involved in immigration enforcement and detention and deportation proceedings. This act included section 287(g), which allowed local police agencies to enter into agreements with Immigration and Customs Enforcement (ICE). Under 287(g), police were authorized to receive training from ICE and became deputized to perform certain immigration enforcement functions. That marked a major shift toward formalizing the involvement of local police in immigration enforcement, revealing the intersections among mass policing, mass incarceration, and mass deportation. After the 1980s, the rise of Black and immigrant populations became a key driver of police budgets.[109]

The 1994 crime act extended prison sentences, helped states build prisons if they adopted truth-in-sentencing policies—those that required people to serve a minimum of 85 percent of their sentence—implemented federal three-strikes laws and mandatory minimum sentences, and flooded already heavily policed communities with a hundred thousand additional officers. Though the prison population was already rising in 1994, the act created a slew of additional incentives that would increase incarceration rates and lengths as well as the policing of Black communities. Notably, the bill provided states that adopted truth-in-sentencing policies with federal funds to build prisons, and many states responded by doing just that.[110] The head of the Civil Rights Division of the Justice Department under President Barack Obama told the *New York Times* that Biden's 1994 act had "created and calcified massive incentives for local jurisdictions to engage in draconian criminal justice practices that had a pretty significant impact in building up the national prison population."[111] The 1994 crime act also expanded the crimes eligible for the death penalty to include sixty additional crimes, including narcotics offenses. As a result, some people were sentenced to death solely because of the 1994 act.[112]

Federal rhetoric and policies shape culture, politics, and public narrative,[113] not just federal laws. The 1994 crime act caused ripple effects[114] on states and cities, which responded by implementing punitive policies and practices in line with the federal tough-on-crime stance.[115] Federal laws affected the commitments and policies of states and cities as mandatory minimums and truth-in-sentencing policies spread to states across the country after the passage of the bill.[116] Not only did the bill aid in accelerating mass incarceration, but it also provided police with more resources to systematically harass, arrest, and brutalize Black communities and other marginalized communities of color through COPS[117]—which Biden has continued to unwaveringly advocate despite a lack of evidence suggesting that it is effective at anything it was allegedly created for.[118] The 1994 crime act helped solidify the obsession with punishment in the United States that is responsible for ruining lives, families, and entire communities.

A long line of Republicans and Democrats alike ardently advocated for draconian punishment that would disproportionately affect marginalized communities of color. While Republican presidents and political leaders advocated for the growth of policing and incarceration from explicitly conservative ideological positions, Democrats did so often to gain political traction against Republicans claiming that Democrats were soft on crime. That climate was peaking at the start of Biden's tenure as chair of the Senate Judiciary Committee in 1988, during the presidential race, when President George H. W. Bush used the case of Willie Horton, a Black man who was charged with sexually assaulting a white woman and stabbing her fiancé, to make his opponent, Michael Dukakis, look soft on crime through racially charged fear-baiting.[119]

The intense carceral climate also contributed to the demolition of public housing, as the sites were deemed inherently criminogenic. HOPE VI, a federal program that paved the way for public housing demolition, became a strategy to address the condemned sites.[120] In addition, punitive one-strike policies across all of public housing would bar people from living in public housing if they had been convicted of certain criminal offenses and mandated background checks and other exclusionary policies. Further, as funding for public housing repairs and upkeep waned, there was a growing investment in policing and targeted punishment.[121] The targeted policing and incarceration of public housing residents puts into sharp relief the role of policing in managing inequality. Rather than investing in public housing and addressing the problems residents were experiencing, governments demolished developments and increased carceral control, surveillance, and policing to manage those that remained.[122]

The intense punitive climate also infiltrated schools. Black and Latinx students were heavily criminalized and punished. The 1994 crime act expanded policing in US schools through the COPS grant office. That collectively fueled in-school punishment, suspensions, expulsions, and arrests on school grounds of young students, particularly Black and Latinx students. That punitive context created the carceral continuum known as the school-to-prison pipeline. Underresourced schools with highly punitive cultures created tracks for young people to be incarcerated within a growing prison system.

Collectively, those developments produced the prison-industrial complex, which the urban theorist Mike Davis conceptualized to showcase how various interests and societal systems rely on policing, imprisonment, and surveillance to tackle our society's social, political, and economic problems.[123] As Davis stated at the founding conference of the abolitionist organization Critical Resistance in 1998, "Each of those prisons is a school or a hospital that will never be built. This California gulag archipelago is more of a direct threat and immediate danger, more of a hazard to the health of the people of California, than the San Andreas Fault. No society since Nazi Germany has built so many prisons in such a short amount of time."[124]

A range of technological advancements also changed policing during the 1990s. DNA databases, surveillance tools, and data-driven policing practices increased. Those tools, supposedly unbiased, expanded the capacity of police to engage in widespread policing and surveillance. The technological advancements of the 1990s also led to new tools that could be used to target particular people and populations for arrest. The proliferation of tools and technology geared toward policing would only increase in the years to come.

POLICING THE TWENTY-FIRST CENTURY

The early 2000s brought a number of changes to policing. The plane-hijacking attacks on September 11, 2001, led to the expansion of policing at all levels as it related to what law enforcement refers to as counterterrorism efforts. Policing and surveillance by entities such as the NYPD targeted wide segments of Muslim and Arabic communities that had nothing to do with the events of that day, revealing historic patterns of widespread discrimination, particularly against marginalized populations. The USA PATRIOT Act—the Uniting and Strengthening America by Providing Appropriate Tools Required to Intercept and Obstruct Terrorism Act of 2001—was enacted on October 26, 2001, by President George W. Bush in response to the September 11 attacks.

The Patriot Act amplified the power and capacity of law enforcement with the stated objective being fighting terrorism. The act paved the way for increased surveillance, including wiretapping, and the accessing of personal records including library histories, medical records, and phone, computer, and bank records. Law enforcement was empowered to bypass judges and constitutional rights through tools such as national security letters and sneak and peeks, which allowed police to get access to various records and search homes and offices without telling the targets of the surveillance. Very few of the searches led to any proof of terrorist activities; most were rather for things such as money laundering, immigration, fraud, and drug-related activity.

In addition to domestic surveillance, the act allowed greater intelligence gathering outside the United States and enabled law enforcement to detain, question, and deport immigrants suspected of terrorism. Since the act was created, civil liberties and constitutional rights groups have objected to its broad, sweeping empowerment of law enforcement. The legislation has been the subject of controversy since its inception due to concerns about its impact on civil liberties and privacy rights. Since 2001, it has undergone several reauthorizations and modifications.[125] In 2003, the Department of Homeland Security (DHS) was founded, and immigration enforcement was divided between ICE and Customs and Border Protection (CBP). The newly founded DHS would have considerable resources for the expansion of border and immigration detention and enforcement. These entities would also collaborate with local and state law enforcement. The formation and expansion of new law enforcement entities was also met with an increase in strategies to police and surveil communities.

In the 2000s and early 2010s, stop-and-frisk, whereby officers stop, question, and pat down people on the street, allegedly based on a reasonable suspicion that they might be involved in criminal activity or in possession of a weapon or illegal substance, was used extensively in New York City and other cities throughout the country. Cops had discretion to determine reasonable suspicion, which meant that police could stop and frisk whoever seemed suspicious to them, which is often motivated by race, class, and gender. Stop-and-frisk was practiced across pronounced racial and class lines. There were such severe patterns of racial discrimination that in 2013 a judge ruled that it was being practiced unconstitutionally.

THE RISE OF TECHNOLOGY AND BIG DATA

Between 2000 and 2010, the emergence of various data and computer systems brought new policing technologies, including the incorporation of data analytics, the monitoring of social media, and facial recognition tools.[126] These technological developments have been funded and advanced collectively by the public, private, and academic sectors.[127] Private companies have accrued massive returns on investments in police technology following high-profile cases of police violence, technology being framed as a means of reform. This technology includes body cameras, "less lethal" weapons, and riot control tools. Building on tools such as CompStat, police also engage in allegedly data-driven approaches that determine where and how police engage in criminal activity.[128]

The digital age has enabled police to engage in discriminatory policing under the guise of being neutral. Since 2010, more tools have emerged, expanding the reach and scale of policing and also following the patterns of the biased systems that produced them. Tools that allow police to spy on phone and computer data, ShotSpotter tools—which summon heavy police presence to places that a device identifies has had a shooting with high levels of inaccuracy—military equipment, and algorithmic tools such as facial and license recognition are now used daily. While these tools are often purchased with money meant for particular purposes, such as counterterrorism, they're used for a wide net of enforcement often unknown to the public. State and federal grants as well as city funding siphoned from other social services fund these tools and have led to increased capacity and expansion among police.

In recent years, "big data" (large quantities of information used to make and study patterns) and advanced surveillance tools have helped police monitor people more closely. This technology-driven approach reinforces patterns of discrimination and leads to a focus on marginalized communities of color.[129] Today, data- and algorithm-driven strategies such as predictive policing, social network analysis, and focused deterrence are seen as racially neutral, but they target communities of color and position punishment and control as answers to social problems created by legacies of white supremacy and capitalism.[130] Moreover, the use of social media to surveil and monitor communities has become increasingly widespread among police.[131] Advances in criminological research that focus on algorithm-driven police tactics, such as focused deterrence, precision policing, and hot-spot policing—all of which rely on the idea of purportedly neutral data analytics to determine lists of people and places to target with heightened police attention—have led to the police use of big data, social network analysis, and geographic analytics.[132] Police maintain a large degree of discretionary control over how these technologies are implemented.[133] They have been used for gang suppression in New York City with little oversight, which violates the rights of communities, casts nets that ensnare people who may not be involved in harmful behaviors, and does not get at the underlying causes of harm and violence within communities.[134] This leads to a continuation of these problems rather than an end to them, as attempts to displace social issues to prisons do not actually address those issues in a sustainable, root cause–focused way.

As social media have proliferated, they have become another means whereby police engage in surveillance, data gathering, and policing. This has led to the widespread arrest and incarceration of individuals and groups who post on social media, even though their posts may not reflect actual incidents of violence.[135] Social network analysis tools are intended to show the networks that people are embedded in. Social network analysis also takes on other forms, including the use of arrest records to see who has been arrested with whom, and is a core component of police-involved gun violence reduction initiatives.

POLICING PROTEST

Since 2010, a number of notable protest movements have either been sparked by or experienced police violence. In particular, policing has been used to quell dissent over economic conditions and exploitation. Most notably, Occupy Wall Street (OWS), inspired by the Arab Spring—a series of protests and uprisings across the Arab world beginning in 2010, driven by demands for political and social transformation—was a protest movement that sprang up in 2011, its participants seeking to combat the economic disparities between the wealthiest 1 percent of Americans and the rest. OWS took place in Zuccotti Park in New York City and was cleared by police after about two months.

Police violence was widespread throughout the OWS movement. Participants, legal monitors, and reporters told of the use of batons and pepper spray, as well as a strategy known as "kettling," a method of crowd control that involves creating large police cordons to confine groups of people. On September 2, 2011, police pepper sprayed a group of protesters who were already encircled by police, leading to attention and criticism. When the movement was cleared from the park on November 15, police also used extensive force and arrests. Many involved in the protests, including legal monitors and reporters, shared accounts of law enforcement officers exerting extreme force. As discussed in chapter 1, a primary driver of police development was the desire to oversee and protect the interests of the wealthy and class elites. The violent police response to the Occupy Wall Street protests showed that this legacy has continued.

A number of high-profile cases of police violence have sparked outrage, protests, and uprisings since 2010. Most notably, significant protests across the country were sparked after the murders of Michael Brown and Eric Garner in 2014 and Breonna Taylor and George Floyd in 2020, during the COVID-19 pandemic. Those moments built the momentum for what organizers and activists would come to call the Movement for Black Lives (M4BL, also commonly referred to as the Black Lives Matter movement) and a movement for transforming public safety through frameworks such as invest-divest and police abolition. While past accounts of police violence typically led to a focus on reform, for the first time in history, the discourse that emerged in 2020 was about reimagining public safety altogether.

The Ferguson, Missouri, uprising following the murder of eighteen-year-old Michael Brown on August 9, 2014, sparked protests and rebellion across the city. The police department responded with military-grade tactical equipment and weapons, which led to national attention to police militarization through initiatives such as the 1033 Program. More recently, the murder of George Floyd by a Minneapolis Police Department officer led to global protests and unrest and to one of the largest social movements in the history of the United States.

Following the murder of Michael Brown, community organizers began to make different demands, particularly for the defunding and abolition of police. Those calls were amplified and took the national stage following the murder of George Floyd. Many were stunned by those demands. But the history of policing reveals continued violence and injustice and the inability of police to be transformed into anything but what they have been from their origin: a tool to manage and control people, particularly dispossessed populations. There was a time without police in the United States. And there can be a future without police.

These shifts have been propelled by organizers who have called for transformation rather than reform. Years before the George Floyd protests, organizations and campaigns such as Safety Beyond Policing in New York City, the #LetUsBreathe Collective in Chicago, Reclaim the Block in Minneapolis, Black Visions Collective in Minneapolis, Defund OPD in Oakland, and the Movement for Black Lives, as well as longtime abolitionist organizers and organizations such as Mariame Kaba and Critical Resistance, had been calling for divestment from policing and investment in communities. The work by organizers launching invest-divest and political development campaigns set the foundation for the nationwide calls for defunding and abolition. Thus, the calls that emerged following the murder of George Floyd did not come without context, as some people felt; they were a product of years of organizing and a refusal of the traditional repackaged reforms.

A significant element underpinning the large-scale evolution of policing is the social construction of crime. Far from being an objective set of rules, a criminal code is deeply intertwined with the sociopolitical structures of the time. Many behaviors codified as criminal are aligned with biases, whether they be racist, classist, sexist, heterosexist, or ethnocentrist. The policies that Presidents Johnson, Nixon, Reagan, and Clinton and other Republicans and Democrats alike advocated for and implemented set the stage for a federal commitment to funding local police departments. Increased spending on policing was often made at the expense of social services such as schools and community programs.[136] Since the 1960s, there has been little evidence to suggest that additional funding has done much to drive down crime or violence.[137] In fact, studies of communities with aggressive enforcement and a hyperconcentration of police found associations with increases in violence, worse health indicators, and adverse educational performance.[138] Governments at all levels have created new threats to safety by failing to develop institutions that address the underlying causes of violence and harm, which are often shaped by legacies of racial and class inequality, instead increasing criminalization, policing, and incarceration.

As a result of the continued investment in policing and the criminal-legal system, police today have an immense amount of power. Since the 1960s, police have been given more power to engage in contact with the public through the criminalization of traffic stops and the emergence of pretextual stops targeting poverty and survival economies, and legislators have passed laws to allow for no-knock and quick-knock warrants such as the one that led to the murder of Breonna Taylor. The rise in power occurred in tandem with rapid increases in police funding: national spending on police rose from $2 billion in 1960 to $16.7 billion in 1980 to $67 billion in 2000 and topped $137 billion in 2018.[139] That expansion of funding over time enabled police to engage in increased surveillance and state-authorized violence. Importantly, public policy since the 1960s also reveals that state violence extends far beyond the criminal-legal system. The unjust welfare system, shaped by divestment in response to anti-Black animus; the criminalization of homelessness and mental illness; defunded public housing; and underresourced schools also form the broader cascade of state violence that structures the lives of Black and other marginalized communities across the United States.

PUBLIC HEALTH AND MOVING BEYOND POLICING

The COVID-19 pandemic, which began in late 2019, ripped through Black, Indigenous, Latinx, and other marginalized communities.[140] Stay-at-home orders were most aggressively enforced in Black communities.[141] As these communities dealt with high levels of transmission,[142] they also had significantly fewer resources to help weather the outbreak, which caused gaping racial disparities in rates of infection and deaths. Poverty and structural inequality were among the biggest risk factors associated with COVID-19. Police pepper spraying couples for allegedly not practicing social distancing,[143] violently dragging people off buses for not wearing masks,[144] and aggressively detaining Black individuals for no justifiable reason without any protective gear caused even more damage to communities already reeling from the devastation of the outbreak.[145] Fears of police violence and harassment made me avoid going outside altogether during the pandemic, even for essentials and mutual aid—a practice where members of a community engage in various forms of solidarity work, such as sharing resources, providing support to those in need, and collectively organizing to ensure the well-being and resilience of the community.

As rates of transmission of the virus among cops increased throughout the country, it was also a matter of public health for them to keep their distance and avoid interactions, yet the violence of policing continued. But it had been a matter of public health before, too, as fewer police interactions mean fewer opportunities for police violence—which has been one of the longest-standing public health emergencies[146] in Black communities throughout history.[147] Abolition is a strategy to address the violence of policing and its implications for public health.[148] Protest has often been the only thing preventing people from dying at the hands of police in silence. Communities were also forced to find new ways of protesting[149] and grieving police violence amid the pandemic.[150]

During the pandemic and after, resources and support were essential,[151] not increased levels of policing.[152] Local and state governments could have intervened by providing free testing and treatment, groceries, clean water, personal protective equipment, shelter for the houseless, cleaning services, permanent rent cancellations and eviction moratoriums, and cash assistance for those being hit the hardest by the outbreak.[153] Skyrocketing unemployment and poverty[154] showcased the need for initiatives such as universal basic income programs and guaranteed housing, as welfare efforts to aid communities were not sufficient. But as the pandemic subsided, most of those temporary efforts were halted. Policing did not solve the COVID-19 pandemic, and it will prove insufficient at solving any other public health emergencies occurring now or in the future. We need to move beyond policing.

Some jurisdictions minimized police contact and interactions for a time during the height of the pandemic.[155] Hopefully, in light of the pandemic, we can move closer to reducing police contact and investing resources in developing community-based approaches to conflict, harm, violence, and public health mandates. In light of what Ruth Wilson Gilmore has called "organized abandonment" by governing institutions,[156] compelling mutual aid organizing, based on mutual solidarity and political commitments rather than traditional models of service, sprang up during the pandemic to show the power of community care. Dean Spade discussed that organizing and the importance of mutual solidarity approaches in building communities of care in *Mutual Aid: Building Solidarity during This Crisis (and the Next)*.[157] Mutual aid organizing, along with commitments to building community-based approaches to safety, is key to moving beyond policing.

The past seventy years of policing have brought heightened levels of surveillance, criminalization, and punishment. Policing has transformed and expanded. Policing has been able to shape-shift in response to protests against it. In moments when the legitimacy of policing is in question, politicians and police leaders propose reforms to quell discontent and convince the public that reform interventions can rein in police violence. Just as in the twentieth century, these reforms continue to expand policing and police power. At times, police may have provided immediate interventions for different communities, especially well-off ones, in the absence of other available responses. And well-off white communities may have benefited from police professionalization and advancements. But the overarching relationship of police with Black, Indigenous, Latinx, and poor communities has been shaped by violence and injustice.

While some past efforts may have been well meaning and intended to reduce harm, they failed to deal with the fundamental problems: policing and police power. Policing is centered on the threat or use of violence. As a result, any time there is an encounter with police, the possibility of violence and coercion will always be present. This is true even when an interaction seems innocuous. The power that police have to engage in violence against other human beings lies at the heart of the issue. Protest in response to the violence of policing prompting reform has become an established cycle.

INTERLUDE II

(PART A) THE HARMS OF CRIMINALIZATION: THE STORY OF ROBERT PEACE

Robert Peace. Peace, as we called him.

It was 2007, and I was in high school at St. Benedict's Prep. We were on the end-of-year fifty-five-mile hike in the Appalachian Mountains that was required for new students — the Trail, as it was called. It was a sunny day in the middle of summer. I saw Peace at a resting point midhike and remember being surprised. He had stopped teaching but was walking the trail as an alumnus — something St. Benedict's alumni often did. Those who knew him revered him. He had grown up where many of us were from, excelled academically, attended Yale, come back to teach at Benedict's, and still walked and talked as if he'd never left Essex County.

His face is still seared into my memory from that sunny day in the mountains. We were surrounded by trees and hills, and Peace, as always, seemed immovable.

The last person from St. Benedict's to go to Yale before me was Peace. In 2014, my first year of grad school at Yale, I walked into the bookstore to get books for the semester. And Peace's face — the same face I remembered seeing in 2007 — was on a pile of books in the front of the bookstore. I froze as I looked upon the title *The Short and Tragic Life of Robert Peace.*

Peace's story has been widely shared since the release of the book. His father was imprisoned for murder and later died in prison. His mother worked endlessly to provide him with opportunities. Peace excelled academically, athletically, and socially — and earned a spot at Yale. But at Yale, like many disadvantaged students, he struggled economically. Peace started to sell weed, becoming one of the most popular providers on campus. It's speculated that he made up to $100,000 during his time as an undergrad.

He had been selling weed at least as far back as Yale and continued after he returned to Newark.

It was suggested by police and in the media that his death was related to his involvement in selling weed. It was suggested in the news that he had made up to $1,000 a day using his background in molecular biochemistry to grow potent marijuana.[1]

After he graduated, Peace began teaching at my high school while I was still there. He came back to teach for four years, then left to work at the airport, traveling far and wide for years. In 2011, he was murdered in the basement of his Smith Street home — not far from where I live as I write this.

The truth is that no one truly knows the circumstances that led to Peace's death, as Peace is not here to tell us and those responsible are unknown. It could have been a dispute over something else. It could have been poverty-shaped jealousy or conflict over territory. Or any of a number of other interpersonal reasons.

There's a piece of Peace's story that is often left out: systems of punishment, incarceration, and criminalization, all of which contributed immensely to the conditions that led to his death. The criminalization of marijuana, in the context of the war on drugs, worked to create conditions in which the use and sale of it were far more dangerous than they needed to be.

The problem that Peace had was not that he sold drugs; it was that drugs were illegal. And perhaps he was protected from certain complications at Yale because elite, predominantly white campuses are not treated by the criminal-legal system and society as criminalized spaces and thus the use and sale of drugs are not made nearly as dangerous. In Newark, New Jersey, the opposite is true.

The police often ascribe motive where there is none to displace any responsibility to find out anything — or to help society find an easy answer or an out to explain away a tragic death. In this case, it wasn't a Yale graduate murdered tragically in his home; it was a drug dealer who was killed. The narrative provides a frame that justifies and explains his death. It's critical not to simply accept the police's narrative of Peace's life — and death.

Peace was simply ahead of his time. And so much of his life—and his death—was structured by conditions shaped by factors far older than he. I don't see Peace as having made any grave mistakes that justified the outcome of his untimely death; just decisions that carried consequences—some of which could have been anticipated, others wildly unpredictable.

It took me more than six years to write this. I started trying to make sense of Peace's story when he was first murdered and later started putting words onto a page after the book was released.

The book, written by his former roommate and friend at Yale, describes Peace's story, and what was framed as the duality of his life, at length. *The Short and Tragic Life of Robert Peace* was read widely, and a professor even mentioned it in a seminar my first year. Every time the story came up, that image of Peace's face up in the Appalachian mountains would surface in my mind.

The book sought to humanize Peace. And in many ways it did. Scores of articles came out after the book was written, a movie, Rob Peace, based on the book, was released in 2024, and Peace's story continues to be discussed widely, including in class during my first year in grad school. Every time I saw an article or new story, I saw Peace's face, heard him talk, saw his walk, imagined him making jokes, and remembered his laugh.

Many people shared their opinions on Peace. The stories and narratives about his life ranged in focus, discussing the conditions of the hoods he had been raised in, his strained relationship with his father after his imprisonment for a double murder, how one is never able to escape the habits and codes of where one comes from, Peace's personal failures, character flaws, or deficits, or the mistakes that he had made that had squandered his privilege—which he and others around him had worked incredibly hard to ensure he had.

But to me, even the most well-meaning writings, essays, and reviews never seemed expansive or capacious enough to capture the fullness of Peace's life and story. All the think pieces, book reviews, and opinions seemed to miss capturing his complexity and humanness, despite the writers' intentions. So I started writing down notes, journaling, and asking a different set of questions.

The writings and opinions never seemed to capture how the criminalization of marijuana, and drugs more broadly, had complicated Peace's life in ways that had exposed him to danger, injury, imprisonment, and ultimately death—danger that those involved in the pharmaceutical industry or the rapidly legalizing cannabis industry never have to consider, let alone worry about. And even more, how the prison and criminal-legal systems—and their obsession with punishment rather than other forms of safety and accountability—robbed Peace of his father at seven years old. Peace worked for years to overturn his father's conviction on a number of grounds, which included the lack of a speedy trial, until his father's death in prison.

Many people who read the book and heard of Peace's story asked the same questions: What went wrong? What went right? How did Peace go from Yale to dying the way he did? I had a hard time making sense of it until I realized that they were asking the wrong questions and were searching for a simple answer to a complicated person's story. Even more, they were projecting morals and hopes onto Peace that Peace himself might have felt differently about. I knew that there was something deeper—more human—about the story that escaped the "structure versus culture versus personal" explanations that were projected onto him.

I spent years working through Peace's story and all that had gone into shaping his complicated, layered, and wondrous life, in part because I yearned for a sense of clarity about Peace's life and death and also because I always saw myself in him, which both scares and encourages me. Then I realized that people—me included—were asking the wrong questions and projecting our dilemmas, questions, and confusion onto Peace's life when Peace had never asked us to do so.

Some may read the story and ask why someone who came so far would make these decisions. Why, after having all the opportunity in the world, would he end up a drug dealer? Only Peace knew exactly why he had made certain choices. But they were his choices to make. And instead of focusing on those decisions—which he might have been happy and content with—it's more important to examine the conditions that gave rise to his story to begin with.

When we ask what went wrong, we begin with the wrong question. First of all, the police speculated that his murder had something to do with his drug sales. But the people who murdered Peace were never found, and police are often wrong about motives, especially when there seems to be a clear—stereotypical—story. Maybe his murder did center on his involvement in selling marijuana. But we don't know for certain why he was murdered, and assuming that the police are correct is misguided and puts faith in a system that hasn't and will never deserve it.

Only Peace knew the financial obligations he had, the routes he saw as reliable, and his rationale for deciding to do what he did. And in life all we have is choices, and even those choices are constrained and, depending on where you're from, may not be choices at all. And perhaps those obligations and stresses were shaped by his losing his father to the prison system and his own work to free him from it.

In the end, perhaps Peace lived a wondrous, complicated life that was tragically cut short. Perhaps to Peace, it wasn't so short and tragic and extended far beyond where he might've thought it would go as a child. Either way, the story, and the power, of Peace's life do not have to be seen through a lens of its being short and tragic. Maybe our metrics of time fail to capture the fullness of Peace and the dynamism of his life, which he held through the complications that he himself did not produce.

The deeper, more important question is why Peace had to experience the conditions that he had to escape from—and was likely scarred by beyond what most will ever know—to begin with.

Peace was wise far beyond what most will ever realize, and he decided to live his life in the way that he chose. What cut his life short wasn't simply his own decisions but the broader context shaped by poverty, criminalization, policing, and incarceration. There were no irreconcilable mistakes in Peace's story, just decisions with consequences largely shaped by factors related to white supremacy, racial capitalism, and a criminal-legal system that harms far more than it helps.

Many people from poor and working-class families and communities matriculate to places like Yale and struggle financially, socially, and mentally once there and after they leave. Some of them end up doing things that are criminalized. People often want to return to where they're from and also to be financially stable—which Peace found a way to do using his background and skills. He did that in addition to inspiring students at St. Benedict's during the time he spent teaching there and participating in school life, including by walking the Appalachian Trail long after he stopped teaching. People live complicated lives, make mistakes, hurt people, are hurt, and navigate trauma and hardship. People such as Peace have more to deal with for reasons completely outside their control than those who come from better-off, privileged backgrounds. But while some frame Peace as having made mistakes, the conditions in which he lived structured a life more prone to premature death.

Why do people have to leave their communities once they achieve some semblance of success? Why is selling weed a cause for some to judge Peace, while pharmacies make billions of dollars today off of medical marijuana? Given the circumstances Peace was born into, he lived a complicated and beautiful life. He certainly left his mark on people, myself included.

If a few things had been different, he may have had a far easier life.

One of the most pressing dimensions of his story, one that flies under the radar, is the harm that stems from drugs' being made illegal. If drugs had been decriminalized, he would have been liberated from a host of complications and things might have been different.

The truth is that drug criminalization does not stop drug use, addiction, or the consequences of the drug trade. When something is illegal, it is pushed to the fringes of society. There, violence becomes a primary way to deal with jealousy, conflict, and violence. And cycles reproduce themselves. Peace was a genius. And he wanted to live within his home community, near his mom, and saw an opportunity to make money using his skills he'd developed. Outside of a criminalizing context, the path seems completely rational.

Mass incarceration has forced a number of survival economies to the outskirts of society and has made it incredibly difficult, and often dangerous, to navigate conflict. Criminalization, mass incarceration, and policing have made illicit economies such as the drug trade and sex work even more dangerous. Even more, the criminalization of drugs robs people of their own stories, as it has done with the way Peace's life is often narrativized.

Nearly ten years later, marijuana is legal in New Jersey. People can grow weed in their homes. Perhaps if people could have grown their own and Peace had been able to start a community business, he could have made money and lived life on his own terms. But the criminalization and policing of marijuana—and of drugs more broadly—throughout history forced it to be regulated by logics that make injury, violence, and death far more likely.

There was nothing inherently wrong with any of what Peace did. From what's known, he made no serious mistakes. Everything that went wrong had to do with the context and circumstances he found himself in. And the fact that he was ahead of his time.

Ending mass incarceration is not enough. The United States needs to repair the harm to individuals, families, and communities that mass criminalization has caused, or the legacy will continue to ring through time. Drugs should be taken out of the criminal code altogether. After decades of aggressive enforcement, people still use and sell drugs, and because of their criminalization, the risks associated with them have remained unnecessarily intense.

In 2021, New Jersey legalized and decriminalized marijuana as part of a broader national shift away from drug criminalization. Similarly, Oregon's Measure 110, enacted in 2020 to decriminalize personal possession of all drugs, initially represented a significant move away from a punitive approach to drugs. However, it faced a rollback in 2024 due to political pressures and war-on-drugs-style disinformation tactics.[2]

While many politicians continue to overlook the needs of those most impacted, and corporations seek to profit from changing drug policies, the lives lost and affected by the war on drugs continue to cast a looming cloud over many families and communities, and we are still reckoning with its profound price.

The harm caused by drugs being criminalized extends beyond people being incarcerated and shapes realities and lives. As a push continues for full drug decriminalization, there's also the need to attempt to repair the harms that structure lives and hardships. And we can never forget all the organized violence of the state that shapes and damages lives and communities —and contributes to premature death.

With love. You continue to inspire me, Peace.

(PART B) FOR CHAZZ: DECRIMINALIZE DRUGS

Chazz, a family member, passed away earlier this week. It wasn't related to the Coronavirus, but because of the outbreak, he wasn't able to have a full and proper funeral service. He lived with me and my sisters for a while growing up, and always looked out for me. The

last time I saw him was in Newark, on South Orange Ave. We talked
for a while and caught up. He asked if I was still on the straight and
narrow, told me to keep in touch, and to stay safe.
'It's not too many real niggas left,' was the last thing he said to me.
Those words have echoed ever since, and now there's one less. But
your energy will live on forever, cuz, through those that you touched.
Love you, bro. Rest In Peace. 🖤🕊️

I wrote those words on March 20, 2020, a few days after I found out
someone very close to my family had died from a drug overdose. We were
only a few years apart in age. The circumstances were unclear, but from
what I know, Chazz had been doing drugs since we were young. He had
begun by snorting various drugs, but a few years before he died, he had
begun shooting heroin, allegedly after he started seeing a woman (who
was white and around his age) in North Carolina who taught him how.

In the days following his death, I talked to people he had been close to.
He hadn't been doing well, and a close friend told me that he was struggling
and wasn't himself. He was in pain.

Chazz had a hard life and had experienced incarceration and struggled
with addiction. Apparently he had come to Newark because he couldn't get
the quality of drugs he wanted in North Carolina.

I also heard that he'd had conflicts with people he'd used to run with
after he had started stealing from them, and perhaps because of the stigma
from his drug use. The same person said that someone might have inten-
tionally given him a bad batch because of the beef.

The last time I saw him, he told me he was selling raw cocaine and
doing all right. He'd had a construction job but had lost it and started selling drugs. A mutual friend had tried to help him get a job to get on his
feet, but it was difficult for Chazz to do so, perhaps because of life, perhaps
because of addiction.

We were left with questions: How? Why? Was it actually heroin? Fentanyl?

The issue wasn't with Chazz using heroin. So many of the complications in his life stemmed from criminalization and his financial struggles.
In an ideal world, he could have had access to unadulterated heroin and to
knowledge about how to use it safely while minimizing potential adverse
outcomes. Injecting any drug tends to be more risky than other methods of

ingestion, but he might have started to shoot it because the quality was low, because it was mixed, or because it was not heroin at all. Even more, in an ideal world, he could have had employment, income, housing, and access to healthcare—including addiction support—to ensure that his basic needs were met, his drug use notwithstanding.

The prohibition model surrounding drugs creates a framework of someone being either an addict or completely sober when it comes to drugs such as crack and heroin. This stands in contrast to attitudes toward drugs such as alcohol or cigarettes that are dangerous but do not carry the same forms of stigma. It also stands in contrast to the use of psychedelics or pharmaceutical drugs to enhance creativity. For many, drugs can enhance quality of life with few negative side effects. Perhaps Chazz felt better and would always feel better using drugs. Access to health care and treatment—and all the resources that help to stabilize people, such as food, water, housing, money, and education—would have made a tremendous difference in his life. Perhaps it would have been helpful to ensure that he could use as safely and responsibly as possible.

We shouldn't center the conversation on whether using drugs is morally right or wrong. This approach can push away those who seek help for their addiction but are hesitant to give up the enjoyment they get from drugs.

Financial hardship, racism, and capitalism in general shaped Chazz's choices and their outcomes. The trauma he experienced over the course of his life—and the pain he might have experienced from being harmed and causing harm—might have weighed on him heavily. Maybe he needed help processing that trauma or a way to cope. Maybe drugs offered him that relief.

If Chazz had had places to test his drugs, a safe injection site, a professional to help inject or teach him how, mental health and trauma treatment as a child, a therapist, addiction support that wasn't tied to punishment or the threat of imprisonment, a job that was guaranteed, and a steady income, things might have turned out differently for him.

PART II

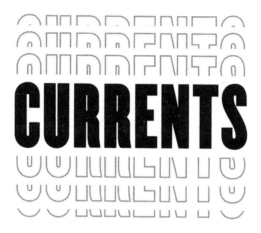

CURRENTS

CHAPTER 3

THE TIDE

The police are honorable, and the courts are just.

It is no accident that Americans cling to this dream. It involves American self-love on some deep, disastrously adolescent level. And Americans are very carefully and deliberately conditioned to believe this fantasy: by their politicians, by the news they get and the way they read it, by the movies, and the television screen, and by every aspect of the popular culture. If I learned nothing else in Hollywood, I learned how abjectly the purveyors of the popular culture are manipulated. The brainwashing is so thorough that blunt, brutal reality stands not a chance against it; the revelation of corruption in high places, as in the recent "scandals" in New Jersey, for example, has no effect whatever on the American complacency.

—James Baldwin, *No Name in the Street*[1]

Somebody was asking me don't you think there are good cops. . . . I think the term *good cop* is an oxymoron. Because the job ain't good. They're all part of a machine that's not good, they are agents of a machine that are not good. Are there good people in those roles? Absolutely. Great people who really thought they would join it to make a difference and make a change, but now find themselves currently fucking up people's days.

—J. Cole[2]

I HAVE DESCRIBED HOW WE'VE GOTTEN TO WHERE WE'RE AT, AND WE'RE stuck in a recurring cycle. Police are said to create a safer society, to prevent and interrupt harm. But police still serve as a key force in managing and preserving inequality. Waves of police violence crash against society and, in a recurring pattern, lead to harm, unrest, and mirages of reform. Depending on who you are, your background, and where you're from, the police respond very differently. The various faces of policing that different people experience explain, in part, why attitudes about policing vary and why abolition may seem unreasonable to some. While the policing state affects everyone, it does not affect everyone the same way. Subjugated communities experience the brunt of police abuse. Better-off communities receive material and psychological benefits. Police, in this way, reproduce unjust inequality by preserving power for those who wield it. But police were never created to bring about a more peaceful society, and they are preventing our collectively working toward one.

There have been recurring cycles of police abuse, unrest, and reform for over a century in the United States. Still, policing over the decades has continued to grow. Since the 1960s, policing has expanded exponentially. At present, there are more than seven hundred thousand police officers in the United States. At least $100 billion is channeled toward policing annually. Approximately 21 percent of US residents sixteen years of age or older had contact with police in 2020—a number that includes traffic stops, street stops, and other forms of contact—which amounts to 53.8 million people."[3] More than ten million people are arrested annually. The Stanford Open Policing Project reports that police stop more than fifty thousand drivers on an average day, more than twenty million a year.[4] More than six million people experienced the threat of force or the nonfatal use of force in 2020.[5] According to Mapping Police Violence, police killed 1,349 people in 2023.[6]

Policing across the United States has swelled and affected social, political, and economic life across the nation. As discussed in chapters 1 and 2, police were historically used to manage and control oppressed communities. Today, that legacy continues. So while the control and contact of police has expanded throughout the country, some people feel the growth of policing far more than others do as it relates to contact, violence, and misconduct.

Throughout history, police have been seen as biased, illegitimate entities by large swaths of the population. But after many periods of reform and cycles of rebranding, perceptions of police have shifted greatly. Today, across many sectors of society, police are said to be the providers of safety. Police have become integrated into nearly every corner of social life, including hospitals and schools, and their presence is mandated after events such as car accidents, on construction sites, and in some medical emergencies. Within communal life, the growth of community and hot-spot policing has led to persistent police presence on city streets, in public housing developments and schools, and at community events. Children are often told that police are the ones who protect everyone from harm. Television shows and movies reinforce these ideas through portraying charismatic, funny, and friendly police stopping crime while normalizing police violence and use of force. News outlets and journalists often default to crime data and police opinion as facts. Policing has inundated all aspects of society.

Police violence, misconduct, and corruption have not stopped after more than a hundred years of reforms. A recurring cycle continues: incidents of police violence occur, some spark national outrage, politicians and police leaders promise reform. At times, policy changes occur, such as the introduction of use-of-force guidelines and departmental shifts. Over time, initiatives such as diversity efforts and the use of body cameras are carried out. Private companies invested in the policing industry — like those that provide technology for police — experience profit boosts and shareholder gains.[7] Police leaders promise community policing and improved relationships. Yet police violence continues, as does resistance to it. The reform promises and efforts are offered in many cases to placate angry communities and either are not implemented or fail to deliver on the promises made. And as discussed earlier, such reforms are not new: as far back as the early 1900s, political and police leaders were offering reforms to get rid of corruption and make police fairer and more just. After widespread protests and uprisings against police violence throughout the 1960s, community policing emerged and police promised to be more diverse, less violent, and more responsive to community needs. But police violence has continued, resulting in recurrent periods of rebellion and unrest.

POLICING TODAY

The United States has the highest rate of incarceration in the world. Average sentences are far longer than in other Western countries, and pathways for furlough and early release have been attenuated over time. Mass incarceration not only affects those incarcerated, it ravages the lives of families and communities that coexperience incarceration. Not only has incarceration ballooned in recent decades, so has policing. There are approximately 787,565 local and state police, according to 2018 estimates, and 137,000 federal law enforcement officers[8]—totaling nearly one million law enforcement officers. The total number of employees at law enforcement agencies, including police and nonpolice employees, clocks in at 1.2 million for local and state law enforcement entities.[9] There are more than 17,000 law enforcement agencies in the United States, which often overlap—and this is all made possible through the influx of federal dollars to local and state police departments. Sheriffs' offices have some of the highest rates of police killings and abuse, and they also enforce evictions and civil orders and run jails in some jurisdictions.[10] State police, such as troopers, are also responsible for widespread discrimination and abuse, particularly as it relates to the roadways, while traffic accidents and deaths continue to be urgent issues that need to be sustainably addressed. The resources involved could be dedicated to providing opportunities and support for the very communities targeted by policing. This would do far more to create effective and sustainable approaches to safety. In rural areas and small towns, police departments can be very small. At times, sheriffs and other county and state policing entities are responsible for policing rather than local departments. It's important to consider how communities can move beyond policing across all geographies, including rural areas. These communities are often in need of resources, and even when small, policing forces can cause harm to poor, marginalized communities.

But what do police actually do today? So far, I've showcased the extensive role of police in managing and controlling marginalized populations. But as a result of police reforms throughout history, crime control became a principal part, at least on the surface, of police functions. In fact, the focus on police being crime fighters rather than being involved with political machines and corruption was a key strategy among reformers during the early twentieth century. In focusing on crime fighting, they were able to shift the perception of police from being illegitimate agents of the state responsible for preserving the status quo to being protectors of society. That shift enabled a level of rebranding that changed the perception of police among more and more people.

Today, while people may not like being pulled over or getting tickets, the overarching perception among many in society is that cops are crime fighters who protect and who are called on when people are in need. This shift, from maintainers of the status quo to agents fighting bad guys, has led to far wider acceptance of the idea that police are a legitimate institution. And today, the main perception the broader public has of police is that they are protectors and providers of safety. And for communities that do not experience systematic surveillance and brutalization by the police, the institution of policing may seem effective. But very little of what police do relates to violence or anything serious. Much of police activity is focused on traffic stops, patrol stops, property crimes, and other nonserious events. Rather than designating funds for those who are not able to afford groceries and other basic needs, companies pay police and private security, often armed, to use the threat of arrest, physical force, and guns to protect their merchandise. Cities such as New York City spend millions on policing public housing rather than developing transformative approaches to safety.[11] In a number of cities, the *New York Times* reported, 4 percent of police calls and activity are focused on violence.[12]

If the police are not addressing violence, as commonly portrayed, what are they doing? It turns out, not much. The vast majority of police time is spent idle. Outside of that, most police activity is focused on nonserious activity and traffic stops. Police also engage in enforcement related to homelessness, theft, and mental health emergencies, which trained, specialized response teams would be much better able to handle. In fact, I argue that all that police are doing—and not doing—in the supposed name of safety can be better dealt with by addressing the root cause of the problems and developing focused response teams and responders trained to address communities' particular concerns.

Data clearly illustrate profound racial disparities in policing. The Stanford Open Policing Project reveals that Black drivers are approximately 20 percent more likely to be stopped by the police than are white drivers, and that following traffic stops, Black drivers are searched about twice as often and Latinx drivers about one and a half times as often.[13] According to the same study, contraband is found more frequently in searches of white drivers. The disparities continue beyond traffic stops. A National Bureau of Economic Research report found that Black and Latinx people are more likely to experience the threat of force or use of force in their interactions with police.[14] The situation is even more stark as it relates to lethal force: data compiled by the *Washington Post* and Mapping Police Violence show that Black people are more than twice as likely as white people to be killed by the police. Native Americans are killed at the highest rate by police.[15]

The effects of police violence extend beyond individual acts of police brutality; there are spillover effects on families and entire communities. High concentrations of policing and surveillance are associated with a number of deleterious effects on health, education, and life outcomes. Living in a neighborhood that is the site of constant police surveillance, which the sociologist Alyasah "Ali" Sewell and their colleagues in a 2021 research study referred to as being "lethally surveilled," is associated with a greater risk of developing high blood pressure and obesity.[16] The study by Sewell and their colleagues showed that associations between health outcomes and lethal surveillance vary by gender. For women in highly surveilled communities, police presence and surveillance are associated with a greater risk of diabetes, high blood pressure, and obesity compared to men. In another study, Sewell and their colleagues found that stop-and-frisk has devastating effects on the mental health of men.[17] The health implications of police violence extend to who is routinely killed: those with mental illness are sixteen times more likely to be killed by the police.[18] Recent studies have also shown the adverse educational outcomes associated with concentrated police presence within communities and schools. Research has shown that following a surge of police within low-income neighborhoods, the educational performance of young adolescent boys suffers.[19] Black girls are often criminalized and policed in schools, which impacts their educational trajectories.[20] Mere contact with the criminal-legal system can cause people to avoid other surveilling systems such as medical, financial, labor market, and educational institutions, potentially serving as a mechanism for exacerbating inequalities.[21]

The body of research surrounding policing and spillover effects makes an important point: policing has a wide range of impacts beyond individual instances of assault and murder by officers.[22] Illness spillovers of policing and surveillance affect entire communities. An important consideration is that all police encounters contain the threat of violence, whether police violence occurs or not. A simple interaction with police can cause those who fear police to experience acute anxiety and stress and trigger associations with violence. Thus, a consistent police presence in communities can have adverse effects, which are exacerbated by moments of unwanted police contact and violence.

Police stop, question, frisk, and use force at disproportionate rates along racial lines. Black people are incarcerated at much higher rates and are much more likely to be subjected to traffic stops than are whites. And Black and Indigenous people are disproportionately killed by police. The targeted policing of Black, Latinx, Indigenous, and poor communities leads to different lived experiences from those of well-off white populations. These diverging experiences can explain, to a certain degree, varying attitudes toward police abuse and sentiments about how to deal with it. Those targeted by policing, surveillance, and imprisonment will likely develop more pessimistic perspectives on the capacity of the police to be reformed, even if they do not believe in police abolition. And even within Black and other marginalized communities, police and political leaders rely on relationships with residents who tend to be of higher class statuses to engage in public relations efforts and garner support.[23]

POLICING MOBILITY

Traffic stops often lead to police engaging in criminal investigations. The fact that these invasive stops and searches are even possible is the result of a special automobile exception to the Fourth Amendment. The amendment guarantees "the right of the people to be secure in their persons, houses, papers, and effects, against unreasonable searches and seizures," which is another way of saying that it protects our right to privacy against the unchecked power of the police. But under the automobile exception, first codified in 1925 and then expanded over the decades by successive Supreme Court rulings, drivers are considered to have a reduced expectation of privacy; the full protections of the amendment are weakened.

The implications of this reduced expectation are many. But among the farthest reaching is the practice, affirmed by the Supreme Court in 1996 in *Whren v. United States*, by which drivers can be temporarily detained[24]—that is, stopped—by officers on the basis of a flimsy pretext, such as a broken taillight, even if the officer's real purpose is to look for evidence of criminal activity. The problem is that such pretexts are an easy cover for rank bias and routine racism. They're a green light for racial profiling. And while some protections are supposed to remain in place to prevent the police from escalating such stops into arbitrary searches (officers, for instance, must obtain consent from a driver before searching a car, unless evidence is in plain view), it's easy for the police to sidestep those protections.

Consider how the process often unfolds, quickly transforming from a simple traffic stop into a search. When police officers pull over a car, they are supposed to allow the driver to go on their way as soon as they are able to verify that the driver can operate the vehicle (and, all too often, as soon as the police give a ticket). But police are also allowed to ask off-topic questions[25] to probe for potential criminal activity or ask the driver to get out of their car and wait in the patrol car while they run a check of criminal records, all in the context of a simple traffic violation. If additional information arises that leads them to have reasonable suspicion of criminal activity—a vague concept that is, once again, easily manipulated by bias and racism—they can extend the stop and request consent to search for evidence. In some states, if officers smell marijuana, they can bypass asking for consent altogether, a potential problem since police have been known to lie[26] about smelling marijuana in order to execute a search without a warrant or consent.

The request for consent, which is supposed to be a safeguard against invasive or abusive searches, is another weak spot in the process. For a consent search to pass constitutional muster, it must be free of coercion. But police power, particularly in the context of the long legacy of police violence and corruption, is inherently coercive,[27] especially for Black drivers. From Philando Castile, Sandra Bland, and Maurice Gordon to countless unknown Black drivers, routine traffic stops have too often turned into occasions of police violence. This reality can make people consent, out of pure terror, to a search they would rather decline, if only to avoid further suspicion and escalation.

The story of pretextual stops, in which police pull people over for traffic violations and begin fishing for criminal activity, and consent searches,[28] in which police use their power to coerce individuals to allowing them to search their vehicles, is similar, in many ways, to the story of stop-and-frisk. In both instances, officers need to have only reasonable suspicion of criminal activity to begin an investigatory stop. And because of the vagueness of that reasonable-suspicion standard, both practices have a disproportionate[29] impact on Black and Latinx people.

Moreover, as with stop-and-frisk, the solution to the problem of consent searches is often framed as a simple matter of instituting reforms such as community policing and procedural justice: if police can just be trained to behave in ways that are professional, neutral, and fair, people will feel better about police interactions and encounters with them will be less likely to go awry. The limits of these efforts are perhaps best illustrated by Minneapolis, a city that implemented all the often-touted progressive reforms, yet in which police still murdered George Floyd.

There are approaches that are at once direct and powerful and are being embraced by a growing number of organizers and activists around the country. The first and perhaps most obvious of these is a judicial one and involves nothing less than challenging everything from the legality of the way stops and searches are conducted to the legal foundations on which they stand. Such cases can be brought in federal or state courts. What is essential is that they "should challenge existing precedent at every turn," as Matthew Segal, the legal director of the American Civil Liberties Union (ACLU) of Massachusetts, wrote[30] in the *Guardian* several years back.

One precedent that must be challenged is the one that allows for pretextual stops in the first place. There are various ways to argue against them, but one critical tool is the equal protection clause of the Fourteenth Amendment. This clause prohibits discrimination on the basis of race and other categories. In the case of consent searches, there is clear evidence in cities and states throughout the country that Black drivers are targeted for stops and searches at disproportionate rates. A strong case can be made that pretextual stops are being carried out in an unconstitutional manner and that this way of conducting them, if not the fact of the stops themselves, must be addressed.

Next, consent searches must be challenged. An argument can be made that in the context of police violence and alongside the fact that police are not always required to let people know that they have the right to refuse a search, many consent searches are not truly free of coercion and thus are not constitutional. The dream in bringing such a case is that a judge would rule against the use of consent searches altogether. But a more realistic outcome might be that officers would be required to state that people are free to refuse the search, as they are required to read people their Miranda rights before interrogating them while in custody.

Versions of both of these approaches were used successfully in New York City in *Floyd v. City of New York*, which famously forced the city to rein in[31] its stop-and-frisk program. In that case, the Center for Constitutional Rights argued that the New York Police Department had violated the Fourth and Fourteenth Amendment rights of thousands of Black and Latinx New Yorkers through a pattern of racial profiling and unconstitutional stops. Judge Shira Scheindlin agreed, concluding in a 2013 decision, "The city's highest officials have turned a blind eye to the evidence that officers are conducting stops in a racially discriminatory manner. In their zeal to defend a policy that they believe to be effective, they have willfully ignored overwhelming proof that the policy of targeting 'the right people' is racially discriminatory and therefore violates the United States Constitution."[32]

Scheindlin's decision was a landmark legal victory for Black and Latinx New Yorkers, but it was also limited. While her ruling forced New York to reform how it approached stop-and-frisk, dramatically reducing its use across the city, it nonetheless allowed the practice to continue under the pretext that it could be done in a constitutional way. To this day, racial disparities persist, highlighting one of the challenges of relying on legal solutions: although essential, they can also be slow and onerous. And at a time when so many of our courts, including the nation's highest, have been stacked with conservative appointees, the judicial system seems an increasingly unfriendly place to seek redress.

In 2020, New York City's anticrime units, long criticized for violent and discriminatory practices, including unconstitutional stops and numerous police killings, were disbanded. These units, which can trace their origins to the contentious Street Crime Unit, known for its aggressive "We Own the Night" motto, faced public outcry after the tragic killing of Amadou Diallo in 1999.[33] This led to their replacement with anticrime units in 2002. Fast-forward to 2022: Mayor Eric Adams, who was a former police officer, reinstated these units as "neighborhood safety teams" in an effort to allegedly combat gun violence. This move, while promised under the guise of reform, continues to align with Adams's broader strategy to escalate policing across New York City, including in areas like train stations, despite ongoing debates about the efficacy and impacts of such police presence. Police-centered approaches stand in the way of alternate initiatives and pilots that deploy crisis responders, community mediators, resource providers, and community-based safe passage approaches to contexts such as transportation.

A 2022 report by federal monitor Mylan L. Denerstein underscored the persistence of discriminatory and unconstitutional stops—particularly in select precincts by these rebranded units, with a staggering 97 percent targeting Black and Latinx communities.[34] The revival and expansion of such units under Mayor Adams, often justified through fear-stoking rhetoric, not only perpetuate fear and inequality but also divert attention and resources from sustainable safety solutions that address the root causes of violence and social disparities. Dismantling these anticrime units and stop-and-frisk practices are crucial steps forward.

Activists and advocates have begun to explore a range of city- and state-level policy changes to mitigate and occasionally even end the scourge of pretextual stops and consent searches. In Texas, for example, Democratic legislators in 2020 expressed that they would introduce a package of criminal-legal measures that includes banning pretextual stops.[35] In 2020, Virginia passed legislation[36] prohibiting police from stopping drivers for such minor infractions as broken taillights or brake lights, tinted windows, and loud exhaust systems. Meanwhile, some localities, such as Durham, North Carolina, have shifted[37] from allowing verbal consent for searches to requiring written consent in an effort to curb manipulation and coercion.

But even with these necessary interventions, organizers, particularly those working toward police abolition and a complete reimagining of public safety, argue that there is a need to go further, to experiment with alternatives to the way we deal with traffic concerns. They have begun pressing for police to be removed from the area of traffic safety altogether.

Today one of the most reliable functions of traffic stops is to provide revenue[38] for cities and states. Another is to serve as a basis for fishing for more serious crimes. But imagine if alternatives were created to address concerns about traffic safety (which remains an undeniable problem) through a public health framework centered on safe-driving education and outreach, as opposed to police stops and tickets.

This vision might have appeared implausible just a few months ago, but it has been gaining momentum in both New York City and Los Angeles, where activists have begun waging campaigns to remove police officers from traffic oversight and replace them with department of transportation workers, among others. In Berkeley, California, in July 2023, the city council approved a plan to remove police from traffic stops and instead use unarmed city workers to deal with traffic safety matters.

We now know that the only way to ensure that police violence doesn't occur is to prevent police encounters with drivers. If someone does need to be stopped for a matter related to traffic safety, that stop can be made by someone who will handle the situation with a public health approach, not by someone with a gun and the license to kill with impunity. The roads might become a lot safer, and many fewer people would have to experience the fear or reality of police violence. People shouldn't have to fear that they will lose their life over a broken taillight.

POLICING AND CRIME

Does policing lead to less crime?

It often doesn't, but it might in certain contexts. But in focusing on that, we're asking the wrong question.

One of the most researched ideas in social science examining the relationship between policing and violent crime data is that in particular instances, certain qualities of the police — namely hypervisibility and persistent presence — have the potential to reduce violence.[39] Studies showing this have been based on methodologically sound social research designs, but it is important to note that there are other studies — including, in New York

City, a quasi–random control study, which is often considered a highly reliable type—that found that policing may actually lead to increased amounts of reported crime.[40] Regardless, even if policing does deter violence or criminalized activities in particular instances, that does not mean it is the only answer to violence and harm. There are far more sustainable approaches that do not center on the violence of policing. We also need reliable ways to measure safety to better understand what helps to cultivate safety.

Crime data is notoriously fraught with issues, and acts that are defined as crimes are underreported. Some acts, such as shootings and killings, tend to be more accurately reported. But even data on shootings can be flawed—including when jurisdictions employ ShotSpotter technology, which is alleged to notify police when a shooting occurs using sound technology. Many notifications end up being false ones, including the one that led to the police murder in 2021 of Adam Toledo in Chicago.[41] So even if police presence or an increase in policing deters reported criminalized behavior, that does not necessarily mean it is reducing all the activities that would be categorized as crime. The concept of crime has become an accepted way to measure and understand anything considered wrong and deviant. But crime is a social and political construct shaped by those with power. The concept of crime, and subsequent police attention, has been shaped by race, class, gender, sexuality, and immigration status and adversely affect marginalized communities.[42]

Flooding an area with police may deter certain activities or perhaps temporarily displace them. But it does not address the roots of activities that harm communities. At times, it displaces those activities to prisons, where cycles of state and interpersonal violence can continue. Moreover, policing comes with a large range of harmful effects, both direct and indirect.

Even more, the framework of "crime" does not capture the complex nature of safety. Throughout history—up to today—a large range of harmless activities has been criminalized. They include survival economies and activities that Black communities engage in routinely as a part of everyday social life. While cigarettes are unhealthy, stores sell them every day. But selling loosies has been historically criminalized, and the criminalization of the practice led to the tragic murder of Eric Garner. Throughout history, criminal law has been used as a tool to police, surveil, and punish along the lines of race, class, and other forms of difference. Thus, safety does not relate directly to crime, which is perhaps why crime reduction in a community often does not lead to residents *feeling* safer.

As sociologist Elijah Anderson described in *Code of the Street*, an unjust criminal-legal system along with structural inequality can make some develop codes that make violence more likely.[43] And as author Ethan Brown details in *Snitch*, the coercive pressure of courts and prosecutors for coop-erators to "snitch" has also led to tension within communities, pushing us further away from fostering safety and accountability.[44] The unjust pressure from the criminal-legal system for people to cooperate has ultimately led to the Stop Snitching movement. Moving beyond policing, prisons, and puni-tive approaches allows us to escape from these dynamics altogether to bring us closer to collectively fostering safety and accountability.

Data and studies on patterns of police abuse can be useful in giving a full picture, tracing trends and patterns, and suggesting potential correla-tions. We certainly need data, but traditional data on policing are plagued by problems of data quality and the frames that inform data analysis, as data can be interpreted in various ways. We need ways to understand patterns of police harm, but our understanding has to be rooted in an ethic of jus-tice. We also need new ways to understand community safety, as the notion of crime misses the mark in a range of ways. A number of crowdsourced platforms have emerged to fill the need for transparent data sources, as the criminal-legal system is not a reliable source. Inevitably, we need to make crime statistics obsolete by pushing for frameworks that measure safety and community well-being in a holistic way. This should include safety from interpersonal, institutional, and state harm.

THE PROBLEMS OF DATA-DRIVEN POLICING

A number of developments within policing and the social scientific research into it have created new paradigms and police strategies. The increasing use of data to drive police tactics across the United States undergirds these developments. The turn to data in policing has been made possible by tech-nological developments as well as academics and data scientists who collab-orate with police to develop their technological capacities. One particular example is hot-spot policing, whereby police flood particular "hot areas" (determined by available data) with policing and surveillance presence, has been a major development that has led to the growth of "problem-oriented policing" as a framework. While traditional models of policing centered on responding to calls, hot-spot policing has justified persistent police presence in neighborhoods, housing developments, and communities throughout the United States—and around the globe. The occupying presence that residents report at times showcases the dominating nature of the presence-as-deterrence strategy, which draws on personnel, visual and sonic cues such as police lights, surveillance cameras, police floodlights, community engagement efforts, patrols, and vehicle placements.

As a result of data-driven, people-and-place-focused policing, police are no longer simply reacting to calls and dispatches. For years, many communities criticized police for taking too long to respond and for remaining largely out of sight. Now police and police technology fill many communities—even though those same communities still experience extensive wait times and harm when police are called, as well as routine police violence because of their continued presence.

In addition to focusing on areas, or hot spots, social network analysis and crime databases have led to a concentrated focus on individuals. The findings within social science that a large percentage of individuals who engage in and experience gun violence exist within small, concentrated networks has led to an intense focus on particular individuals who are typically seen as "gang" or "group" affiliated. The individual and group focus has led to the widely used, yet not widely understood, tactic of focused deterrence, or group violence intervention. This model is applied in a variety of ways throughout the country, but its central features are the use of social network and data analysis by academic partners to identify those deemed most likely to commit gun violence. Focused deterrence works by identifying those involved in violence through arrest patterns, surveillance, and legal system data. Then program administrators provide social services that they deem useful to those identified; advocacy by members of the community of an end to gun violence; and a series of threats made by prosecutors and law enforcement not only to those who may engage in gun violence but to the entire group in which those people are embedded. Making these threats is referred to as "pulling levers."

The initiatives often fall apart as communities withdraw their support. In addition, findings as to their effects are inconclusive. Some studies suggest that such interventions do work, at least in the short term, while other studies have shown no reductions in violence following their implementation.[45] But the individuals and groups who receive extra attention from local, state, and federal prosecutors and amplified sentences for charges still face extended sentences despite the programs' not even living up to the promises of violence reduction. And even when they do work, there is a central question: Are there other ways to reduce violence that will not lead to anyone languishing in a cage?

I first witnessed these initiatives up close at Yale as a graduate student, through professors involved with partnerships that helped steer such work and analyze data to determine who would be targeted. I was alarmed. Seeing focused deterrence initiatives up close showed me its harms—specifically its framing as the solution to gun violence. The work relies on punitive models of public safety and unjustly targets entire networks of people with criminal-legal punishment if anyone in the group is involved with gun violence. While reducing gun violence should remain a goal, there are ways to achieve it without harmful activities centered on punishment and surveillance that are rhetorically framed as "fair" and "just." Despite a growing number of academics that identify as abolitionists,[46] academia remains deeply embedded in violent policing practices. The police violence and carceral harm that academics help to enable often go unspoken, concealed by the veneer of scientific objectivity.

In cities across the United States, enthusiasm is building around focused deterrence. In the 1990s, Operation Ceasefire began in Boston under the criminologist David M. Kennedy's guidance. The operation's focus was on reducing violence among young men, and it came to be known as the Boston Miracle. It became the model for various other initiatives funded by governments and private sectors.

However, this model doesn't seem to deliver on its promises. The social service component often has no measurable effect on reducing violence.[47] Even more alarming, the focused deterrence strategy may lead to mass arrests, as evidenced by a 2013 study in Cincinnati in which 75 percent of identified group members were arrested.[48] While the approach might temporarily reduce violence, the impact fades over time. A 2018 meta-analysis by Anthony A. Braga, David Weisburd, and Brandon Turchan concluded that the focused deterrence initiatives they had evaluated had had only a modest effect on violence that was even lower in more rigorously designed studies.[49] The authors acknowledged that the nonexperimental designs used in some studies to evaluate focused deterrence initiatives—as opposed to randomized experiments—have the potential to overstate outcomes and lead to more positive effect sizes. Beyond the questionable effect sizes and the collateral impacts in affected communities, there are cities in which focused deterrence shows no evidence of efficacy,[50] such as Newark, Boston, Cincinnati, Los Angeles, and New Orleans.

Oakland's experience with Operation Ceasefire is telling. Initially praised for reducing violence, it became unstable in the face of increased homicides and police violence, revealing the inherent instability in such initiatives.[51] A report notes that Operation Ceasefire took several iterations to get off the ground as community groups and social service providers were bypassed in favor of police-centered implementation. And Oakland saw 133 homicides in 2021,[52] its deadliest year since 2006, while the city had fewer than ten people on its violence interrupter staff during much of the pandemic up until the end of 2021. (In November 2021, the city's Department of Violence Prevention more than tripled its violence interrupter staff to thirty-one.) Operation Ceasefire almost crumbled again[53] in light of police violence in recent years, with some community groups and service providers leaving the initiative, revealing the unstable nature of police-involved violence reduction initiatives such as focused deterrence.

Oakland is proof that while focused deterrence may temporarily suppress particular forms of violence, its impact will wane over time, revealing the program's inherent instability. One evaluation from 2012 found that "the success in violence reduction" in several cities that had implemented focused deterrence, including Chicago, "appears to be short-lived."[54] Evidence on the supposed effectiveness of the "Boston Miracle" was based on two studies,[55] both of which failed to isolate which aspects of the intervention were the driving forces of its success. This means that it isn't clear if punitive threats, heightened surveillance and incarceration, social services, or select community involvement were the drivers of the seeming decline in violence, which is essential information for understanding how focused deterrence operates. And focused deterrence can be profoundly punitive: sociologist Nikki Jones wrote in her 2018 book *The Chosen Ones: Black Men and the Politics of Redemption* that a young person allegedly involved in a gang in Boston received a sentence of nineteen years and seven months in federal prison without the possibility of parole for possession of a single bullet.[56]

An important question lingers: Is focused deterrence just, even if effective? While it's presented as a community-partnered solution, the social services component often falls short. Skepticism grows as the initiatives seem to rely more on punishment than on community support and intervention. What's needed is a focus on addressing the root causes of violence, including structural racism, poverty, and trauma. Resources should be shifted to building community capacity and addressing the underlying problems. The complexities of violence go beyond what focused deterrence can solve, and its punitive nature may only make matters worse. The real solutions are likely to be found in deeper, community-centered initiatives that take account of violence's true nature and address it at every stage.

One of the central ideas of focused deterrence—that a small percentage of people are responsible for the majority of shootings—is useful. But resources should be directed to those who have shown promise for violence reduction without the coercive elements of the state. These initiatives are often led by those directly affected, including those formerly involved with gangs. Having deep ties to communities allows them to prevent and de-escalate violence in ways law enforcement never can.

Rather than working with the criminal-legal system, some argue for empowering community-based organizations that can disrupt violence without coercion. The House of Umoja in Philadelphia, for example, reduced gang related deaths without law enforcement involvement.

Community-based groups that focus on antiviolence work are often undermined or underfunded, especially those that explicitly choose to not work with or receive information from the police and center on noncoercive avenues of violence reduction. The House of Umoja is one such community-led effort that has received just a fraction of the attention and financial support of programs based on focused deterrence.[57] As the political scientist Vesla M. Weaver noted, a decade after its implementation in 1968,[58] "Umoja was serving 400 boys from 73 different gangs, and gang-related deaths had fallen from 40 a year to just one in 1978."[59] But government funding streams have largely bypassed Black-led community groups such as the House of Umoja in favor of law enforcement efforts and organizations.[60]

The House of Umoja demonstrates that community-based antiviolence work that does not include collaboration with the criminal-legal system runs the risk of being delegitimized, undermined, and targeted by police and the criminal-legal system.[61] The adversarial stance by state and political entities is rooted in the fear that if communities can manage violence and other harms without the criminal-legal system, its existence will be hard to justify.

Resources should be redirected to building the capacity of community organizations and institutions that can intervene in and disrupt flows of violence—including gender-based and state violence—in all its forms. These interventions include uprooting structural racism; developing peace and healing centers; addressing and providing reparations for the legacies of slavery and colonial and state violence; ensuring quality housing, dignified jobs, and a guaranteed income; developing and funding community organizations; empowering political organizing; and increasing green spaces and youth programs, including summer jobs and after-school programs.

Violence is much deeper and far more complicated than focused deterrence—or hot-spot, community, and problem-oriented policing—can ever address, and these initiatives render the problems of violence more intractable by presenting punishment as a solution. People know they can be incarcerated for shootings, yet they commit violence despite the criminal-legal system's gratuitous and endless capacity for punishment.

Violence reduction work requires going to the root of why violence occurs, including grief, fear, poverty, toxic masculinity, status, trauma, wealth extraction, the desire to be seen—and addressing these things at all stages. Violence interrupters can be helpful in disrupting networks of violence before they arise. But violence interruption initiatives that rely on threats by police and the criminal-legal system lack the trust of communities, as they are both ineffective in the long run and seen as extensions of police and the state.

Community-based violence reduction initiatives are not simple or easy. But they're what will be required to stem the tides of violence.

THE MIRAGE OF REFORM

Why is abolition—rather than reform—necessary for safer communities? Why are nicer, more professional cops still not the answer? Would

prosecuting the police end police violence and harm? How do the police create violence far beyond individual cases of brutality and murder? Why does
police violence in particular spark rebellion? What are the steps we need to
take on the road to abolition? What would it mean to live in a world free of
police violence and terror? Trying to answer these questions led me to the
conclusion that in order to create a new paradigm of public safety, it is necessary to abolish all systems of policing, the entire criminal punishment system more broadly, and the culture of fear, punishment, and violence these
institutions have promoted.

Interventions such as consent decrees—whereby the Department of
Justice sues local police departments for patterns and practices of abuse and
racial bias and requires particular reforms—may be effective at reining in
particular patterns of abuse. But patterns can shift and change over time in
terms of the use of force, stops, arrests—and the subjective experiences and
perceptions of policing during and after the onset of a consent decree. This
shape-shifting is often motivated by public outrage over specific police tactics and technology. Thus, a consent decree may coerce police to alter their
behavior, but it does not change the core functions of police, who are focused
on those deemed worthy of protection and are tools of race-class control.
For example, since Newark enacted the consent decree—which has been
hailed as a beacon of police reform—there have been more documented
cases of police stops, which disproportionately happen with Black people, as
well as more documented incidents of use of force.[62] There have long been
use-of-force restrictions in police departments, but the criminal-legal code
allows police to engage in violence despite these policies. Even when they do
violate the policies, police are rarely fired or prosecuted. Traditional reforms
also pour more money into policing under the illusion that policing has the
capacity to guarantee safety and justice.

Police training is also framed as a panacea for the violence of policing,
but it has not stopped tides of policing violence. Procedural justice, which
stresses the importance of fair and just interactions between civilians and
legal agents, and legal cynicism, seen as the primary issue between police
and Black and other marginalized communities of color, are two frameworks used for police training. Together, these ideas enable those invested in
maintaining the carceral state to gain legitimacy, while stifling the growth
of innovative strategies for community-based safety models. Procedural

justice training initiatives have grown in popularity among reformers and political leaders in connection with other academic-led strategies, such as focused deterrence, emphasizing community policing. These strategies are said to enhance community relations by centering on interpersonal dynamics, yet some critics, such as Stuart Schrader, rightfully contend that they ultimately foster coercive control and solidify police dominance.[63]

Measuring the effectiveness of these reforms depends on the outcomes being evaluated, such as reducing police shootings or use of force. The results might appear positive, even if marginal, leading us to believe that the existing model is the only viable option for community safety. This leads to an approach that relies on using a mathematical formula and tweaking variables to reach specific goals such as altering the use of force, arrests, stops, and public perception. Such a formulaic approach becomes a trap, as efforts to stabilize police legitimacy during crises tend to focus on manipulating the equation to achieve desired outcomes. However, the issue goes deeper; it's not about changing inputs and outputs but rather challenging the whole model of the approach itself. The cycle of reforms and adjustments to policing hasn't addressed the core problem; it has merely masked it, preventing us from looking beyond the existing paradigms.

Over the past ten years, the number of people killed by US law enforcement has been relatively consistent. There have been more than a thousand police killings every year,[64] and many more people have been harassed, brutalized, and sexually assaulted. Yet the number of police officers charged for criminal offenses, including murder or manslaughter, remains incredibly low. Those convicted of murder or manslaughter have yet to reach double digits in a single year.[65] While it may seem that the individual police who were involved in police killings are the criminals, the truth is that the whole system is guilty.

Qualified immunity is one of the main reasons police can act as if the law doesn't apply to them — because, by and large, it doesn't.[66] Qualified immunity was first established by the 1967 Supreme Court case *Pierson v. Ray*. The case began with a racist arrest in Jackson, Mississippi, while a group of Black and white clergymen on a "prayer pilgrimage" to advance racial desegregation sat together in a Jackson bus terminal waiting area.[67] The Supreme Court used qualified immunity as the rationale for protecting law enforcement officials from lawsuits and financial liability in cases where they acted in supposed good faith. In 1982, it was expanded to protect police and government officials from criminal and civil repercussions unless their conduct is "clearly established" as unconstitutional and unlawful.[68] In 1986, it was reinforced to protect "all but the plainly incompetent or those who knowingly violate the law."[69] It was then further reinforced by Supreme Court decisions in 1991, 2001, and 2009. Today it largely means that police can be held liable only if a federal court of appeals or the US Supreme Court has already found that someone previously violated the Constitution by engaging in exactly the same conduct under exactly the same circumstances.[70] In other words, in order for a police officer to be convicted, there has to already be a court decision showing that a different cop was convicted of doing essentially the same thing.

In recent years, the Supreme Court has upheld a police officer's right to use lethal force if they *think* a person might be a threat.[71] This is one of the main reasons why, despite the 6,800 civilians killed by police between 2013 and 2018 documented by Mapping Police Violence,[72] only 1.7 percent of police officers were charged with any crime.[73] This provides a base of criminal procedural law that allows police to largely do whatever they want without ever going to trial. For context, in 2019, the US Court of Appeals for the Sixth Circuit held that Tennessee cops who allowed their police dog to bite a surrendered suspect did not violate clearly established law.[74] Why? Because even though there was case law making it illegal for police dogs to attack individuals who had surrendered, in this instance, the man had surrendered by sitting on the ground and raising his hands rather than lying down. Qualified immunity has also covered police officers who stole $225,000 from local businesses;[75] an officer who shot a ten-year-old while trying to shoot a nonthreatening family dog;[76] and officers who destroyed an Idaho woman's home with tear-gas grenades and other projectiles (when they had the keys) while looking for someone who wasn't there.[77]

The Supreme Court has made it practically impossible to prosecute the police, even when clear and gratuitous harm is done. In effect, police disproportionately brutalize, assault, terrorize, and kill Black and Indigenous people, as well as other marginalized communities, with the full support and protection of the criminal-legal system.

Even when officers are charged by prosecutors, the likelihood that they will actually see a jury and be convicted is close to zero. It's highly uncommon for police to be jailed when they brutalize or kill people. Even when such a decision is sustained, it is often overturned by police leaders or appeal boards, which are largely structured by police unions. Between 2006 and 2017, the largest police departments in the United States fired at least 1,881 officers for various forms of misconduct and violence, including lying about overtime, sexual abuse, and unjustified shootings, as the *Washington Post* reported.[78] At least 451 of those officers were reinstated after they won appeals mandated by union contracts. This is why even when police are investigated and charged, it usually means nothing and is often a symbolic attempt to alleviate tensions with those calling for accountability.

Firing violent or abusive officers is almost as hard as prosecuting them. An investigation by the *Chicago Tribune* found that officers in Chicago were fired in only about 0.5 percent of cases in which there was confirmed misconduct.[79] Police unions and departmental procedures make it incredibly difficult to fire officers. Police usually investigate themselves, and when an independent body does investigate, it often sides with police as well and rarely sustains misconduct claims. In Chicago between 2011 and 2015, the Independent Police Review Authority reviewed 10,500 complaints of police misconduct filed by Black people. Of those, only 166 cases—a mere 1.6 percent—resulted in a "sustained" finding or led to disciplinary action following an internal investigation.[80] In a broader context, out of all 29,000 complaints filed during that period, the authority sustained only 2.6 percent, indicating a very low rate of disciplinary action across all complaints.[81] A review resulting in an unsustained decision means that the review board decides that there is insufficient evidence or lack of clear proof to either prove or disprove the allegation, leading to no definitive conclusion or disciplinary action against the accused officer. When an independent civilian review board does decide on disciplinary measures or firing, it's largely a suggestion and is often ignored or appealed by police leaders and unions.

Police are rarely fired, despite police misconduct and violence being rampant.[82] When they are, they tend to be rehired through police union adjudication or simply move to other police departments. Police unions often write firing and appeal processes into contracts, allowing police unions to appeal and arbitrate decisions to fire police. And people can't sue police directly because of their qualified immunity, so city settlements, which are drawn from tax dollars, have become the norm.

In Minneapolis, where George Floyd was murdered, nearly 50 percent of police who were fired got their jobs back during arbitration processes stemming from union appeals.[83] Police have managed to insulate themselves with more and more immunity. The model is set up to protect police and police power, which is in part why organizers in Minneapolis have been calling for the defunding and dismantling of the department, which the city council voted in agreement with before the decision was rolled back by the Minneapolis Charter Commission and members of the city council.[84]

Even if qualified immunity ended and it were easier for police to be charged, that still wouldn't be the answer. Even though people want justice when police kill Black and other marginalized people,[85] using the same criminal-legal system responsible for mass incarceration and the devastation of communities across the country will not end the violence or bring about justice. First, the police killings we see on camera that become sensationalized are not all the violence perpetrated by the police. Most incidents of violence and terror that police commit, including sexual assault, the second most commonly reported claim against police, are never reported, and it's likely that nothing would happen even if they were. Studies have found that at least 40 percent of police officers' families experience domestic violence, compared to 10 percent of the general population.[86] Victims of domestic abuse at the hands of police should not be expected to be helped by their abuser's coworkers, who often dismiss and cover up the violence.[87]

Despite more than a thousand killings by police each year in the United States, the number of officers charged or convicted remains remarkably low. This reveals a systemic issue, not just the failure of individual officers. The truth is, the criminal-legal system itself is culpable, and we must recognize that mere punishment and imprisonment are not solutions to police violence or any other societal problems. Policing and the broader carceral systems that collaborate with and support it are not capable of holding police accountable on a large scale. The notion that we can fight for the system to hold each and every officer accountable is not logical or supported by history or present-day evidence. The focus on trying to make the criminal-legal system capable of holding police accountable and stopping police violence is a distraction because outside of occasional exceptions, police will not be tried and prosecuted by the criminal-legal system: the system itself is set up on the basis of complaint review processes, police-led disciplinary procedures, police union involvement, and prosecutors and judges who work with police every day to allow police to operate with relative impunity. If the criminal-legal system were to hold all police accountable for any infraction or act of violence that police committed, the system would crumble from a lack of personnel.

The United States is the world leader in incarceration, accounting for nearly 25 percent of all those incarcerated globally despite only making up 5 percent of the world's population,[88] and the prison system will never be an answer to the police system; they are all different sides of the same prison-industrial complex. We must break free from the reform trap that has confined our imaginations, invest in community-based approaches to safety, and move beyond policing. By nurturing community-led efforts and moving resources toward genuine community support and interventions, we can address the root causes of violence and create a more just and sustainable approach to safety.

The focus should be on transcending punitive approaches of all forms, working toward the development of community-oriented models that do not depend on the coercive elements of the state, and ensuring that all people — in the territory now known as the United States and everywhere — have what they need to thrive. By channeling resources to communities rather than doling out punishment, we can build a society in which safety and justice are attainable without mechanisms of punitive control.

Calls to end qualified immunity or prosecute responsible officers after tragic incidents such as the murders of George Floyd, Michael Brown, and Breonna Taylor might seem logical. Society has conditioned us to use arrest and imprisonment as forms of justice. Prosecution seems like a logical approach to addressing police violence. We're conditioned from a young age to believe that when people do heinous and harmful things, they should be arrested, prosecuted, sentenced by the court, and incarcerated. We're told that that's what justice looks like and that the criminal-legal system guarantees that justice will be served. But we have to move beyond the idea that policing, punishment, and imprisonment are the solutions to anything, let alone police violence. The focus on criminal-legal approaches to respond to police violence points to a need for a deeper conversation about what justice really entails.

The issue is not individual police or bad apples. It's policing and police power itself. From slave patrols in the South to labor strike busting in the North, policing has long been based on racial and class domination and criminalizing the marginalized.[89] We can't reform or prosecute our way out of this. Ending qualified immunity may weaken police power and legitimacy in some ways, as well as making it easier for survivors of police violence and the families of those who have lost loved ones to police violence to sue police officers directly.[90] But defaulting to imprisonment, while it may feel satisfying, is not justice. When you're taught that punishment is justice, you crave it. It feels like the only option. But there can be no justice for the murdered when the system is still creating more victims. This approach also relies on and legitimizes the same system that is responsible for the violence to begin with.

While police reform has not stopped the flow of police violence and misconduct, it has served key functions. One, periods of reform following outrage over policing have legitimized the idea of policing as an institution that is capable of being reformed. This is central in a society that relies on policing for social control. Principally, if the broader population does not believe that the police are legitimate, people are more likely to resist police power and rule. If the state cannot rely on ideology to control its population, governments resort to force to coerce consent. The Italian Marxist philosopher Antonio Gramsci theorized how *hegemony*—the widely accepted political, moral, and intellectual beliefs of a society—is fundamentally shaped and wielded by those in power in order to maintain the status quo.[91] The sociologist Stuart Hall later expanded on the concept, showing how ideas were wielded around a mugging crisis—which was racialized, exacerbated, and used to cause a moral panic—to justify an intensification of policing and punishment.[92] In a society that is positioned as free and democratic, the need to rule through brute force poses a range of concerns. So for civil society, the police need to be seen as legitimate crime stoppers. This is why so much is invested politically in maintaining the image of police as providers of safety, especially in light of widespread unrest. The state relies on police to enforce its rule. If more than three hundred million people begin to resist police in various ways, it will pose a major threat to the nation-state and its power over its citizens.

Two, the history of reform reveals another important pattern: periods of reform following unrest over policing have almost always led to expansions of police power, capacity, and scope. Promises of police who are more diverse, more equipment and technology such as body cameras and Tasers, and more resources for training do not stop police violence; they expand police capacity. This expanded capacity then enables police to engage in efforts that can harm the broader public, and dispossessed communities in particular. If reforms and investment in training and technology had the ability to end police violence, they would have ended it long ago. But the cycle of policing, outrage, and reform has continued far too long.

Given the long-standing tensions between police and race-class-subjugated communities, attempts to engage in reforms such as community policing can also occur outside of particular incidents of police violence, though the efforts are tied to the broader history of police violence. The 1994 crime bill, for example, led to a surge of police in communities — as well as schools — in the name of safety and community policing. Politicians looking to expand police presence have done so under the guise of meeting community needs and improving police-community relations. While many people from marginalized backgrounds feel as though police do not provide safety and are unjust, some may feel that the police are capable of substantive reform. And throughout history, as James Forman Jr. articulated in *Locking Up Our Own: Crime and Punishment in Black America*, some members of Black communities — especially those who have greater social, political, or class capital — have advocated for more policing and punishment.

One of the most salient mirages of reform is the promise of community policing. In response to Black uprisings throughout the 1960s, politicians and police leaders made a push toward expressed commitments of community policing. The deaths of Eric Garner, Rekia Boyd, and Aiyana Stanley-Jones; the countless Black bodies that the state has disappeared to prisons; and the millions of people stopped, questioned, harassed, brutalized, and frisked are evidence that the state's investment in community policing did nothing except attempt to legitimize police and provide them with increased resources. Community policing is meant to conjure up images of police and communities in harmony with each other, a return to the golden era, when police were known and a part of community life. But as history shows, that time never existed in the way it's often framed — especially for any group that has experienced oppression in the United States. As Keeanga-Yamahtta Taylor rightfully pointed out,

"There is no 'golden age' of policing to which elected officials can point, and there is little reason for optimism that American police can truly be reformed."[93]

The sociologist Forrest Stuart detailed the rise and practice in Los Angeles of therapeutic policing in *Down, Out, and Under Arrest: Policing and Everyday Life in Skid Row*, which focuses on using police to route people—in this case those who are homeless—into treatment and mainstream life and institutions. Therapeutic policing functions as a tool to make police appear more benevolent while ultimately serving as a veneer for punitive, criminalizing behaviors by police and the criminal-legal system. As Stuart wrote:

> The police thus constitute an important, though surprisingly overlooked, pathway by which neoliberalism's disciplinary enterprise breaches the walls of welfare organizations and suffuses the streets and sidewalks of marginalized communities. Therapeutic policing operates as a form of outreach social work that aims to transform and reintegrate residents as productive, self-governing citizens. Equipped with new legal tools and expanded discretionary authority, officers use coercive ultimatums—enter a rehabilitative program or go to jail, look for employment or suffer monetary fines—to instill residents with new habits, attitudes, and dispositions. Deployed as "tough love" for residents' own good, this street-level mode of poverty governance legitimates elevated levels of repression while widening the net of coercive control. As a result, additional (and previously noncriminal) behaviors and populations are subjected to ubiquitous surveillance and intrusive regulation.[94]

Therapeutic policing, community policing, and similar approaches are symbolic approaches with real outcomes: they reinforce the idea that police are reformable, that with a different approach, they can help transform communities. Police and politicians—and even members of Black and marginalized communities themselves at times—can use this to justify more police resources, training, and diversity.

THE DESIRE FOR SAFETY

People want safety. And those living without it are often looking for any and all ways to cultivate it. In a society that constantly communicates that police are the providers of safety, some will instinctively advocate for more police as a way to address safety, albeit while hoping for more community-oriented, fair, and just police. This is also why some people from oppressed communities will advocate for more police—if one's neighborhood feels unsafe and police are said to be the primary providers of safety, how else would a community become safer? As a result of decades of politicians and police leaders framing increases in policing as the way to decrease crime under tough-on-crime platforms that are mobilized for political support, this notion has become widespread, and even people who feel that the police are illegitimate still desire police protection when they see no other pathway for developing a safe community.

Racism is baked into the origin of policing. While the idea that police are the stewards of public safety is dominant, history reveals that this is simply not true. As a result, in Black, Latinx, immigrant, Indigenous, and poor communities, perceptions of police don't track perceptions among the broader public. As a result of targeted enforcement and contact among these communities, perceptions tend to be focused less on crime control—since communities experiencing harm and violence often feel that police are failing at crime control—and more on the brutality and harm that police subject communities to. And while some people, especially those with more conservative beliefs, believe that police are a central facet of community life and are capable of reform through efforts such as community policing, diversity, and use-of-force guidelines, a growing number of oppressed communities are embracing alternative visions of the future in which safety is actualized in sustainable ways rooted in repair and community. And increasingly, those who are not particularly targeted by police in their everyday life are moving away from views of police as mere crime fighters. One reason for this shift may be a result of activists from all backgrounds experiencing police violence and suppression during protests.

Police are the only fully funded institution that has been granted full power and responsibility over public safety. So the fact that there is so much conflicting data on when, where, and if police lead to decreases in crime should speak volumes. But even if they do provide immediate interventions in certain situations, we must reframe the question: Are there other entities that can provide interventions without the violence of policing? Violence is real and affects many communities across the country. So why rely on police and policing? We have seen over time that (1) policing was not designed for public safety, (2) police reinforce racial, class-based, and gendered injustices, (3) police violence sparks unrest, and (4) despite decades of police reform, police continue to engage in rampant violence and misconduct and preserve and expand their power.

We need to change how we approach safety altogether. Some interventions may lead to reductions in police abuse or misconduct, while others may reduce violence, but that is not sufficient. In addition, these reforms often reinforce the idea that modern policing is in fact capable of being transformed into something that it fundamentally is not. There are approaches that can reorient our society altogether that can cultivate safety and accountability, approaches that can address the roots of violence and remove opportunities for police violence. There is a need for testing and being open to change when necessary, but in focusing on marginal improvements and evidence-based interventions that tweak established systems, social scientists have reinforced current institutions and approaches to safety. To truly find a way out of the dark, we need to change it all. We also need data and evidence of a different type—rooted in an ethic of social justice and radical theoretical approaches. Data are currently used to preserve and expand policing and systems of punishment in the name of piecemeal improvements to fundamentally unjust systems.

Policing in the United States is a behemoth. The sheer size and scope of policing lend themselves to a level of control over American life that is so far reaching it is hard to imagine a United States before there were police—and even harder for many people to imagine a future without the massive policing infrastructure that exists today. Reforms from the twentieth century till now have not solved the problem of police abuse. Abolition is a vision that breaks from the current formulas—and formulaic thinking more broadly—that continue to produce recurring cycles of organized violence, harm, and abandonment.

FROM REFORM TO ABOLITION

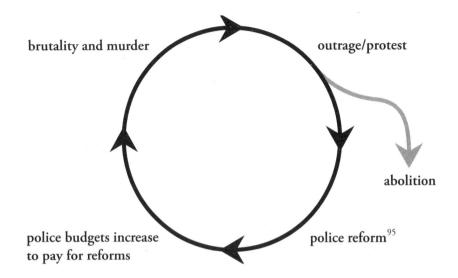

Through community relations initiatives, procedural justice, implicit bias training, and reforms that focus on rooting out "bad apples," police are taught to engage in ways that make communities feel heard and listened to while doing nothing to fundamentally reduce police violence and contact. Academics and social scientists often help develop and legitimize the police and the criminal-legal system without enabling shifts that will lead to meaningful reductions in police violence. Other reforms, such as review boards that have little to no decision-making power, are symbolic rather than transformative and have little effect on reducing police contact, arrests, and violence.

Academics, politicians, and police leaders posit use-of-force standards, force report requirements, and mandate licensing as solutions to police brutality and misconduct. The police reform era began over a hundred years ago, and procedure, professionalism, and training were framed as a solution to the problems of policing. Minneapolis had implemented all the progressive reforms—body cameras; de-escalation, implicit bias, and mindfulness training; reconciliatory efforts with communities of color; use-of-force standards; requirements that police intervene in misconduct; and community policing[96]—leading its police department to be held up as a model of progressive police reforms. Yet the police still murdered George Floyd.

Reducing contact and investing in community resources and institutions, as well as using alternatives to conflict in cases such as mental health crises, will guarantee that police violence does not occur and also help reduce violence, conflict, and harm within communities. It's also critical to remember that police brutality and killings are not the only form of police violence — sexual violence and domestic violence are among the most commonly reported police misconduct.[97] The violence of policing affects all Black people, including Black women,[98] despite most of the attention on this issue focusing on Black men who experience police violence. Moreover, the terror that many communities experience as a result of police presence and interactions is also a form of police violence.

―――――――

While many elected officials criticized demands to defund the police and reinvest in communities, some progressive-leaning mayors, such as Ras Baraka in Newark, implemented invest-divest proposals. In the heart of Newark's evolving public safety landscape, Mayor Ras Baraka's strategic decision to propose a 5 percent reduction in the police budget emerged as a pivotal moment.[99] This reduction signified a tangible shift of resources toward community-led safety efforts and led to the establishment of the Office of Violence Prevention & Trauma Recovery (OVPTR) in June 2020. The shift signified an institutional commitment to redefining public safety beyond the confines of traditional policing. In 2015, Baraka also helped to found the Newark Community Street Team (NCST). Through initiatives such as violence intervention and prevention programs that rely on credible messengers, community-based mental health and trauma services, and the Public Safety Round Tables, NCST is committed to advancing community-based safety. These efforts are distinguished by their focus on community engagement and support over punitive measures, aiming to mediate disputes and prevent violence proactively.

Mayor Baraka's initiatives to redirect police funds toward community-led efforts represents a meaningful stride toward reimagining community safety. But despite Baraka's commitments to community safety approaches, he also has remained deeply committed to policing.[100] In his critique of the defunding movement, Baraka stated, "Most of our residents want police officers. They want police officers in our neighborhoods, they want safety, they want security."[101] But Baraka, in his focus on criticizing defunding,[102] misses an important opportunity for a nuanced understanding of what is at the heart of the issue: people desire safety and are told that police are the only ones that can provide it, as Baraka signals.

Public statements by the mayor and City of Newark and media portrayals of these initiatives in Newark often highlight that they maintain collaborative relationships with the police and serve as a bridge to help build trust for policing.[103] However, the reality of these initiatives' engagement with law enforcement actually contrasts the police partnership depictions in some ways. While OVPTR is a city entity, NCST in particular is an independent, community-based organization. NCST operates under a philosophy that prioritizes a clear demarcation from law enforcement, emphasizing that they do not share any detailed information with police. This stance is rooted in a commitment to safeguarding the well-being of their outreach workers and communities, as well as in light of an unjust history of police in Newark that ultimately led to a federal consent.

The contrast between NCST's work and the perceived or suggested partnerships with police underscores a critical dialogue about the essence of community safety work and its relationship with law enforcement agencies. Despite the public discourse that often suggests police collaboration, the actual practices and philosophies of organizations like NCST challenge this narrative. They strive to redefine public safety from a community-centric perspective, offering solutions that emphasize healing, support, and prevention over conventional policing methods. Recognizing the unique and independent contributions of community-based organizations without tethering it to police involvement is essential in reshaping approaches to safety. Moving beyond oversimplified narratives of police-community partnerships, often wielded for political capital, is crucial to fully appreciate the depth and potential of these community-based safety approaches. Elected officials have the opportunity to challenge the false equating of policing and safety by not engaging in practices where they use community safety initiatives as ways to reentrench policing.

The national landscape also reveals how the discourse surrounding community safety often becomes entangled with policing. This intertwining becomes particularly evident in the approach taken by the Biden administration through the American Rescue Plan of 2021. While ostensibly aimed at bolstering community safety, a significant portion of the $10 billion allotted to public safety and violence prevention allocated resources that favored initiatives that increase police capacity and partnerships with police.[104] Notably, much of this funding was channeled to police for capital expenses and equipment—including tasers, rifles, cars, shooting ranges—as well as police dogs, squad cars, jail equipment, and infrastructure.[105] This allocation strategy underscores a preference for models that incorporate police involvement in approaches to safety, whether due to a genuine belief in the efficacy of such partnerships or as a maneuver to navigate the political landscape without alienating certain constituencies.

The favoring of police-community partnership initiatives raises key concerns about current and future community-led safety approaches. By promoting programs that are either directly associated with law enforcement or that rhetorically align with policing, there's a risk of perpetuating the narrative that effective community safety is inseparable from police involvement. This perspective not only narrows the scope of potential solutions but also risks alienating those within communities who are skeptical of police and the criminal-legal system. The implication that community safety initiatives must operate in conjunction with police forces can undermine the autonomy and efficacy of truly community-centered approaches, potentially deterring engagement from those who might benefit most.

The intense, favorable presence of police portrayals throughout mainstream media and culture is often referred to as "copaganda"—media propaganda favoring the police that shapes public opinion about policing in a positive way.[106] Copaganda also confines public opinion around how safety is defined and the means by which it can be achieved.[107] The positive portrayals of police in media, the news coverage that reinforces the police as fixed, unbiased providers of public safety, as well as the widely shared images of police engaging with communities at playgrounds, giving out ice cream, hosting barbecues and giveaways, and in other contexts have become important aspects of constructing the police within broader society as an ostensibly legitimate institution. The emphasis on police-community relations and the rhetorical merging of community safety with policing serve to reinforce copaganda and the notion that police are an immutable and necessary fixture in society. This narrative overlooks the potential for community-based approaches to independently manage and address safety issues. For community safety initiatives to be genuinely transformative, they must be sustainable and operate with independence from policing. This means not only reducing explicit partnerships with police but also carefully navigating the language and rhetoric used to describe and promote these strategies.

Moving forward, there is a pressing need to reenvision how community safety is conceptualized and implemented. Efforts should focus on empowering communities to lead these initiatives, fostering environments where safety solutions are developed and managed by those directly impacted by them, without defaulting to police involvement. By prioritizing community engagement and management of safety issues, it is possible to challenge prevailing narratives of copaganda and demonstrate that effective, sustainable safety strategies can exist outside policing frameworks. This shift requires a deliberate reevaluation of funding priorities, program designs, and the broader discourse on safety, ensuring that community-led approaches are recognized and supported as viable and necessary off-ramps from policing.

Reforms that do not reduce police power and scope will not lead to the end of police harm and the reimagining of safety and justice. For instance, Camden, New Jersey, which is often praised as a case study in police reform, is not an example of reimagining public safety.[108] In 2013, the local government replaced the local police department with a more resourced county-level department that has created an intense surveillance culture in the city. The model still rests on punishment, surveillance, and control when there are ways to foster safety and accountability that do not center on policing and prisons.

ENDING THE WAR ON DRUGS: TOWARD DECRIMINALIZATION

On December 10, 1986, in a speech titled "The View from Here," James Baldwin stated:

Now if you want to get to the heart of the dope problem, legalize it. That destroys the profit motive, and may save our children. Nobody that has a habit who can afford it is going to go to jail. So it is a law, which in operation, can be used only against the poor. And a law like that is a bad law. And it has not stopped anybody from his fix. It just puts some people in jail and some people under the ground. Because a whole lot of money is being made on the anti-dope law, which does not work.[109]

The war on drugs has had disastrous impacts and has not solved problems related to drugs; in many ways it has inflamed them. Problems often attributed to drugs in many cases actually stem from structural inequality. A lack of public education on responsible drug use, compounded by the proliferation of poor-quality and counterfeit drugs, makes drug use far more dangerous than it needs to be. It's also essential to distinguish between those who use drugs and those who are addicted to them. As the neuropharmacologist Carl L. Hart highlighted, 70 to 90 percent of drug users aren't addicted.[110] Issues such as mental illness, poverty, and socioeconomic challenges often drive problematic drug use more than the drugs themselves do. Hart also pointed out that the harms associated with drugs are amplified by the fact they are criminalized. In his book *When Crack Was King: A People's History of a Misunderstood Era*, Donovan X. Ramsey noted that the crack epidemic was damaging, but in often misunderstood ways. Many of the problems attributed to crack cocaine had roots in a racist criminal-legal system and anti-Black politicians who scapegoated crack use for unrelated problems.

Labeling people addicts and using derogatory terms such as *fiends*, *crackheads*, and *junkies* stigmatizes people and flattens their complex experiences and identities. In the process, stigmatizing people who use drugs also leads to the broader problems surrounding drug use, such as systemic inequality and injustice, being overlooked. People are not seen as complex humans who may need support and who may be dealing with a range of realities shaped by an unjust world; they are simply addicts. This kind of labeling, which also can lead to people who use drugs being unfairly treated, disproportionately targets marginalized communities, despite members of the affluent segments of society using similar substances.[111] Members of better-off communities who use drugs that are considered serious do not experience intense stigma and social ostracization. This societal branding doesn't deter drug use; it weaponizes it, perpetuating existing inequalities. The stigma associated with particular drugs, such as crack cocaine, along with their criminalization, simplifies the image of many people who use drugs, particularly those who are marginalized from society: those who use the stigmatized substances are automatically seen as drug addicts.

The stigma of drugs has largely been shaped by the use of the substances by marginalized communities of color and poor people. The narratives surrounding drug use and sale are influenced by campaigns to stigmatize them, even as pharmaceutical companies and health care providers distribute other drugs that people become addicted to on a grand scale—a major cause of the opioid crisis. Even more, big businesses benefit from the sale of alcohol and cigarettes even though they can be very dangerous and harmful. Comparatively, major pharmaceutical firms rarely face legal consequences for wrongdoing and practices that cause harm.

The criminalization associated with the war on drugs targets Black and Latinx communities disproportionately, revealing the underlying racial and class dynamics in play. The stereotypes around drug dealers are often driven by racial and class scripts. They often view their trade as a path to stability, at times amid chaos. If given the resources and opportunities, many people who sell drugs might pursue different lines of work that would feel meaningful. Large pharmaceutical companies provide narcotics every day in a multibillion-dollar industry—at times with harmful outcomes—and are not criminalized in the ways that Black, Latinx, and other marginalized drug dealers are. People should be accountable for causing harm by engaging in practices such as knowingly giving someone different drugs from what they wanted or adulterated drugs. But the draconian criminalization of the war on drugs has had everything to do with race and class, rather than a genuine interest in safety. Research has shown that prohibition approaches and aggressive drug enforcement increase violence and harm, making drug economies more volatile and dangerous.[112]

Nationally, trying to enforce sobriety through criminalization has failed. Due to criminalization, lack of drug testing, and inadequate education about responsible drug use, many users turn to low-quality or adulterated drugs, increasing the risks of overdose and death. Drug use, which is ultimately a personal choice, can indeed become a serious concern, but in the case that it does, it requires a public health approach, not draconian punishment. The way forward involves a significant paradigm shift. Current drug criminalization policies harm more than they help. Decriminalization, which removes laws and excessive regulations driven by capitalist interests and punitive politicians, is the solution. While drugs can be harmful, it's vital to separate the drugs' effects from societal factors such as poverty that produce and intensify problems.

Drug addiction is real and destabilizing. None of this is to say that drugs themselves can never cause harm. The crack epidemic had real impacts, despite many of them being propaganda. The harm actually stemmed from poverty and precarity, which led to higher rates of addiction, and a conflation of the effects of poverty and those of drug use that stemmed from racist and classist narratives. Drug stigma, especially for the use of substances considered to be "hard drugs," has also paved the way for alienation and punishment.

The central concern should be safe use and ensuring drug quality. But the United States has proven incapable of regulating drug use in a just and equitable way that does not lead to criminalization of marginalized communities. The criminalization of drug use, far from being a remedy, has caused more harm than it has alleviated. The solution lies in decriminalization. This involves not only ending the criminalization of drugs but also stepping away from excessive regulation, which often arises from capitalist motives rather than genuine public safety concerns. A decriminalized landscape that emphasizes education would prioritize safe use and the assurance of drug quality, increasing safer outcomes for anyone who decides to use substances.

While drugs can cause harm, much of the damage caused during eras such as the crack cocaine epidemic was shaped and amplified by poverty and systemic inequality. Effective treatment for substance abuse would involve holistic support, encompassing mental, social, and financial aspects. Relying on law enforcement in drug situations only escalates potential harm.

Treatment for people struggling with substance abuse can take the form of wraparound services including all mental, social, housing, and financial needs. When emergency support is needed, a nonpunitive team of at least a social worker, a psychologist, and a medical doctor can help oversee treatment. What does police presence in cases of alleged drug use or misuse do other than create the potential for harm? Drug safety workers who are informed with a public health approach, medication to counter overdose, and the tools to educate and reduce the potential for adverse outcomes from drug use offer a much more reliable strategy.

We must shift from a punitive prohibition stance and adopt a framework that recognizes the multifaceted nature of drug use and respects the people involved. By prioritizing education, support, and public health, we will pave the way to a healthier society.

IN DEFENSE OF DEFUNDING

Following the tragic police murders of George Floyd and Breonna Taylor, campaigns advocating defunding the police and reallocating their funds to community investments surged. Those calls, however, were met with sharp resistance. Texas governor Greg Abbott, for instance, signed into law HB 1900, which threatened to penalize cities with populations over 250,000 if they pursued significant divestment from police.[113] Critics ranging from media outlets to politicians and even some academics accused defunding advocates of increasing violence and political polarization.[114] There were accusations that the calls for defunding directly led to the rise of conservative politicians and that activists were causing chaos. When Eric Adams campaigned for mayor of New York City, he used his pro-police stance and identity as a Black man to appeal to voters and repeatedly criticize calls to defund the police. The rhetoric of Black individuals supporting the police provides a compelling counternarrative to creating transformative perspectives around safety and justice. As antidefund critiques gained traction nationally, some previous supporters distanced themselves from the defunding movement. The critiques failed to account for the precarity and crisis caused by the government's overall failure in response to the COVID-19 pandemic. Marginalized communities were left reeling economically, as well as in terms of health, both of which can increase violence and harm. But rather than examining the root causes, the focus became fearmongering and focusing on protests against police violence. Calls for transforming approaches to safety and justice cannot be the scapegoats for issues of violence and harm within society.

To address concerns about increased violence in the wake of calls to defund and abolish police, it's essential to note that these arguments are hardly novel. After protests sparked by Michael Brown's death, claims about low police morale resulting in spikes in crime emerged. In some cases, the claim of increasing crime was inflated and untrue. In other cases, violence did increase during the early years of the pandemic—but there were likely a range of reasons for those changes, largely the COVID-19 crisis and the subsequent fallout resulting from governments' poor handling of the pandemic.[115] There may be times when police presence can deter crimes, but the central question remains: How can we address the root causes of these behaviors? Proponents of defunding argue for a shift from policing to community investment, noting that there are diverse ways to tackle violence and that policing doesn't necessarily prevent incidents such as intimate partner violence.

Furthermore, the argument that protests against police violence result in increased community vulnerability creates an unjust framing that implies that communities must either tolerate police violence or pursue age-old reforms that haven't eradicated police misconduct. This dilemma underscores the need for a comprehensive shift beyond policing. To address these challenges, there's an urgent need for community-based safety measures and resources that are accountable and transparent and can adapt to feedback. Community safety initiatives not only are less likely to harm people than modern policing but are not likely to cause the kinds of conflict and tension that arise in the forms of protests and uprisings. The problem of policing is at the root of all of these issues, and we need to move beyond it.

Critics of defunding are drawing from a familiar playbook, framing the debate as a choice between being "soft" and being "tough" on crime. This is effective because it taps into a fundamental human desire: the desire for safety. Many Democratic and Republican politicians alike chastised the demands to defund the police. Former president Obama stated in 2020, "I guess you can use a snappy slogan like 'defund the police.' But, you know, you lost a big audience the minute you say it, which makes it a lot less likely that you're actually going to get the changes you want done."[116] However, calls to defund the police aren't a mere rhetorical slip or framing mishap; they are a challenge to the deeply entrenched notion that policing is the only means to ensure safety. The objective isn't necessarily to change everyone's perspective but to catalyze a broader transformation toward genuine safety and justice, even if some remain staunchly pro-police.

It is essential to critically examine the notion of Black-on-Black crime, a trope that has been constructed and utilized by both liberal and conservative factions. Drawing upon the work of David Wilson in *Inventing Black-on-Black Violence: Discourse, Space, and Representation*,[117] this examination reveals how the trope has been employed to various ends, often overshadowing genuine concerns about safety and harm within Black communities. The concept of Black-on-Black crime is frequently presented as a unique and "racial" problem, which paradoxically serves to both minimize the significance of harm experienced within Black communities and to portray such harm as inherently racial. This framing dismisses the broader socioeconomic and structural factors contributing to crime, instead reducing it to a simplistic racial narrative.

Liberals have sometimes employed this trope to advocate for a stronger social welfare state, yet without adequately addressing the punitive aspects embedded in the current social welfare system. This approach risks perpetuating a narrative in which increased social welfare is viewed primarily as a crime prevention measure, rather than as part of a broader goal to create a more humane and equitable society for all.

Conservatives, on the other hand, have often used the Black-on-Black crime trope to undermine discussions about systemic racism and police brutality, suggesting that internal community issues rather than external systemic factors should be the focus. This perspective deflects attention from necessary policing reforms and broader societal inequalities. The trope of Black-on-Black violence requires a nuanced critique. Its political use must be understood and challenged, particularly in how it influences discussions about policing, social welfare, and community safety.

One common response to the calls for defunding is politicians' and police leaders' claiming that Black people want more cops in their communities. James Baldwin's words are instructive:

> The Black Panther Party for Self Defense.... It is a need which no black citizen of the ghetto has to have spelled out. When, as white cops are fond of pointing out to me, ghetto citizens "ask for more cops, not less," what they are asking for is more police protection: for crimes committed by blacks against blacks have never been taken very seriously. Furthermore, the prevention of crimes such as these is not the reason for the policeman's presence. That black people need protection *against* the police is indicated by the black community's reaction to the advent of the Panthers. Without community support, the Panthers would have been merely another insignificant street gang. It was the reaction of the black

community which triggered the response of the police: these young men, claiming the right to bear arms, dressed deliberately in guerrilla fashion, standing nearby whenever a black man was accosted by a policeman to inform the black man of his rights and insisting on the right of black people to self-defense, were immediately marked as "trouble-makers."[118]

Black people—all people—want safety. In today's society, people are socialized to believe that police are the only ones who can provide it, because nearly every institution within society—schools, media, politicians, and mainstream institutions—reinforces the idea that police are the only ones who can protect us. Some people may benefit from policing because of their identity, leading them to feel a semblance of protection from police rather than feeling targeted. But police do not do a good job of increasing safety. And there are other ways to bring about safety that do not come with the violence of policing. When people ask for more police, they are really asking for more safety. But community-based approaches to safety and ensuring that people have what they need are the answers to that desire.

The Black Panther Party's efforts to counteract state power and police power with community patrols and survival programs provide valuable lessons. They faced intense opposition and warfare from the state, underscoring the importance of studying history, building coalitions, and enacting transformative methods of community care. We must study, learn, build coalitions, act, and develop institutions and transformative approaches of relating and caring for one another, such as with mutual aid, that will render policing obsolete. This will also show the capacity for communities to handle problems autonomously, particularly when they have the necessary resources.

A pivotal aspect of the discourse surrounding police abolition concerns the varied perspectives within Black communities on law enforcement. Black individuals hold diverse views on policing, ranging from critiques of police response times to broader systemic issues. This complexity is further entangled in political debates about Black support for abolitionist movements. While some argue that Black communities desire more policing due to concerns about crime, violence, or police neglect, these assertions often fail to address the safety and experiences of harm within these communities.

Historically, campaigns such as Officer Friendly and various police-community relationship initiatives that have specifically targeted Black communities reveal a deeper, more insidious narrative. In a society in which anti-Black ideologies persist, these campaigns often operate under the assumption that Black people require more policing than other racial groups. This belief is not only rooted in racist stereotypes but also serves to weaponize the need for policing against Black people, purportedly in their own interest.

Critiques of abolition frequently draw on anti-Black ideologies, even when claiming to represent the desires of Black communities. They often intertwine with narratives about a "culture of poverty" or "Black-on-Black violence," racializing violence as inherently a "Black" issue. This perspective not only misrepresents the realities within Black communities but also perpetuates the notion that policing is an essential, even benevolent, presence in these communities.

In addressing these facts, it becomes clear that police reforms have often targeted Black people, exploiting their critiques and concerns to bolster pro-policing stances. Such reforms, while claiming to be in the interest of Black safety, seldom confront the root causes of interpersonal and community violence. A genuine investment in the safety of Black communities involves a thorough examination of how these forms of violence are intricately linked to broader structural violence. It is centrally important to challenge the narrative that Black communities inherently "need" policing and advocate for approaches that truly prioritize their safety and well-being, beyond the limited and often harmful scope of policing.

THE ILLUSION OF TRUST

The discussion of police reforms, especially those targeting Black communities, highlights a critical aspect of how responses to critiques of police abuse, racism, and neglect often take the form of initiatives aimed at "building trust" or improving police-community relations. These reforms, while purportedly addressing the concerns of Black communities, can inadvertently reinforce the notion that these communities require more policing, rather than fundamentally rethinking the role and nature of policing itself.

Programs such as Officer Friendly, which attempted to introduce a positive image of police among young children, illustrate this approach. While appearing beneficial, they often operate under the assumption that building a friendly rapport with police can mitigate systemic issues of abuse and racism. Such programs do not address the root causes of mistrust but rather focus on superficial relationship building.

Another notable example is the D.A.R.E. (Drug Abuse Resistance Education) program, established in 1983 as a joint venture between the then LAPD chief of police, Daryl Gates, and the Los Angeles Unified School District. Throughout the 1980s and '90s, the program spread across the country. D.A.R.E. aimed to educate young people about drug abuse prevention. However, it maintained a draconian, racialized approach to drug use. The program also involved students in surveillance activities, essentially encouraging them to report on family members' drug use. In increasing stigma and racist narratives around drugs, D.A.R.E. helped create a context in which drugs were used as a scapegoat for a range of social issues. Research has suggested that the initiative had no measurable outcome effects.[119]

The underlying assumption in many of these reforms is that Black communities inherently require more policing, a notion deeply ingrained in societal and institutional perspectives. This assumption not only overshadows the legitimate critiques and demands for change from Black communities but also perpetuates a cycle in which reforms serve to enhance and refine policing methods, rather than dealing with alternatives that move beyond policing.

Such reform efforts fail to acknowledge the systemic nature of policing issues. They do not challenge the premise that more policing is the solution, thereby stalling broader efforts toward abolition and societal transformation. This approach implicitly suggests that Black communities are in constant need of policing, reinforcing harmful stereotypes and diverting attention from the need for more profound structural changes. The specific targeting of Black communities with policing reforms under the guise of building trust and improving relations underscores a deeper issue: the persistent belief that policing is an essential and irreplaceable component of these communities. This belief underpins the continuation and reform of policing practices, hindering the progress toward abolition and the realization of a society that genuinely prioritizes safety, justice, and equity for all.

Narratives about Black culture and family structure are embedded in policing and police reforms. This is particularly evident in programs such as D.A.R.E. and police athletic leagues, where police organize sports and recreational activities and extend their roles beyond law enforcement to include being "father figures," friends, or mentors. These programs embody a discourse that often specifically targets Black communities, suggesting a need for external authority figures or role models to prevent crime and delinquency. These programs operate on the premise that police can fill voids in family structures or provide mentorship that is supposedly lacking, particularly in Black communities.

The portrayal of police as substitute family figures or mentors in programs such as D.A.R.E. and police athletic leagues is more than a community outreach strategy; it is a reflection of deeper societal narratives about race, family structures, and the supposed role of law enforcement in "correcting" perceived social and cultural deficits. Understanding this dynamic is essential to a thorough critique of policing practices and the ideologies that underpin them. This perspective aligns with broader anti-Black ideologies prevalent in social sciences, political discourse, and policy. It reflects a narrative that Black communities require intervention by law enforcement to compensate for perceived deficiencies in family and community structures. This is in stark contrast to narratives surrounding other racial groups, such as Asian Americans, who are often subjected to the "model minority" myth, a stereotype that suggests inherent cultural predispositions toward success and law-abiding behavior.[120]

Anti-Black ideologies in social sciences and policy not only inform the ways Black people are targeted with police reforms but also shape perceptions of these reforms as "beneficial." This illustrates the underlying logic in defenses of policing by those who argue that abolition would harm Black people, who are presumed to "want" or "need" policing. Initiatives aimed at "building trust," a concept prominently featured during President Obama's administration, remain central to popular police reforms. The President's Task Force on 21st Century Policing, established in 2014, epitomizes this endeavor.[121] The task force's objective was to strengthen community policing and foster trust between law enforcement agencies and the communities they serve. While the initiative acknowledged issues of police violence and racial discrimination, it also paved the way for pro-police narratives that subtly integrate civilians into policing roles.

Critically, these "building trust" initiatives, while recognizing critiques of racism and police violence, often propose surface-level engagement strategies that do not address the deeper systemic problems in policing. This approach can be interpreted as a strategy to placate public outcry rather than instigating substantial reform within policing practices. While initiatives such as the President's Task Force on 21st Century Policing and programs such as D.A.R.E. and Officer Friendly were developed to bridge gaps between police and communities, their underlying implications and effectiveness warrant critical examination. These programs, in their expressed efforts to build trust, perpetuate pro-police narratives and involve civilians in policing activities in ways that do not fundamentally address the systemic issues of racism and violence of policing.

ADDRESSING GENDER AND SEXUAL VIOLENCE

The National Intimate Partner and Sexual Violence Survey (NISVS) provides insights into both sexual violence and intimate partner violence, which cause lasting harm and trauma, emphasizing the pervasiveness of these issues across the United States. According to the most recent survey's findings from 2016/2017, approximately 54.3 percent of women and 30.7 percent of men report experiencing some form of contact sexual violence in their lifetime, often perpetrated by someone they know.[122] This challenges the traditional "stranger" narrative around sexual violence harm doers and highlights the need for community-based prevention and education that starts early and addresses the root causes of sexual violence. Nearly one in three women and one in ten men also report facing harassment in public spaces, reflecting the pervasive and varied nature of sexual violence across different contexts.

The NISVS also uncovers the alarming extent of intimate-partner violence, with nearly half of women and over two in five men reporting experiences of contact sexual violence, physical violence, or stalking by an intimate partner[123] The data show a high incidence of severe physical violence among survivors, with significant impacts on their physical and mental health, underscoring the necessity for accessible support systems and early intervention strategies. Notably, many survivors first experience violence before the age of twenty-five, further stressing the importance of targeting preventive efforts at younger populations. There is a need for community resources and engagement to effectively address these realities across populations. The findings from the NISVS point to a need for a shift away from punitive measures toward more comprehensive, preventive, and transformative strategies. These should include enhancing education about healthy relationships, integrating support services into community programs, and fostering environments that empower survivors and prevent future violence. This holistic approach can potentially offer a more effective alternative to the often-inadequate responses provided by the existing criminal-legal framework.

A critical examination of the criminal-legal system reveals a disturbing reality: that policing and prison systems are not only inadequate in addressing sexual and gendered violence but are, in fact, environments in which such violence is often perpetuated and normalized.[124] The first point of contact in the criminal-legal system, policing, often fails survivors of sexual and gendered violence in a range of ways. Research indicates that incidents of sexual violence are significantly underreported, partly due to survivors' distrust of the police and the legal system.[125] When cases are reported, they frequently encounter systemic challenges such as victim-blaming attitudes, inadequate training of officers in handling sensitive cases, and a lack of resources for comprehensive investigations. Moreover, instances of police committing acts of sexual violence further illuminate why some survivors do not turn to the police after experiencing sexual harm.

Within prisons, sexual and gendered violence is alarmingly common, with incarcerated people often facing abuse by both fellow incarcerated individuals and prison staff. The Bureau of Justice Statistics has reported that thousands of incarcerated individuals experience sexual victimization in prisons and jails annually in the United States.[126] This environment of violence is exacerbated by a culture of silence and retribution, making it difficult for survivors to receive healing and justice. The punitive nature of the criminal-legal system, with its focus on incarceration over transformative approaches, fails to address the underlying causes of violence. This approach neglects the needs of survivors and does little to transform the behavior of harm doers. As a result, the cycle of violence and recidivism persists, where individuals, once released, often lack the support and resources to break free from patterns of abuse and aggression.

Policies in housing, public assistance, mental health, and addiction services intersect with the criminal-legal system to create a punitive landscape. For instance, individuals with criminal records face significant barriers in accessing stable housing, public assistance, and essential services, increasing the potential of both experiencing and perpetuating violence.[127] This punitive approach extends the reach of the carceral state into various aspects of life, perpetuating vulnerability and harm. As the organizations Critical Resistance and INCITE! have made clear, the criminal-legal system is not capable of ending cycles of sexual and gendered violence.[128] The system's inability to protect survivors, transform the behavior of harm doers, and prevent future violence underscores the need for a radical rethinking of how society deals with these issues. The focus should shift from punitive measures to preventive and transformative strategies to address the root causes of violence and offer comprehensive support to those affected.

CREATING SOLUTIONS FROM THE GROUND UP

How did we arrive at this moment of crisis surrounding policing? Moments of national outrage and rebellion over policing have occurred throughout history and were a major contributor to the uprisings of the 1960s. Police violence against marginalized communities has occurred since the onset of policing, but in 2024 we find ourselves at a critical juncture in history. There has been a resurgence of the Movement for Black Lives, and over the last ten years, organizers have been building and developing politically to bring us to a moment where we see the push for a much different set of demands. In 2020, the nation saw the injection of abolitionist language and demands into popular discourse in a way that was unprecedented. Abolitionists, as well as those calling for a dramatic reduction of the scope and power of policing, have grown increasingly skeptical of the popular, seemingly progressive reforms that have been implemented as solutions in recent years and decades. Bias training, procedural justice, community policing, diversity efforts, use-of-force guidelines, civilian review boards, body cameras, focused deterrence, and training centered on police legitimacy have all been called into question, as many cities have enacted these reforms, and while the impacts of the various strategies vary—from negligible to some impact on particular metrics—they have proven ineffective in stopping cycles of police violence.

Increasing numbers of community-based approaches center on areas such as antiviolence work. These initiatives require resources and capacity development in order to effectively build community-based safety approaches on a large scale. The resource hub TransformHarm.org has developed strategies for transformative justice and alternative approaches to community violence and harm. The Oakland Power Projects, a project of Critical Resistance, has advanced community-based safety, health care, and emergency preparedness models that do not involve policing.[129] The Health Alliance for Violence Intervention supports hospital and community collaborations to advance equitable, trauma-informed care for violence intervention and prevention programs. Violence interrupters use personal outreach by community members to mediate and diffuse neighborhood conflict.[130] In California, the Bay Area Transformative Justice Collective (BATJC) works toward developing and supporting transformative justice approaches to child sexual abuse.[131]

There are many ways to reduce violence and intervene in conflict that do not rely on an incredibly expensive, archaic, and violent model that actively harms and kills Black and other marginalized people. Largely because of the culture of punishment that animates the criminal-legal system, most people do not report events that are defined as crimes. Existing violence intervention models have shown to be effective and do not center on police and systems of punishment.[132] There is also a substantial body of evidence suggesting how other civic and community-based organizations and initiatives can build safe communities without the costs and violence that accompany police and prisons.[133] Possible solutions include conflict resolution teams, summer jobs,[134] after-school programs,[135] addiction and mental health treatment, well-resourced community-based violence interruption teams—including for gender-based violence—more green spaces within communities,[136] and the meeting of the basic needs of all residents. A major intervention is removing police from traffic safety, which seems likely to be implemented in Berkeley, where an unarmed civilian entity will manage traffic safety. This idea is gaining momentum in New York City and Los Angeles, as many instances of police violence start during traffic stops and spiral out.[137]

In 2020, after the murders of George Floyd and Breonna Taylor, there was tension between those calling for traditional reforms and those with more transformative demands. In the summer of 2020, Campaign Zero, a project launched in 2015 to address police violence, launched 8 Can't Wait, a set of policy recommendations based on faulty data science that failed to address the scope of police power. 8 Can't Wait had the potential to undercut the transformative demands emerging from the Movement for Black Lives, and in response, organizers developed the #8toAbolition campaign, which put forth the following recommendations: defund police; demilitarize communities; remove police from schools; free people from jails and prisons; repeal laws that criminalize survival; invest in community self-governance; provide safe housing for everyone; invest in care, not cops.[138] After the release of #8toAbolition and criticism of the faulty data and the fact that the proposed reforms undercut the momentum of the transformative demands being made,[139] Campaign Zero removed the specific data claims from the 8 Can't Wait platform and added a framework of invest-divest and abolition to the platform.

Across the country, organizers are building political power to challenge the century-long reforms that have been recycled and repackaged time and time again for a transformative shift away from police and prisons. Instead, we can prioritize building safety interventions and designing models of responding to conflict, harm, and violence rooted in frameworks such as restorative justice, which focuses on healing and reconciliation within communities, and transformative justice, which seeks to address harm through a focus on the root causes of social issues and change underlying social conditions, rather than relying on punishment, vengeance, and control.[140] In 2018, the Movement for Black Lives outlined a policy platform on invest-divest initiatives, a part of the broader Vision for Black Lives policy platform, arguing for *investment* in safety for Black communities through access to education, health care, jobs, and domestic infrastructure such as housing and transportation and *divestment* from "exploitative forces including prisons, fossil fuels, police, surveillance and exploitative corporations."[141] The platform presented an encompassing vision that addressed police violence as well as the social, political, and economic realities that emerge from legacies of racial and class inequality. The invest-divest section of the Movement for Black Lives platform states, "We demand investments in the education, health and safety of Black people, instead of investments in the criminalizing, caging, and harming of Black people. We want investments in Black communities, determined by Black communities."[142] This platform is the first national push toward an invest-divest campaign. It has influenced many policy efforts in Black communities across the country operating within the larger Movement for Black Lives landscape.

Schools throughout the United States, however, have also been investing in more police and security presence in previous decades. In 2019, Governor Brian Kemp of Georgia unveiled a $69 million security plan[143] for schools that included a $500,000 antigang initiative, as well as a $30,000 budget for police, security cameras, and metal detectors. Due to the pressures and coverage of Black[144] and Latinx[145] organizers' efforts across the country, police presence is decreasing in public schools. More community members are speaking out. In California, many students have police on their campuses but no counselors[146] to provide social and mental health support. Black communities are organizing across the country to push city leaders to listen to calls for community investment rather than pour more money into policing and punishment. In the process, they are contending with police unions and city leaders deeply opposed to divesting from the $100 billion[147] spent annually on policing in the United States, but still they are pushing forward with invest-divest campaigns.

Building on its 2018 policy platform, which set forth a series of invest-divest initiatives, the Movement for Black Lives proposed the BREATHE Act,[148] a sweeping omnibus bill that advances a invest-divest framework and would significantly reduce criminalization, institutionalized punishment, and police surveillance. The bill is perhaps the largest proposed by a Black movement since the Civil Rights Act. The four sections of the bill are Divesting Federal Resources from Incarceration and Policing & Ending Criminal-Legal System Harms; Investing in New Approaches to Community Safety Utilizing Funding Incentives; Allocating New Money to Build Healthy, Sustainable & Equitable Communities for All People; and Holding Officials Accountable & Enhancing Self-Determination of Black Communities.

The BREATHE Act proposes eliminating tactics that are disproportionately used to target Black, Brown, and Muslim communities by prohibiting predictive policing, facial recognition technologies, drones, and similar tools; eliminating the use of electronic monitoring, including ankle monitors, smartphone applications, and any other tool used to track location; ending civil asset forfeiture, where law enforcement agencies can seize assets such as cash, vehicles, and real estate suspected of being connected to criminal activity, often without requiring a criminal conviction or even charging the owner with a crime; abolishing mandatory minimum sentencing laws; ending life sentences; abolishing three-strikes laws; developing a time-bound plan to close all federal prisons and immigration detention centers; repealing federal laws that criminalize human movement and border entry; repealing the 1994 crime act and replacing it with noncarceral, nonpunitive investments in communities; and decriminalizing and retroactively expunging drug offenses.

The BREATHE Act also calls for eliminating federal programs and agencies used to finance and expand the US criminal-legal system, such as the Department of Defense's 1033 Program, the Edward Byrne Memorial Justice Assistance Grant program—one of the largest grant-giving entities for law enforcement administered by the Bureau of Justice Assistance, a component of the Office of Justice Programs in the US Department of Justice—COPS, the Drug Enforcement Administration, and ICE. The bill would ensure that nonpunitive, noncarceral elements of these programs are identified so they can be transferred to another funding source. The BREATHE Act also makes the recommendation to dramatically reduce the Department of Defense's budget. The act is the most sweeping bill offered to date to fundamentally reduce the size and power of police and the broader criminal-legal system.

The only guaranteed way to reduce police violence is to eliminate contact with police altogether. Communities with the necessary time and resources can develop approaches to deal with violence, conflict, and harm. In many ways, aggressive policing and incarceration make communities worse and cause devastating effects that ripple across the social fabric of communities. The criminalization of poverty and survival economies—such as the drug trade and some sex work—further fuels issues and inflames communities through criminalizing conditions that cannot be solved by policing and punishment. As the United States continues to experience political shifts at all levels of government, participatory budgeting,[149] a strategy whereby communities are directly involved in budget decisions, may be the key to invest-divest campaigns. Allowing people to decide how funds are allocated in their communities is an alternative, sustainable way to cultivate safety and prevent politicians' deciding on budgets that do not adequately address the needs of the public.

Activists and organizers have made compelling arguments for abolishing policing, jails, and prisons, and these arguments have been injected into the popular discourse in an unprecedented way. Organizers have made clear that their efforts are not centered on abolishing safety and help but on making a decision—as was made in Minneapolis—to uproot what currently exists. As part of that process, organizers are calling for reimagined models of public safety and transformative models of justice that create safer communities that have the resources they need to thrive. The current model of punishment is not making us safer, and it often leads to cycles of harm and violence that devastate communities.

Abolitionists such as Angela Y. Davis, Ruth Wilson Gilmore, and Mariame Kaba; organizers from Critical Resistance; and so many others have offered visions of a world that sees the utter and complete dismantling of systems of imprisonment, policing, and surveillance—and the creation of new ways of relating to and caring for one another, rooted in transformation and ensuring that communities have their basic needs met and the resources they need to thrive. These visions have been critical in bringing us to the moment we find ourselves in, where we can have very different kinds of conversations. Organizations such as MPD150, Creative Interventions, Anti Police-Terror Project, Generation 5, and the BATJC have also been on the front lines of experimenting with, creating, and developing alternative ways to approach violence, harm, and crises that exist entirely outside of policing and the criminal-legal system.

THE CLIMATE CRISIS BEYOND POLICING

In the quest for sustainable environmental solutions, the challenge often lies not just in identifying what needs to be done but also in finding viable ways to fund these initiatives. Here, the concept of invest-divest strategies becomes relevant, particularly in the context of transitioning toward a regenerative economy. A regenerative economy moves beyond merely reducing our carbon footprint or conserving resources; it's about fundamentally reshaping our economic systems to prioritize renewable energy, sustainable agriculture, and green infrastructure. This holistic approach acknowledges that environmental health is inseparable from societal well-being, especially for those in marginalized communities, who bear the brunt of environmental degradation.

However, to make this vision a reality, significant investment is required. Traditional funding streams and budget allocations often fall short, especially when governments are facing competing priorities such as policing and military expenditure. This is where the invest-divest strategy comes into play: by divesting from sectors such as fossil fuels and reducing funding for traditionally overresourced areas such as policing and militarism, we can free up substantial resources. These funds can then be reinvested into environmental initiatives that will foster a healthier planet and, by extension, healthier communities.

The invest-divest approach is not just about reallocating funds; it's a strategic shift in priorities. It recognizes that long-term environmental sustainability is inextricably linked to social equity and justice. Investment in clean energy and eco-friendly infrastructure is not just an environmental necessity; it's also a pathway to building more equitable societies.

Activists, especially young people in movements such as the climate justice movement and groups advocating for racial and social justice, are increasingly drawing connections among these issues. They see the parallel paths of fighting for a healthier planet and advocating for equitable social structures. The realization that the challenges of climate change cannot be addressed in isolation has led to a broader understanding of the need for systemic change.

The move toward a regenerative economy requires both vision and practical funding strategies. The imaginative envisioning is symbolized in platforms such as the Green New Deal, a term first used by journalist Thomas Friedman in 2007 in an article in the *New York Times*[150] and later developed by politicians and political parties such as the Green Party, and the Red, Black, and Green New Deal, crafted by the Black Hive, an environmental justice initiative of the Movement for Black Lives that seeks to address climate change and ecological destruction particularly as it relates to Black communities in the United States and globally. The invest-divest approach offers a promising pathway to gather the necessary resources while aligning our economic practices with the goals of sustainability and social justice. It's about creating a future where environmental solutions will be adequately supported, not just envisioned, enabling a transition to an economy that will truly nurture our planet and its inhabitants.

It's also crucial to remember the continued environmental disasters Black and Latinx communities live in every day. Land populated by marginalized people of color, including sites where public housing is built, is far more likely to be polluted and contaminated by emissions, factories, and industry pollutants and waste, leading to a range of continued health crises.[151] Demolishing public housing has also wreaked havoc, as the particulates from the demolition sites have caused respiratory problems. Black people also tend to live in overpopulated neighborhoods and cities—largely as a result of government policies such as redlining and colonialism—and experience continued ecological emergencies as a result of high concentrations of pollutants. Addressing environmental racism requires resources and prioritization. But policing, criminalization, and militarization are siphoning off a large share of the resources that could be channeled to addressing and preparing communities for ongoing and emergent ecological disasters.

Our present challenges concerning climate change create opportunities for abolitionist organizing and efforts to flourish, as they reveal that policing and police power are not inevitable, all powerful, or immovable. The safety concerns that have emerged as a result of climate change cannot be addressed by police, and ecological emergencies have the capacity to diminish police capacity and infrastructure, along with any other aspect of society. They also create opportunities for people to show up and be in communities with one another that center on support and care, as the state, including police, continuously shows how unprepared and incapable it is of dealing with, and attending to, the needs of people as they experience routine crises that are amplified in moments of ecological emergency. Defunding and abolishing policing and criminalization can pave the way for a new way of relating to the environment. Climate justice requires resources. Policing and militarism are central places to find them.

STOP COP CITY AND THE ROAD AHEAD

Local, state, and federal governments endeavor to preserve and expand police power, even when it means destroying the environment and people's lives. The most recent example of this is the construction of the Atlanta Public Safety Training Center, or, as activists call it, Cop City, in Atlanta. The Atlanta City Council voted to build a police training facility in the forest where the Old Atlanta Prison Farm, a site of violence, atrocities against those who were incarcerated, and labor exploitation, used to be.[152]

The plans for Cop City were approved by the city of Atlanta in September 2021, after 1,166 Atlanta residents called in and voiced seventeen hours of comments that were played during the city council meetings.[153] Seventy percent of residents opposed the project.[154] Collectives and organizations concerned with the building of the $90 million training facility spanning eighty-five acres cited ecological concerns and the range of unmet needs in the community. A third of the costs were to be paid by the City of Atlanta, with the rest to be paid by the Atlanta Police Foundation, an organization dedicated to increasing funding and resources for police in Atlanta.

Organizations, abolitionists, Atlanta residents, and public figures have joined the protests, demanding the halting of Cop City. Police have arrested and charged large numbers of organizers involved with the Defend the Forest/Stop Cop City movement, who have staged tree sits to prevent trees from being cut down, barricaded the area, attempted to destroy equipment being used to destroy the forest, and taken other actions. At least five have been charged with domestic terrorism by the Georgia Bureau of Investigation.

On January 18, 2023, police officers with the Georgia State Patrol shot and killed one activist, Manuel Esteban Paez Terán, also known as Tortuguita, during a raid on an occupied encampment. Police claimed that Tortuguita had shot at them and found a handgun that Terán had legally bought in 2020, but there is footage suggesting that the police may have shot at one another instead, with an officer being heard saying "Man, you fucked your own officer up."[155] In March 2023, Terán's family released results of an independent autopsy that found that Terán had been shot fourteen times while sitting cross-legged on the ground with his hands in the air.[156]

The case of Cop City is instructive. Various levels of government organized to surveil, arrest, and use violence to repress the Stop Cop City movement, all while climate change and ecological emergencies continue to intensify. This movement is reminiscent, as Benji Hart wrote in a 2023 article, of the No Cop Academy movement from 2017 to 2019 in Chicago, which attempted to stop the construction of a $95 million police training facility in a Black neighborhood on the West Side of Chicago. Hart noted, "The Atlanta City Council—and the state more broadly—cannot define 'loss' or 'victory' for everyday people." Ultimately, these movements serve as sites of political development and base building that result in stronger future efforts against police expansion and toward abolitionist visions.[157] As of January 2024, fights to stop Cop City continue and have garnered widespread support from various coalitions and individuals after protests collected enough signatures—more than a hundred thousand—to put up the matter of stopping Cop City as a referendum. In response, the city of Atlanta announced an intricate signature verification program, seemingly as a way to halt the momentum.[158] That caused organizers to reassess strategies to proceed.[159]

In an alarming trend across the United States, plans to construct Cop Cities are gaining traction. So, too, is resistance to them.[160] These developments represent a concerning move toward more militarized, authoritarian policing methods. A notable instance is unfolding in Atlanta, where the bringing of RICO charges against individuals protesting the construction of such a facility signals a disturbing use of power. The application of RICO—a law designed to tackle organized crime and later used to dismantle Black gangs while failing to address the systemic issues that had produced them—against peaceful protesters is indicative of the use of authoritarian and fascist approaches to preserve police power and quell dissent.

This strategy exemplifies the characteristics of a police state, where resistance to governmental policies, especially those challenging the status quo, is met with excessive legal force. The case in Atlanta, where individuals distributing flyers were arrested[161] and a bail fund was accused of money laundering for assisting those arrested,[162] is a stark example. Moreover, the backdating of charges to the time of George Floyd's killing insinuates a direct attack on movements that challenge the power and scope of policing,[163] framing it as the origin of criminal activity.

Such actions by the authorities are not just acts of intimidation; they represent a clear instance of coercion against those pushing back against oppressive systems. Despite hundreds of thousands of people peacefully voting against the construction of Cop City, the government's response has been one of forceful preservation of police power. The situation in Atlanta is critical, with organizers continuing to demand the halting of the construction of Cop City. Protesters, both local and from other regions, are mobilizing en masse at the proposed site, resisting the creation of a militarized urban training ground for police. This site, intended for practicing urban warfare, has significant implications for the future of policing and environmental justice.

The construction of Cop Cities and training facilities, such as the one proposed in Atlanta, illustrates a concerning trend where land is seized and resources are spent to advance criminalization, rather than being allocated to more beneficial societal uses. This approach by the prison-industrial complex is geared toward control, not the sustainability of our planet. In fact, such efforts contribute to pushing us closer to an environmental crisis, clearly demonstrating the intertwined nature of environmental justice and the fight against an expanding, militarized police state.

Understanding the state's determination to maintain and grow police power is clarifying. It underscores the repressive tendencies of American political systems. Additionally, it highlights the challenges people face in trying to develop safety measures that move beyond traditional policing and incarceration within the context of a modern nation-state. Organizers, movements, and the public must understand the political strategies and frameworks necessary to create a society that is safe, not just controlled. A part of that is deciding on governing approaches that lie beyond the boundaries of the modern nation-state, which emphasizes violence work and socialization strategies to preserve the power of the elites despite the wishes of many communities. I advocate for community-based solutions that focus on developing capabilities and systems that move beyond policing and government control. I believe that communities have the ability to govern themselves and keep one another safe. We have the capacity to create political frameworks that ensure direct democracy, influencing the well-being of both residents and the environment. Waves of police violence continue to ravage communities. Moving beyond policing will help us arrive in calmer waters. I want to live in a world where people are safe, and where there is no possibility of being murdered or brutalized by the police.

The abolition of any oppressive system has never been gained without struggle. Looking forward, we can turn to the words of one of the most prominent slavery abolitionists, Frederick Douglass:

> If there is no struggle there is no progress. Those who profess to favor freedom and yet depreciate agitation, are men who want crops without plowing up the ground, they want rain without thunder and lightning. They want the ocean without the awful roar of its many waters.
>
> This struggle may be a moral one, or it may be a physical one, and it may be both moral and physical, but it must be a struggle. Power concedes nothing without a demand. It never did and it never will.[164]

The only way out of this cycle—the demand—is to move beyond policing and toward visions of transformative community safety. Moving beyond policing is critical if safety and justice are to thrive.

INTERLUDE III

(PART A) COMMUNITY POLICING IS NOT THE ANSWER

Investing billions of government dollars into programs that embed police in Black communities will not reduce police violence, nor will it repair years of injustice.

I was fifteen when I first had a gun pointed at me. The kid holding it must have been around my age. I had just left a party in Brooklyn with my godbrother, Terrell. The police had shut the party down, which was routine after a certain time of night in that neighborhood. After we left with a few friends, a group of kids came out of another building in the housing project we were in and started to follow us down the street.

I had a sense that they wanted to jump or rob us, so I told my godbrother to cross the street. "If they follow us, run," I said. Halfway across the street, I turned around and saw one of the kids raise a gun at me. "If you run, I'll shoot you."

We all ran, but Terrell and I got separated, so I went back. Terrell wasn't there, but he called a few minutes later and we met up, laughed, and rehashed the story. This is just one of the experiences of navigating violence that marked much of my childhood. Throughout all of those experiences, I never thought to call the police. Growing up in the Bronx and later in New Jersey, I learned not to trust or rely on the police. I was assaulted by the police when I was thirteen and harassed more times than I can remember. And more people in my family and community were arrested, harassed, or brutalized than I can count. Instead, I relied on myself and a few people I felt I could trust, such as my godbrother.

Proponents of community policing argue that embedding police, particularly in Black communities, can build trust and partnerships that would have changed my calculus. But the strategy is flawed and has drawn resources away from communities that need it and instead directed them toward policing. Time has shown that community policing is merely an expensive attempt at public relations after a long history of racialized police violence and injustice and does little to reduce crime or police violence.

Community policing, strategies that center on creating officer diversity to better reflect the demographics of the community, and initiatives that focus on trust, reconciliation, and procedural justice between communities and police have become popular with some city leaders, including former mayor Bill de Blasio in New York City[1] and mainstream reform organizations such as the Vera Institute of Justice. At the national level, to take one example, the Department of Justice launched the National Initiative for Building Community Trust and Justice[2] in September 2014.

On the surface, community policing sounds like an ideal way to reform policing. But police violence[3] toward Black people has persisted. A study examining the strategy around the country suggested that community policing does not significantly reduce crime or make communities safer.[4] Community policing may also deter people from participating in local programs that police are involved in, as one study suggests that avoidance of police[5] is a common strategy among marginalized groups such as Black youths. The positive publicity that may come from giving kids ice cream and playing basketball with them does not make communities safer. On the contrary, the strategy further floods communities with police and legitimizes an institution that is centered on punishment and control.

As a PhD candidate at Yale, I wrote a dissertation that examined safety, poverty, and policing in public housing in Brooklyn. I found that residents have to deal with police harassment, deployments into the building, and the stress and anxiety that come with constant police presence. Heightened presence and contact, such as the addition of officers often called beat cops to continuously patrol the building and area throughout the day and night, are often framed as community-oriented policing efforts, which ultimately fuels police expansion.

The NYPD argues that community or neighborhood policing will increase trust and cohesion between police and communities. On its website, the department states, "Neighborhood Policing greatly increases connectivity and engagement with the community without diminishing, and, in fact, improving the NYPD's crime-fighting capabilities. The NYPD has long encouraged officers to strengthen bonds with the communities they patrol."[6] But the disconnect is palpable, and police appear more as an occupying force, surveilling residences as opposed to protecting them.

Structural racism and poverty also force people to employ strategies that are often criminalized in order to navigate incredibly difficult and complex situations, such as with fare evasion.[7] Thus, as long as poverty and racial inequality exist, policing will always expose Black people and other marginalized communities to higher rates of surveillance, arrest, and violence. Community policing creates the false idea that police can solve structural problems through building partnerships, but policing has only made those problems worse.

Police do not speak to the wide range of concerns about safety that residents have, nor should they try to. Marginalized communities need resources to thrive. Investing in community policing—or policing more broadly—will not change the underlying structural context that leads to a lack of safety. Nor will it change the laws that criminalize people for being poor and disadvantaged. The solution to public safety lies in negating the idea that policing equals safety.

The real work lies in developing alternatives to punishment and policing, not producing nicer cops.

The billions of dollars channeled through the COPS Office and the 1994 crime act to expand police resources and power could have been invested in community institutions and programs that foster safety and wellness, such as arts and athletic programs, violence interruption initiatives, high-quality schools, community-led domestic violence support, hospitals, and drug treatment facilities.

Federal funding could also go toward alternatives to policing that may actually cultivate safety. If I could have called people I trusted within the community who were trained to help manage violent situations, I might have done so that night in Brooklyn. Trained and well-resourced rapid response teams that can address a wide range of emergencies without police presence may be the future of cultivating safety and solving the problem of policing.

Hundreds of millions of dollars are being funneled to police departments that agree to make efforts to repair the supposedly broken relationship between Black people and police. But the relationship was never whole.

Many people I know have irreparable relationships with the police. No number of conversations or events will fix the relationship or make them comfortable calling 911 in an emergency. Divesting from policing and investing in communities will ultimately make people far safer than police ever will.

(PART B) A WORLD WITHOUT POLICE

I'll never forget that day: the fear of losing my life shadowed the excitement of getting into college. The body has a way of remembering. I was paranoid for days. But I never thought of calling the police.

"There's a target on ya head."

I was seventeen and hauling ass, trying to get home after a group of kids from a well-known Crip neighborhood in Newark tried to jump me. After I'd lost them, my phone vibrated. I looked down at my phone and discovered that I had received an email from a university I was waiting to hear back from: I had gotten in.

A friend called me right after I briefly saw the email notification and said that I had a target on my head.

The situation had started because of hearsay. The word on the street was that I didn't like a dude my girlfriend used to date. He and the kids I was running from were from the same neighborhood.

I had spent time in that neighborhood over the years because a close friend that I'd known since middle school, who later became a Crip, also lived there. I knew people there, and they knew me. And I also knew a lot of people in the neighborhood and throughout Newark who had guns. So I knew exactly what it meant when I was told that I had a target on my head.

"Yeah, bruh, it's green light on you in the hood. It's out of my hands now" was what my close friend said.

It was sparked by something silly, but it could have cost me my life.

I told my friends first. One of them suggested that we escalate — that we find the people who had tried to jump me after school and "trip on them." Thankfully, when we went searching for them, we didn't see them.

Next I called my cousin, who was from a different neighborhood but well connected. He knew a high-ranking member of the Crip set the kids were from and was able to defuse the situation. "Damn, I didn't know that was your cousin," one of the members said. "Tell him he good." And that was it.

Thankfully, because of my cousin and his connections, a few months later I left for college. Most of my classmates had no idea of what I had gone through to get there.

Many people may not understand why I chose not to call the cops. At the time, it was a simple reason.

I knew that in a moment of grave danger, Newark police would only exacerbate the situation. As a teen, I was only somewhat aware of the rampant patterns of police corruption and violence that would later require the city to undergo a federal consent decree. My experience is not unique. Many Black youths from my community and those like mine feel similarly and are forced to find other ways to manage their own safety.

My analysis is not anecdotal. After starting my PhD in sociology and African American studies at Yale, I immediately began to research safety, inequality, and policing.

I quickly learned that police do not stop violence and harm; they perpetuate it more than they seem to stop it. Emerging research indicates that the intensive policing of Black neighborhoods may contribute to increased incidents of criminalized behaviors and heightened violence.[8] Yet there remains a commitment to policing. The carceral state controls the resources and dominates the narratives about public safety. But the evidence is clear: police are not the solution. Community programs, good-quality education, good hospitals, jobs, and opportunities help make neighborhoods safe. Not police.

Still, more than $100 billion a year is spent on policing in the United States annually. Those same billions of dollars could be invested into the community-based programs and institutions that are shown to make communities such as Newark safer.

In my own work surrounding policing and public housing, I have found that while police may make some people feel safe in certain situations, that doesn't translate into long-term experiences of safety. In addition, police do not speak to the range of concerns residents have. Residents across public housing and other disadvantaged housing contexts tend to feel unsafe due to a variety of factors, such as lead-tainted water, exposed pipes, broken elevators, lack of gas and electricity, and malfunctioning heating systems, just to name a few. The concerns that residents in my fieldwork experience far exceed the scope of policing. But still, they are given more police, more cameras, more surveillance.

The countless cases of police violence and corruption, from the beginning of modern policing as slave patrols to the murders of Atatiana Koquice Jefferson, Breonna Taylor, and Eleanor Bumpurs in their own homes, have shown that no amount of reform will fix the problem of policing. I want to live in a world with safety, not policing. Of course, we won't get there overnight. But the real work of fostering safety lies in developing alternatives to policing and prisons and ultimately in working toward a world in which we do not need or think we need policing.

Working toward a world with safety beyond policing is indeed a long-term struggle. But there is hope. Organizers across the country are challenging mass policing and focusing on community-centered programs and initiatives. Examples include the Kings against Violence Initiative (KAVI) in Brooklyn,[9] No Cop Academy in Chicago,[10] BYP100's She Safe, We Safe former national campaign,[11] and invest-divest campaigns such as LiberateMKE in Milwaukee.[12] Organizers with the Durham Beyond Policing coalition in North Carolina successfully organized to divert funds for additional police personnel toward community-based safety and wellness initiatives.[13]

Violence interrupters, arts and athletic programs, initiatives centered on domestic violence support, treatment facilities, and safe spaces for LGBTQ+ youths all work to create community-centered safety, but they're often defunded.

People often question the practicality of police abolition. Some of the skepticism is warranted. We live in a violent society. The United States has more guns than any other nation in the world. Domestic violence, murders, human trafficking, and sexual assault are all concerns that need immediate attention. But what I turn to instead of leaning into skepticism is the realization that police do not stop or guarantee safety. So what might?

Imagine if people had the option to call a service—with the number 333, for example—that could respond to violent or potentially harmful

situations; if all neighborhoods had well-trained and well-resourced violence support, interruption, and prevention teams for various forms of
violence—including domestic violence and sexual assault; if there were
dedicated conflict resolution specialists throughout communities capable of
managing the wide range of issues that are often exacerbated or criminalized by the criminal-legal system.

Imagine if my cousin had been paid to do the work he did for me,
full-time.

And imagine if those kids chasing me had had something else to run to.

CHAPTER 4

SOLUTIONS FOR A NEW WORLD

Some people may ask, "Does this mean that I can never call the cops if my life is in serious danger?" Abolition does not center that question. Instead, abolition challenges us to ask, "Why do we have no other well-resourced options?" and pushes us to creatively consider how we can grow, build, and try other avenues to reduce harm.

—Mariame Kaba, *We Do This 'til We Free Us: Abolitionist Organizing and Transforming Justice*

AN ABOLITIONIST VISION OF A POLICE-FREE WORLD IS THAT THERE WILL BE safety and help when it's needed. When I was young, I didn't think much about the police unless they were stopping or harassing me. When I was concerned for my safety, the idea of calling 911 never entered my mind. I grew up trying to avoid the police (and arrest) as well as traversing violence. I knew that the police were rarely helpful to people I knew, and when they were present, they often made matters worse. So I tried to not think about them much unless I was forced to. Had there been community-based approaches to safety that I could have called on, there were so many times that I would have done so.

We are in a time when notions of safety are being reconsidered. Police have assumed responsibility over a wide range of problems that arise within communal life. But an endless number of possible safety responses do not involve the violence of policing. There are areas of safety and emergency response that have extensive histories, others that are new, and a number waiting to be imagined and implemented. To move beyond policing, we need to start creating a society in which police departments are obsolete. How can we change how we think about issues of safety and who responds to crises? How can we live in a safe world without certain people or communities finding themselves routinely oppressed? When you look at your community, what are the things you dream of seeing when the police aren't there? We can build a safe world. But it requires moving beyond policing.

We need a paradigm shift toward community-based safety. Public safety as a concept emerges from the idea that the state can produce safety for its population. Community safety emphasizes the community as the focus of safety work and as the determiner of who is responsible for safety. As a framework, community-based safety allows us to rely on a different approach — not one that centers on the framework of public safety, which is commonly dominated by discourses of police, prisons, and the criminal-legal system, but a framework that centers on community safety, accountability, and belonging. There is also a push toward reclaiming the term *public safety* in a way that aligns with community-centered safety. As the name of one abolitionist organizing principle proclaims, "We Keep Us Safe."

So how can we go about imagining a tapestry of safety, crisis, and emergency response approaches that allows us to see a world in which moving beyond policing is possible?

A major factor in the experimentation with community safety models is the availability of resources. Many localities' available funds are limited. But given that policing often takes up a large portion of city budgets, one viable option for developing alternatives is to divert funding from policing toward community-based safety strategies. Reducing funds for policing and channeling them into community resources and institutions is a key strategy. We need to explore new ways of handling emergencies, moving beyond just calling 911. Many people across the country feel that police are not the answer to safer communities. To the contrary, policing is often associated with police violence for many. As communities look for solutions beyond policing, it will take a commitment to actualize alternative visions for community safety. As localities across the country vary widely, the specifics of the provision of safety in any given location will also vary. Thus, one first step is to create task forces and committees that can look into community-based safety and plan experiments with new emergency response systems that will build beyond policing. Then research will be needed to investigate the efficacy of alternatives and constantly make suggestions for improvement.

Endless response approaches to a range of crises and concerns can be developed. While innovation has marked almost all aspects of society, the archaic approach of police managing concerns about safety has remained intact. So if a community were looking to develop a range of emergency response approaches beyond policing, how would it do so? I always recommend starting from square one: What are the main concerns that you and those in your community have? Be as extensive and thorough as possible. Make sure to listen to a range of voices—including those that are typically not prioritized—and consider all the concerns that come up. These can include intracommunity violence, domestic violence, street harassment, sexual assault, child abuse, theft, carjackings, concerns about animals, feeling unsafe in school, shootings—it can be anything and everything. Ask: If police were not around, how could society organize itself in a way where these things would be less likely to happen? How can a range of pertinent responses and approaches to concerns surrounding safety be developed? And how can communities respond to such encounters in ways that give healing to the people experiencing the harm and reduce the likelihood that it will occur in the future? These questions and deep listening can help develop preventions, interventions, and responses to each scenario that emphasize accountability and community.

COMMUNITY MEDIATORS

People navigate and resolve conflict with one another every day. At times, conflict resolution is not simple or straightforward. In these cases, having community mediators who can facilitate dialogue, accountability, and resolution can be essential. In many places, people feel that they have only the police to call during disputes. If the police show up, they have the potential to make things worse. Even more, they often do not have the tools or training necessary to de-escalate the situation. Rather, they rely on the threat and use of violence. Communities need mediators for times when people are having trouble resolving conflict by themselves. Mediation can help build community bonds as well as keep situations from escalating and potentially becoming dangerous. We need trained community mediators who will facilitate conflict resolution and support people as they navigate everyday conflict.

A community mediator is anyone who has the experience to navigate community concerns. In some cases, community mediators can be designated by the broader community for particular forms of mediation work. Others can be trained in community mediation and de-escalation and, while it may not be a primary or consistent area of work, rise to the occasion to help manage concerns in a peaceful and solution-oriented way.

For community-based mediation and dispute resolution to be successful, there must be proactive involvement and autonomy among communities. This approach will enable communities to prevent and address conflicts, from minor neighborhood disputes to broader disagreements over shared community resources. This strategy centers on effective communication, facilitation, and mutual understanding. In doing so, it can cultivate a communitywide sense of stewardship for peace and cohesion. A crucial aspect of community-based dispute resolution and mediation is strengthening community connections. Through internally and peacefully resolving disputes with community mediators — or through skills and training shared with communities by mediators — residents can develop resilient relationships with their neighbors, fostering an atmosphere of unity and mutual respect. These bonds will be invaluable, as strong, cohesive communities are often better prepared to confront larger challenges.

Additionally, community-based dispute resolution acknowledges that there are unique cultural and social dynamics in every community. In contrast to traditional punitive models, community-based mediation strategies are tailored to fit the specific requirements, values, and traditions of each community. This context-specific strategy can lead to more sustainable resolutions. What kinds of problems could community mediators manage? All kinds: arguments, disputes, fights, conflicts among friends and neighbors, beefs between individuals and groups; unresolved conflicts; conflicts over money; ensuring that people act according to community wishes on late nights and nights out; mediating conversations in schools among students, teachers, and guardians. As an alternative to civil or criminal court processes, which are lengthy and expensive and break interpersonal bonds, community mediators can both intervene during situations that need intervention and serve as pathways for responding to problems and conflicts that have already occurred. In doing so, they can help provide solutions that do not rely on an archaic, punitive, and exploitative criminal-legal system.

Of course, there are cases when people simply might not be fond of one another. But when trust is broken or the cohesion of a community is being challenged, community mediators can intervene. They can also help train people in conflict resolution, peace building, and restorative practices to build and restore communal bonds. Central to community mediation is the idea that communities can manage their everyday problems and conflicts on their own when they have the capacity to do so. Community mediators can be present in communities and also available by rapid response through a specific phone number. Upon being called, mediators with expertise relevant to the situation can respond. Community mediators can be active in schools to help manage problems without disciplining, suspension, and school police; to help de-escalate and resolve community concerns such as thefts and arguments; to make sure people have mediation processes if they are experiencing problems they are not able to resolve themselves; and to train others in peacefully navigating conflict and concerns on their own. Community mediators can be equipped with tools such as restorative justice and transformative justice in order to help with peacemaking and healing after conflict and harm.

DESIGNING PEACE

Mediators can draw on different models of mediation and resolution.[1] They often do street outreach, working with trusted people in the community to try to de-escalate tensions before they become violent. Restorative justice practitioners focus on bringing parties together to repair harm and engage in community mediation efforts. Other efforts integrate design and conflict resolution practices, such as the work of Deanna Van Buren, the executive director and design director of Designing Justice + Designing Spaces (DJDS). Van Buren and DJDS work against punitive frameworks of justice.

The design collective focuses on the development of spaces and structures that encourage restorative justice and community bonding, in addition to providing housing for those transitioning from incarceration. This trailblazing approach aims to modify the locations and environments in which justice is carried out, thus steering society away from a punitive system toward a restorative model of justice. DJDS envisions a world in which communities have centers dedicated to finding peaceful solutions to any and all conflicts that arise in surrounding neighborhoods. This is an important strategy in making sure residents avoid being arrested and ending up in prison.

Guided by the philosophy of restorative justice, the organization states, "Our bold idea is that by transforming the spaces and places where we do justice, we can help our society make the shift from a punitive justice system to a restorative justice system. We hope to see peacemaking centers in every community in this country and end the age of mass incarceration."[2] Peacemaking centers have the potential to serve as spaces for healing and conflict resolution and as hubs for spreading community mediation and peacemaking practices throughout the community. Practitioners can be housed and trained at these centers, and there can be training available for everyone in the community to increase conflict resolution and peacemaking skills. In addition to engaging in healing and accountability for serious cases of harm, peacemaking centers can serve as spaces to mediate all forms of community conflict before it escalates and environments in which more serious problems are made less likely through ongoing community and peace building.

The work of DJDS aligns with the abolitionist and geographer Ruth Wilson Gilmore's thesis that freedom is a place.[3] We have to design the spaces and environments in which freedom, justice, and safety can thrive. There have been decades of investment in carceral geographies and environments of confinement.[4] From prisons to the use of bars, barbed wire, and built environments designed to facilitate surveillance and control,[5] policing and punishment aren't just stand-alone institutions; their logics and meanings have been incorporated into everyday life and modern design. Thus design and geographic approaches that prioritize visions of a free, just, transformative world need to flourish so abolitionist visions can be manifested in the places and spaces that we all navigate every day.[6]

MEETING NEEDS AND MEDIATING CONCERNS

Community mediators can be trained with a range of skills and frameworks. This will increase communal capacity to mediate a wide range of issues while reducing reliance on policing. There can be different teams within a broader community mediation institution that all focus on different issues, or there can be one entity with different people who have both generalized training and different specialties. Ultimately, community mediation also prevents more serious events from transpiring and helps build safe, stable, accountable communities that are able to address problems as they come up. These efforts can and should be separate from government entities to remove political influence and the bureaucracy and problems that come from modern American politics. It's also important to ensure accountability among mediators to ensure that the approach remains productive and useful for everyone within a given community.

Community mediators can also be allocated resources to help people in need. Say someone's bike was stolen. Mediators can draw on community networks to try to learn who did it, with the aim of finding and returning the bike. But also, mediators can be allocated resources to make sure the person has access to a bike or other transportation in the meantime. In addition, community mediators can facilitate processes between parties and also ask justice-oriented questions, such as why people in a particular community are stealing bikes to begin with and how this can be addressed through direct efforts, resolution, outreach, and system transformation. Or take a case where two people have a fight. Rather than allowing it to escalate, both parties can come to the table and engage in a culturally specific process that will allow them to receive what they need—whether healing or growth—and prevent escalation.

Imagine another scenario, a robbery. Someone takes something from someone else and leaves the other person feeling alone and violated. A team of emergency responders can respond shortly after. Right away, the person can be compensated. In the long term, responders can provide immediate social support and mental health care. Most important, a transformative role would center on attempting to understand what gave rise to the incident and abolishing the unjust conditions that give rise to such incidents to begin with. So if someone breaks into a car because they are poor or otherwise struggling, there can be a process whereby that person can be accountable while the needs of all involved can be addressed. And if they are stealing because they are unable to meet their basic needs and are thus engaging in actions that may be harmful to themselves and others, moving beyond policing means looking for ways to ensure that they have their needs met so they don't feel as inclined to steal.

VIOLENCE INTERVENORS

A desire for safety lies at the heart of the human experience. People generally seek lives that are free from violence and instability. Mainstream society positions police as the providers of safety. But as discussed in previous chapters, policing and the criminal-legal system have not been overarching sources of safety. To the contrary, they often do little to protect people and can even make matters worse. In some cases, in the absence of any other response, police can and do provide people with immediate interventions. But as I mentioned in chapter 3, just because police provide interventions in particular situations does not mean that they are the only ones who can do it or are the best to do so. Policing has come to incorporate social service components, seemingly performatively, such as mental health responders and caseworkers, as Forrest Stuart discussed in his book *Down, Out, and Under Arrest: Policing and Everyday Life in Skid Row*. But this alienates all those who are skeptical of police initiatives and attempts to merge violence work with service provision. We need approaches to safety that work, approaches that are rooted in justice and accountability, not violence.

Violence is widespread in American society. Violence is multidimensional, as described by the antiviolence organizer Mariame Kaba: people can experience violence from within and outside their communities as well as from the state.[7] One of the biggest justifications for policing is that it protects society from violence. Police actually attend to violence much less than they do to other trivial activities. And despite widespread policing, cycles of violence continue, and policing contributes to the violence that many communities experience. In order to address violence, one has to see the particularities in patterns of violence while also addressing the root causes of those patterns. In many cases, violence is centered around dominance and a desire to control. It also stems from fear, pain, grief, a desire to belong, a desire for respect, and trauma.

The best-known form of violence intervention is for issues that center on gun and street violence. The focus on gun violence is largely shaped by the damaging effects that this form of violence has on entire communities. Research shows that cases of gun violence can affect children's performance in school and a community's overall health and sense of peace and comfort, among other consequences.[8] Violence intervention focuses on community members' becoming actively involved in reducing violence before it occurs and de-escalating it when it does. Importantly, while some interventions draw on police support and collaboration, others reject police involvement and take an entirely community-based approach. The benefits of a fully community-based approach lie in the fact that these initiatives are less likely to alienate people in the community who are cynical about the police.

Violence intervenors can intervene in arguments, street issues through street outreach work, and more. These early interventions can help stop violence before it intensifies. Violence intervenors can also respond to cases of violence from a trauma-informed perspective, looking to engage in psychological first response where the short-term and long-term mental health of those experiencing trauma is prioritized; this can be applied to other emergencies and disasters as a strategy to promote safety, stabilize survivors of disasters, and connect people to long-term support and resources.

BALTIMORE'S SAFE STREETS

Violence interruption initiatives exist in various forms in the United States and beyond. Violence interruption has existed for some time, but in recent years the initiatives have garnered more attention while not being very well understood. While they vary depending on the context, the programs rely on respected members of the community, many of whom have been involved in incidents of violence themselves. These respected members use their relationships and knowledge to intervene in networks of violence as well as de-escalate encounters. This work can bring together groups in conflict or involve a more one-on-one approach. One notable example is Safe Streets in Baltimore. In a recent report, researchers noted that the five areas that had been in operation the longest had experienced a significant drop in homicides—an average of 32 percent over the initial four years of program implementation.[9] However, the six more recently established sites didn't show any significant shifts in homicide rates during the evaluated period, which indicates that such initiatives need time to become established and effective. Across all eleven program locations analyzed in the study, Safe Streets was linked to a noticeable decline in nonfatal shootings over the duration of the program, with a predicted reduction rate of approximately 22 percent.

Even within Baltimore, the specific implementation of violence inter-ruption can vary across neighborhoods. In the Belair-Edison neighbor-hood, Dante Johnson, a site director of Safe Streets, has shared his thoughts about working directly with the police, telling NPR, "We don't oppose law enforcement, but understand—we can't work with them doing this work, because people have to trust us."[10] Mayor Brandon Scott, in the same article, stated, "I never, ever, ever, ever want our violence interrupters to lose that authenticity in the things they are able to do. But we have to evolve in a way that the totality of gun violence workers in the city, from our hospitals, from Safe Streets, from the police department, from everyone else...have some sort of working relationship that does not invalidate any of those partners." Here we see that politicians, often appealing to police departments and police unions—which wield a great deal of power in many locations—for political support, can attempt to steer violence intervention work in favor of police involvement. Some violence intervention models feature police cooperation and collaboration, but the most promising initiatives have been proven, or have the promise, to reduce violence without police involvement, as that involvement almost always delegitimizes the efforts given the history and present realities of policing.

Interrupters can also experience a range of challenges, such as resource limitations, limited training options, unsustainable structural models, and violence within the community and from police. In addition, violence inter-ruption programs can face pressure to produce results deemed desirable by nonprofit and government funders, as well as pressure to professionalize in ways that do not support the interrupters in their efforts to engage in their work.[11] Violence interrupters can face their own challenges, especially given their own life experiences, and may also have faced interference from law

enforcement. Recently, in Baltimore, three Safe Streets workers were murdered over the course of a year, although little is known about the context
of their deaths and any potential motivations.[12] Violence workers put themselves into high-risk situations and have their own backgrounds that can
make them vulnerable to violence. Interrupters in Baltimore continue to
take risks to try to prevent gun violence from happening. But the tragic
deaths point to a need to evaluate and consider ways to safeguard workers
as much as possible while allowing them to continue engaging in the transformative work they remain committed to.[13] They also point to the need for
increased support and resources for violence interrupters.

HOSPITAL-BASED VIOLENCE INTERRUPTION

Hospital-based violence interruption programs are a promising approach
to antiviolence work. They are initiatives aimed at preventing retaliation
and recurrent violence among those admitted to hospitals for violent injuries. These programs seize the critical moment when a victim is in the
hospital and receptive to intervention. Trained violence interrupters, often
with personal experience of violence or neighborhood ties, engage with
patients, providing immediate support and longer-term guidance. They
may offer resources such as counseling, social services, and assistance
navigating legal processes. These programs focus on breaking the cycle
of violence and fostering safer communities. These interventions have
seen success in many urban hospitals. The Health Alliance for Violence
Intervention (HAVI) supports hospital and community collaborations to
advance equitable, trauma-informed care for violence intervention and
prevention programs.[14]

With thirty-four member programs across the United States and in
three other countries, including Oakland's Caught in the Crossfire and
the San Francisco Wraparound Project, HAVI involves more than 350
practitioners and many developing programs. To place the work of HAVI
and hospital-based violence interruption programs into perspective, we
can look at an example of a trauma-informed, hospital-based intervention.
Say there is a shooting between two groups. One person is injured, and
that person's group is looking to retaliate. Violence interrupters, with a
trauma-informed perspective, can come to the hospital, talk to the family,

and de-escalate the situation. By intervening in the flow of violence, interrupters can use the respect of their community to reduce the likelihood that the other group will retaliate. They can do this through sharing wisdom, allowing people to talk and share their feelings—and grieve—and pointing out the potential consequences of retaliatory action. Most people in such moments are looking for support, and they receive it from those in their community.

As Karenna Warden wrote in an article on community-based violence interruption,[15] there are a number of hospital violence intervention programs (HVIPs) across the United States. HVIP models across the country are showing promising results. Warden showcased three standout examples, Oakland's Youth ALIVE! program, the San Francisco Wraparound Project, and the University of Maryland Medical System's Violence Intervention Program. Here's a closer look at each.

In 1994, Oakland's Youth ALIVE!, a violence prevention organization, launched Caught in the Crossfire, the first hospital-based intervention program of its kind in the nation. The inspiration for this innovative program came from the personal experience of a young man named Sherman Spears who suffered a shooting in 1989 that left him paralyzed. During his time in the hospital, Spears felt overwhelmed. His family was in distress, his friends were consumed by thoughts of revenge, and he found it challenging to connect with the medical staff. Despite those pressures, he made the decision not to seek vengeance.

After connecting with a support group under Youth ALIVE! that focused on violence, Spears began a new chapter. He started visiting the hospital to engage with other young victims of violence. His journey and efforts paved the way for what eventually became the HVIP model. But Youth ALIVE! didn't stop at Caught in the Crossfire; it expanded its mission to provide a broad array of prevention, intervention, and healing programs that reach beyond violence intervention. The results have included a 70 percent reduction in arrests and 60 percent less criminal involvement as compared to a control group,[16] as well as significant savings in hospital costs through reduced hospitalization for violence-related injuries.

Founded in 2005 by Dr. Rochelle Dicker, the San Francisco Wraparound Project has successfully reduced reinjury rates and connected patients with essential services such as education and mental health support. The program was designed to curb the ongoing cycle of youths returning to the hospital with violent injuries. The goal is to break the pattern of violence in the lives of participants. The program helps patients find alternatives by linking them with opportunities in higher education, mental health support, and supportive services. The approach works to engage in ways that are culturally competent. Successes include a 400 percent decrease in reinjury rates and savings of around $500,000 per year in hospital costs.[17]

In the last case, Baltimore's Violence Intervention Program has made considerable progress in community-based safety. Since 1998, Dr. Carnell Cooper's program has made significant strides in the prevention of reinjury and saved an estimated $1.25 million in incarceration costs.[18] The program is founded on the understanding that patients who have experienced intense trauma are in the midst of psychological crisis. It thus centers its approach on four essential stages: first stabilizing the person, then aiding in recovery, followed by helping with community reintegration, and lastly fostering self-reliance. Only 5 percent of participants have been rehospitalized after intervention, compared to 36 percent of nonparticipants.[19]

HVIP initiatives, a form of community violence intervention, demonstrate effective prevention, intervention, and healing strategies. They not only address the immediate needs of the victims but contribute to overall community well-being. Importantly, they rely on noncoercive ways of disrupting flows of violence rather than mass policing and imprisonment.

FIREARM HARM REDUCTION

A transformative approach that does not fit into popular violence interruption models is that of a Chicago organization, Stick Talk. Stick Talk is focused on creating responses to gun violence that do not criminalize gun possession or entirely forbid the use of firearms.[20] Stick Talk puts forth a strategy known as firearm harm reduction to transform on-the-ground responses to gun-related incidents. Drawing inspiration from other successful harm reduction interventions that have positively influenced public health and safety, such as those for drug use, Stick Talk's firearm harm reduction strategy centers on those affected by gun violence. The collective prioritizes young Black and Brown people who have survived gun violence and who often carry firearms for self-protection in the absence of other reliable safety mechanisms. Stick Talk doesn't endorse or stigmatize firearm possession. Rather, it nurtures support networks in which illicit gun users can embrace healing, educational, and leadership opportunities that meet their survival requirements. The organization also provides them with a platform they can use to grieve for their murdered loved ones, comprehend their own trauma and harm, learn about gun safety, and cultivate practices to reduce the risks they face—regardless of their decision to retain their guns or not.

Since 2020, Stick Talk has been working on its firearm harm reduction approach in Chicago, within prisons, and in communities that experience high levels of gun violence and gun-related arrests. Black and Brown young people who both engage in and experience gun violence often describe carrying guns as a survival strategy in neighborhoods where firearms are pervasive and law enforcement isn't trustworthy. Young people say that this approach provides them with the practical skills and knowledge they need to survive, including first-response training for gunshot incidents. Participants learn about the gravity of gun ownership and how to respect the damage guns can do. Stick Talk theorizes that once guns become less of a taboo, people will behave more safely around them. The group is hopeful that consistent engagement with firearm harm reduction hubs will eventually lead to a decrease in harmful gun use.

Stick Talk aims to reduce the number of young Black and Brown people arrested and jailed for gun possession offenses and to challenge the criminalization of their survival tactics. It posits that if provided with the right support and sufficient time to evolve, the firearm harm reduction approach will lead to a decline in gun violence and enhance community safety more efficiently than the criminalization of firearm possession and abstinence-based approaches.

As described by Cristian Farias in a compelling overview of violence intervention from an abolitionist perspective,[21] Stick Talk echoes the principles of earlier radical movements such as the Black Panthers. Stick Talk views the right to bear arms as a crucial aspect of community survival and mutual support. Its education initiatives include enlightening participants about historical self-defense tactics within Black communities, the perpetual impact of aggressive gun policies on Black and Brown individuals, and how these defensive strategies have often enhanced the nonviolent dimensions of the civil rights movement.

In its mission, Stick Talk collaborates with a collective called Ujimaa Medics, a consortium of Black organizers, community residents, and health care professionals. This alliance facilitates training across Chicago, enabling people to provide vital first aid to gun violence victims during the crucial moments before medical professionals arrive. These lessons, which are shared with high school students and community groups in high-risk areas, include techniques for treating gunshot wounds, ensuring airway security, and managing severe bleeding. While such a hands-on approach deviates from the traditional model of violence prevention, the group leaders firmly believe in empowering bystanders to intervene, citing the lack of adequate safety and healing provided by police services.

Regarding the significant influx of government funding and efforts into community violence intervention, Stick Talk's cofounder and co-director, ethan ucker, is more concerned with building robust infrastructure and sustainable funding for the initiative's work rather than government funds, as he pointed out to Farias in the article "On Both Sides of the Gun." He maintains that transparency with donors about Stick Talk's mission and ensures that the resources received go primarily toward maintaining operations and providing direct aid to participants and their families. When speaking to Farias, ucker warned against the overprofessionalization of community safety and violence prevention efforts, emphasizing the vital need for workers to establish sincere, enduring relationships with the people they serve.

SAFETY PODS

A promising strategy to address violence is the formation of pods, an idea developed by the Bay Area Transformative Justice Collective (BATJC), which focuses on child sexual abuse. Pods are networks of support. A cofounder of BATJC, Mia Mingus, wrote:

> During the spring of 2014 the Bay Area Transformative Justice Collective (BATJC) began using the term "pod" to refer to a specific

type of relationship within transformative justice (TJ) work. We needed a term to describe the kind of relationship between people who would turn to each other for support around violent, harmful and abusive experiences, whether as survivors, bystanders or people who have harmed. These would be the people in our lives that we would call on to support us with things such as our immediate and on-going safety, accountability and transformation of behaviors, or individual and collective healing and resiliency.…

We knew that across the board, people who experience violence, harm and abuse turn to their intimate networks before they turn to external state or social services. Most people don't call the police or seek counseling or even call anonymous hotlines. If they tell anyone at all, they turn to a trusted friend, family member, neighbor or coworker. We wanted a way to name those currently in your life that you would rely on (or are relying on) to respond to violence, harm and abuse.

POD

Your pod is made up of the people that you would call on if violence, harm or abuse happened to you; or the people that you would call on if you wanted support in taking accountability for violence, harm or abuse that you've done; or if you witnessed violence or if someone you care about was being violent or being abused.[22]

Pod building is central to the BATJC's approach. It involves creating a network, or pod, of people around an individual that can help address harm, accountability, and healing. This pod is typically composed of friends, family, or community members who are selected based on trust and shared values. The aim of a pod is to create a supportive and effective environment in which harm can be addressed without punitive measures such as incarceration or the involvement of law enforcement. Pods focus on communication, understanding, healing, and transformative justice, a process that not only addresses the harm but also works to change the underlying conditions that led to it. This process is mutual, meaning that everyone involved has a pod, including the person who was harmed, the person who caused harm, and other community members. Together, these pods work to address harm, encourage accountability, and promote healing. By prioritizing relationships and community, those who practice this approach seek to create long-term, sustainable change in behavior and social conditions.

People can have a number of pods for different matters. Pods can assist in preventing and dealing with various types of harm, such as personal disputes, domestic issues, community conflicts, and even problems caused by the government. Additionally, they can help by creating a network that holds people responsible for their actions and offers support to everyone involved. At a community level, there can be pods trained in trauma-informed responses to support a range of community members, teams that conduct regular community check-ins for everyone's well-being, teams that provide training and dedicated groups for mental health crises, teams that offer quick support for housing needs, and teams that use a health-focused approach to help people dealing with drug-related problems, including overdose. Pods and collectives can also focus on mutual aid, shelter and food support, and emotional and mental wellness and healing, and they can serve as political organizing bases. Now is the time to make the transformation.

Many different tools and technologies can be used for these efforts. But they have to have a just container—and the approaches that form a tapestry of safety systems can allow the appropriate tools to be used in ways aligned with community desires and interests.

Communities can draw on secure, encrypted technology and apps to facilitate communication and immediate intervention dispatch, as well as long-term support and preventive work. Those in a person's pod can be immediately alerted if that person is in an emergency. The kind of emergency can be relayed, which can also dictate who responds and with what resources. There can be a loud ringer alert mechanism for pod members to alert those who are close by and have access to rapid transportation. But these tools must be situated in frameworks that are secure regarding technology and privacy and not be used for profit or to punish or surveil people at any step of the way. Collective resource pools can also help with navigating and intervening in crises.

Importantly, investments in violence intervention must include all forms of violence, which means increasing capacity and resources for addressing gender violence within communities. This includes sexual violence, intimate-partner violence, and other forms of abuse. In applying a range of responses to these issues, carried out by those who have training and experience in addressing conflict, communities can tackle a large share of the harm that exists in contemporary society. These approaches would benefit from prioritizing the interconnected components of prevention, safety interventions, and transformative responses as a holistic approach to managing community concerns.

CRISIS RESPONDERS

We need to begin scaling back police presence and contact in everyday life. To that end, it's necessary to develop alternatives for mental health emergencies, homelessness, drug-related concerns, and other crises. Antiviolence organizers don't want to reduce the likelihood of police violence occurring; they want to reduce the opportunity for it to occur in the first place. The only way to do this is to remove police from communities. The development of various mobile crisis response models represents a groundbreaking community-based safety approach, which aims to provide on-the-spot assistance to individuals dealing with mental health, drug, or alcohol-related health crises. This innovative model relies on multidisciplinary teams of mental health professionals and health care providers who are dispatched to the scene to provide immediate care and intervention. These teams are expertly trained in crisis intervention and de-escalation techniques, with a commitment to offering compassionate, person-centered care. Rather than approaching the situation with a law enforcement lens, team members focus on understanding and addressing a person's immediate needs, providing supportive care, and creating a plan for follow-up services if necessary. These teams play a critical role in linking people to community resources and services, serving as a bridge between crisis moments and longer-term support. This model is designed to reduce the likelihood of unnecessary confrontations with law enforcement and incarceration, instead emphasizing therapeutic interventions and support.

Nearly half of all incarcerated people have been diagnosed with a mental health disorder.[23] Those with mental illness are over ten times more likely to experience police use of force,[24] and at least a quarter of fatal encounters with law enforcement involve a person struggling with mental health problems.[25] A significant number of police calls and arrests involve the homeless, with a glaring disparity in places such as Portland, Oregon, where the city's houseless made up 52 percent of arrests in 2017 despite making up less than 3 percent of the population.[26]

CAHOOTS

CAHOOTS (Crisis Assistance Helping Out on the Streets) is a community-based public safety program in Eugene and Springfield, Oregon, that began in 1989 and has received considerable attention since 2020. It emerged from the work of a community-centric, activist-oriented health clinic founded in 1969, the White Bird Clinic.[27] The clinic recognized the urgent need for alternatives to traditional law enforcement, specifically in cases tied to mental health crises, substance use, and homelessness, which are predominantly health and social concerns rather than law enforcement matters. CAHOOTS offers mobile crisis intervention 24/7 in the Eugene-Springfield metro area. The program is dispatched through the Eugene police-fire-ambulance communications center and the Springfield nonemergency system.

CAHOOTS provides support in response to urgent medical needs, including psychological crises, as well as information, resources, referrals, advocacy, and transportation to the next step in treatment in some cases. CAHOOTS' focus areas include but aren't limited to: crisis counseling; suicide prevention and intervention; conflict resolution and mediation; grief and loss support; substance abuse; housing crisis; first aid and nonemergency medical care; resource connection and referrals; and transportation to services. CAHOOTS is unique in its approach to safety, as it focuses on harm reduction and crisis intervention rather than law enforcement. Instead of armed police officers, its teams consist of a medic (a nurse, EMT, or paramedic) and a crisis worker who has substantial training in the mental health field.

Something that sets CAHOOTS apart is its nonpunitive, empathetic, and de-escalation-focused approach. This strategy has been notably successful in reducing the reliance on police for social issues. The outcome has been a significant decrease in confrontations that could potentially escalate to violence. This approach successfully diverts a large number of nonemergency incidents away from the traditional emergency medical services system, which can free resources to be used in other ways. Furthermore, CAHOOTS puts a premium on continuous engagement and follow-up, not just immediate crisis resolution. This ensures that people are not left without support at the doorsteps of social service agencies but receive ongoing support in their journey toward healing and recovery if needed. Above all, CAHOOTS is about community; it's embedded in the philosophy that every community member deserves dignity, care, and the chance for a better life. This is why CAHOOTS has been embraced by the local community and serves as a model for other crisis response approaches.

CAHOOTS responders wear plain, casual attire, including a CAHOOTS shirt or jacket, and engage in a care-driven, calm manner. They serve as crisis responders in a range of situations: they evaluate situations, provide immediate assistance, and direct individuals to further care or services if needed. Despite handling nearly 24,000 calls in 2019, they required police backup less than 1 percent of the time, demonstrating their ability to manage crises effectively.[28] The model also prevents violent police coercion, saving the community money, as the teams handle situations that would otherwise lead to police-injured people in emergency rooms, which can be costly. Roughly 20 percent of 911 calls, particularly those involving homelessness, addiction, intoxication, or mental health crises, are directed to CAHOOTS.[29] CAHOOTS team members do not carry weapons and discreetly listen to police radios through earphones.

The journalist Rob Waters spent time with CAHOOTS and reported on his experiences witnessing calls and CAHOOTS team responses.[30] He told the story of a thirty-two-year-old man named Spencer who had had a frightening night. He thought that he might have ingested a veterinary drug, ivermectin, and was troubled by thoughts that his dog, Lulu, had been harmed, though Lulu had died the previous year. Hearing voices, feeling sharp pain, and feeling he might be having a seizure, Spencer reached out to his friend Brandon and shared his fears on Facebook Live, with more than 150 viewers seeing the stream. First, EMTs arrived to check his health. He was physically okay and said that he felt that the EMTs did not attend to the concerns he was having about his mental state. A CAHOOTS team then arrived and offered calm, supportive guidance. He was in the midst of a mental health crisis, and he received the support he needed to navigate the experience rather than the situation's being exacerbated by police. Spencer later expressed gratitude for the immense community support and for living in a city that values mental well-being.

As Waters wrote, the most common type of call that CAHOOTS receives is for someone in crisis or someone who needs a check-in to see if they are okay. Another common type of call is specifically for someone who may be suicidal; CAHOOTS receives an average of four such calls a day.[31] Waters, who spent time with two CAHOOTS teams, reported that the calls varied widely. In one instance, someone who was houseless had fallen into a stream. CAHOOTS responded and helped the person deal with the difficulty and shock of the experience. The CAHOOTS team brought the young man clothes, food, and support, as he was cold and could have developed hypothermia.

Waters wrote further on the varied cases of CAHOOTS calls and responses:

> Another man called and said he was feeling suicidal and was found face down on the sidewalk. The team flipped him over, and he revived, walked to the van with assistance, and accepted a ride to Willamette Family Inc.'s Buckley's Sobering Services.
>
> Not all of the calls involved homeless people. A pleasant older woman came out of her house when the CAHOOTS team arrived and asked whether machines and sand were coming out of her head. Reassured that they were not, she thanked the team and went back inside. . . .
>
> Perhaps the most dramatic call came in the afternoon and brought a response from both police and CAHOOTS. The mother of an eighteen-year-old man called 911 to report that he had posted a video showing him pointing a gun at his head. The mention of a gun required police to go to the house where he was living with his godmother, while the CAHOOTS team hung back until the officers radioed an all-clear. The team members then joined the officers on the porch and quickly took charge, telling the police they could leave.
>
> The young man acknowledged posting the video but denied that the gun had been pointed at him or anyone else. His godmother said that she saw the video and agreed there had been no

real danger, adding that the gun was now locked up. The young man chatted amiably with the CAHOOTS team, accepted a business card with crisis phone numbers, and then excused himself to go back to sleep.[32]

These varied responses to moments of crisis show the importance of crisis responders who can respond to a range of issues with resources, care, and support. In all the instances Waters listed, the presence of police could have resulted in tragedy, as it often does with people in crisis.[33] The CAHOOTS model holds potential for other communities. There's room to expand and improve this model, particularly as its jurisdiction is currently limited to noncriminal calls, meaning that police officers may still be tasked with situations that CAHOOTS personnel are better trained to handle. One way to expand CAHOOTS' jurisdiction could be to decriminalize situations such as addiction and homelessness. Presently, police response to homelessness is driven by city laws that criminalize it. Changing the laws that criminalize such behavior could broaden the scope of what a mobile crisis response unit such as CAHOOTS can address. Another potential strategy for initiatives such as CAHOOTS is developing an alternative number that the public can call for crisis intervention. Finally, crisis responders can respond along with violence interrupters, community mediators, and other community safety workers equipped with community-based safety approaches to accountability and justice, removing the threat of police violence, increasing the likelihood of amicable outcomes given that a police presence can exacerbate problems, and allowing more specialized responses.

MH FIRST

Another crisis response model is being pioneered by the Anti Police-Terror Project (APTP), which has been engaged in a number of efforts to build community-based models of safety outside systems of policing and punishment. One example is APTP's MH First, a cutting-edge model for nonpolice community-first response to mental health crises. The goal of MH First is to respond to mental health crises including, but not limited to, psychiatric emergencies, substance use problems, and domestic violence.

Currently, MH First operates in Oakland and Sacramento and has its own hotline number. APTP has also led the Defund OPD campaign for the past five years, seeking resource reallocation into community resources and alternative models of public safety. Specifically, the campaign is calling on Oakland to "Reduce OPD's allocation from the General Fund by 50% (roughly $150 Million); disallow unauthorized overtime by OPD; invest in housing, jobs, youth programs, restorative justice, mental health workers and other services that actually keep the community safe."[34] Linking this work to a broader vision, APTP states, "50% is only the first step. Our ultimate goal is to disband and abolish OPD."

APTP describes MH First this way:

> Our purpose is to interrupt and eliminate the need for law enforcement in mental health crisis first response by providing mobile peer support, de-escalation assistance, and non-punitive and life-affirming interventions, therefore decriminalizing emotional and psychological crises and decreasing the stigma around mental health, substance use, and domestic violence, while also addressing their root causes: white supremacy, capitalism, and colonialism.[35]

MH First Sacramento began in 2020 and offered services throughout the week. It was followed by MH First Oakland.

The journalist Emily Nonko has profiled MH First in detail.[36] As discussed in a 2020 Next City article, during the months leading up to the COVID-19 pandemic, groups of three volunteers made up the response team. The "contact person" was ideally someone who could draw upon personal experience to connect with the caller. Accompanying this person was a medical professional who handled on-site dispatches and a "safety liaison," whose role was to engage with community members and the police at the crisis scene.

APTP cofounder Asantewaa Boykin, who was a psychiatric nurse for more than ten years, emphasized to Nonko the importance of the liaison's role given the significant involvement of law enforcement in medical and emergency situations. The collective pays particular attention to having safety liaisons manage interactions among volunteers, those they serve, and any police presence from beginning to end. And rather than using leading questions often found in emergency response, such as "Do you want to harm yourself?" or "Do you plan on harming others?" volunteers ask, "Are you safe?" Boykin and MH First workers developed the Mental Health First Aid Handbook as an adaptable framework to ground their work in community care–driven mental health crisis response. MH First is run entirely by volunteers, meaning that Good Samaritan laws protect responders while they are acting to the best of their abilities in their areas of expertise. Good Samaritan laws provide legal protection to people who give reasonable assistance to those who are injured, ill, incapacitated, or facing significant danger, ensuring that volunteers acting to the best of their abilities in their areas of expertise are not held legally liable for unintentional harm, as long as their actions are not grossly negligent or reckless.

If police were already present or en route or community members reported feeling unsafe, MH First dispatched a team. During the pandemic, on-site dispatches were temporarily suspended due to COVID-19, with the free hotline remaining operational. The team also coordinated transportation services when necessary. According to Boykin, the Sacramento team fielded around thirty to forty calls per month and successfully de-escalated most situations without the need for police or emergency services.[37] In one case that likely represents a common reality, responders provided transportation for a young man who needed to go to the hospital but was apprehensive about calling 911.

During the pandemic, MH First further developed its technical infrastructure, including ensuring that all its records are digital and compliant with the Health Insurance Portability and Accountability Act of 1996 (HIPAA). The organization still employs a three-person team structure, with two managing the call and the third serving as a consultant. In the absence of on-site dispatches, the team will contact emergency services as a final resort if de-escalation attempts are unsuccessful and no community alternatives are accessible. After hundreds of Oakland residents expressed interest in backing a local program, APTP was convinced that the model could be replicated, so it created MH First Oakland.

There are endless ideas for crisis intervention response teams. Ultimately, someone experiencing a drug-related medical emergency—as well as food and water insecurity—needs an immediate, trauma-informed response. A holistic approach to crisis intervention can address the complexity of mental health crises, prioritizing empathy, dignity, and respect. With a focus on supporting people within their communities and linking them to necessary resources, mobile crisis response units represent a paradigm shift in crisis response, putting human welfare and health at the forefront.

It's also critical to center on noncoercive, care-driven approaches, especially for those who require ongoing, long-term support. Due to the coercive and punitive nature of some mental health approaches, which the abolitionists Mariame Kaba and Andrea J. Ritchie refer to as "soft policing," many people avoid seeking help or refuse help out of fear. It's crucial to help stabilize people by providing them with nonpunitive, transformative approaches to mental health. Ensuring that people have treatment options early on and outside of crises can prevent situations from worsening over time.

SAFE MIAMI

Safe Miami, a coalition comprising Dream Defenders, the Circle of Brotherhood, Dade County Street Response, and Touching Miami with Love, represents a transformative approach to public safety in Miami.[38] In a city where Black individuals disproportionately fall victim to gun violence, Safe Miami's work is pivotal in shifting the focus from increased policing to community-based solutions.[39] The collective's Healing and Justice Center is at the forefront of this change. It's a community-based public safety program centered on violence reduction, mental health improvement, and diverting individuals from the criminal-legal system.

The Healing and Justice Center operates under a holistic philosophy: addressing not just the symptoms of violence but its root causes, which often lie in poverty, inadequate housing, and lack of essential services such as health care and education. A key component of its work is the Freedom House Mobile Crisis Unit. This initiative provides an alternative to police intervention in mental health crises, currently operating as a pilot program for residents within a five-mile radius of Liberty City. The service is set to expand to 24/7 coverage, demonstrating a commitment to accessible, community-led crisis management.

The Trauma Recovery Center (TRC) is another essential service offered by Safe Miami. This nationally acclaimed organization focuses on providing free mental health services to survivors of violence aged fourteen and older. The TRC tackles barriers to accessing mental health care and legal resources in the aftermath of trauma, offering in-person counseling and case management for a range of violent experiences, from physical assault to domestic violence. Additionally, Safe Miami has partnered with BetterHelp to provide free online counseling, extending mental health support to those who might not otherwise have access. Their Doctors Within Borders initiative provides free urgent care services, further cementing the collective's commitment to holistic community health.

Beyond health care, Safe Miami emphasizes the importance of skills and knowledge for emergency situations. Its Stop the Bleed and CPR training programs empower community members to respond effectively to gun wounds, a critical skill given the slow ambulance response times in many neighborhoods. Recognizing that young people often bear the brunt of systemic failures, the collective provides safe spaces and supportive guidance, helping them navigate and process trauma.

Safe Miami's response to violence goes beyond immediate aftermath support. When shootings occur, its team actively engages with the community, offering emotional support and connecting individuals to their wide range of services. This proactive approach contrasts starkly with typical police responses, which often focus on punitive measures rather than on healing and preventing future violence.

Additionally, Safe Miami provides conflict resolution services, afterschool youth programs, and support for survivors of violence, emphasizing community care and intervention over punitive measures. These initiatives align with the collective's broader political activism, challenging the allocation of resources in Miami Dade County, where nearly a third of the county budget is spent on police and corrections.

Underpinning all these initiatives is a broader political commitment. Safe Miami advocates for a reallocation of resources, arguing that real safety comes from investment in housing, jobs, education, and health care, not increased policing. Its work is a testament to the power of community-led initiatives in creating safer, more resilient neighborhoods. Safe Miami's approach echoes the legacy of the Black Panther Party's survival programs, blending activism with essential services such as health care clinics. This collective represents a tangible example of community-led public safety, demonstrating the efficacy of resource allocation to empowering and healing communities, rather than criminalizing them.

TRAFFIC SAFETY WORKERS

Traffic stops are among the most frequent occasions of police contact, abuse, and violence. Police systematically stop drivers, and the resulting interactions are typically unobserved. As discussed in previous chapters, cars have been one reason for large-scale police expansion. A range of laws and rulings allows police to engage in pretextual stops and searches that disproportionately affect Black and other marginalized drivers.

The roads are sites of tragic accidents, injuries, and deaths. According to the National Highway Traffic Safety Administration, there are more than 6.8 million automobile accidents each year in the United States, and nearly thirty-eight thousand people die from such accidents each year. In recent years, accidents have been surging to the highest they've been since the 1940s.[40]

If policing stopped crashes and accidents, these numbers would not be so bleak. There is a clear need for a new paradigm of traffic management that moves beyond punitive interventions by the police and criminal-legal system and leads to large-scale reductions in road tragedies while simultaneously reducing contexts in which police violence can take place. Organizers and advocates have made gains around reducing police involvement in traffic safety, particularly in banning pretextual stops and searches. And while the initiatives are still in their nascent stages, the most powerful visions are being put to the test: traffic safety approaches that are free from police involvement and center on traffic safety workers and design as means of making the streets safer — from both accidents and police.[41]

THE BERKELEY APPROACH: BERKDOT AND RACIAL JUSTICE

In July 2020, the Berkeley City Council passed a novel measure to establish the Berkeley Department of Transportation (BerkDOT).[42] This entity is designed to handle parking and traffic problems using a strategy explicitly designed to tackle racial bias and abuses stemming from routine police stops. It proposes an alternative vision for traffic safety management that other municipalities could adopt. This shift is intended to minimize overall police-civilian contact and subsequently reduce the potential for racial bias and police brutality. Notably, it foregrounds a racial justice lens to prevent the perpetuation of systemic racism. Additionally, it suggests connecting the reimagined traffic safety approach with greenhouse gas reduction initiatives, which recognizes the broader environmental impacts associated with vehicular and traffic safety.

BerkDOT is not merely a shift in the organizational chart; it's a novel approach to traffic safety. Its mission is focused on a cooperative model that people adhere to rather than one rooted in punishment. This represents a significant change in the culture of enforcement, emphasizing equity and community engagement over penalties and punitive measures. The responsibilities of the new department are wide ranging and reflect a comprehensive approach to traffic safety. They include traffic enforcement, parking enforcement, crossing guard management, collision response, and reporting. Each of these areas, traditionally under the purview of the police, represents a distinct point of interaction between law enforcement and the public. By shifting these tasks away from the police, Berkeley is actively working to reduce potential friction points and foster a more trusting relationship between residents and the city government.

Additionally, BerkDOT recognizes the role that transportation plays within the city. Its mandate not only addresses immediate traffic safety issues but also acknowledges the importance of transportation in meeting Berkeley's broader greenhouse gas reduction goals. This reflects a nuanced understanding that traffic safety and environmental sustainability are not separate issues but interconnected aspects of a city's well-being. Further, it explicitly identifies a commitment to racial justice. Having recognized that traffic stops are one of the most common points of interaction between police and the public—and a significant source of stress for Black and other marginalized communities—Berkeley is attempting to eliminate this potential source of conflict.

As noted in the Berkeley proposal:

[The City is in the process of creating] a Berkeley Department of Transportation (BerkDOT) to ensure a racial justice lens in traffic enforcement and the development of transportation policy, programs, & infrastructure. . . .

One way of addressing these issues in Berkeley is by creating a Department of Transportation (BerkDOT), shifting traffic and parking enforcement responsibilities away from the Berkeley Police Department and coupling it with the work currently housed in the Transportation Division of the Public Works Department....

Berkeley can lead the nation in refocusing its traffic enforcement efforts on equitable enforcement, focusing on a cooperative compliance model rather than a punitive model. A Department of Transportation in the City of Berkeley could shift traffic enforcement, parking enforcement, crossing guards, and collision response & reporting away from police officers—reducing the need for police interaction with civilians—and ensure a racial justice lens in the way we approach transportation policies, programs, and infrastructure. It would also ensure a focus on transportation that is separate and apart from public works issues, fitting for the importance of transportation as an issue of concern to Berkeley and as a key component of our greenhouse reduction goals.[43]

Los Angeles; Portland, Oregon; and Minneapolis are also exploring the possibility of removing police from traffic safety.[44] This is one way to minimize unnecessary police contact and address systemic problems in traffic safety and beyond. As the Berkeley model continues to unfold, it may serve as a case study for communities across the nation. Its impacts on racial justice, community trust, and traffic safety will be closely watched and could shape the future of traffic management in cities across the country and even globally.

While Berkeley is looking to break new ground with its approach, there are some challenges, the main one being that state law does not currently allow civilian traffic safety management.[45] A recurring trend with novel approaches is laws that prevent these approaches and center on policing as the only possible option. Given the complexity of local, state, and federal laws and politics, a central priority is collective strategizing around how communities can challenge and move beyond state power in developing community-based safety models. As state and federal governments often fail to provide safety and actively impede transformative efforts, communities must find ways to build and meet their own needs.

A NEW PARADIGM OF TRAFFIC SAFETY

A key component of reshaping traffic safety lies in the need to devise alternative approaches for driving-related incidents that might escalate into dangerous or harmful situations. In our quest to reimagine public safety frameworks, it's essential to establish bodies capable of delivering safety interventions. Emergency response squads and professionally trained mediators who are not associated with the police and can be swiftly mobilized can offer solutions that don't depend on legal, punitive actions. Local jurisdictions can ultimately decide on the optimal use of such responder teams, which must be capable of defusing and de-escalating potentially violent situations that may exceed the capacities of regular traffic safety mediators.

Reconstructing roadways to discourage speeding and other traffic infractions, as well as fostering alternative entities to manage traffic safety, can contribute to road safety while circumventing the hazards associated with police-led traffic control. Reengineering city roads can involve constructing speed humps, tapering streets, installing traffic circles, and planning traffic paths to curtail unsafe driving behaviors. Self-regulating roads can aid in reducing police interactions with motorists while providing an alternative to cameras and other tools that may infringe on civil liberties and escalate the government's use of punitive, revenue-driven methods.

A number of other proposals have emerged in places such as New York City;[46] Cambridge, Massachusetts;[47] St. Louis Park[48] and Brooklyn Center, Minnesota;[49] the state of Florida;[50] Montgomery County, Maryland;[51] and Los Angeles.[52] But government entities other than the police can still practice racial discrimination and financial extraction. In order to ensure a transformative approach, we need fail-safes to prevent new traffic control entities from becoming complicit in government processes that extract wealth from oppressed communities—and the broader public—in order to generate revenue.[53] Punitive or financially driven traffic control will not increase safety and will contribute to predatory extraction, especially from subjugated communities.[54] We need to move beyond paradigms of enforcement to center on safety and accountability, not punishment and extraction. One way to prevent predatory government practices is to create nongovernmental entities driven solely by the desire to produce roads that are safer overall—from police violence and accidents—to oversee the everyday management of traffic safety with the guiding principles of justice, safety, and accountability.

A public health approach to traffic safety would rely on a multifaceted framework focused on enhancing health and safety rather than a punitive, criminal-legal one. Key strategies and structures for successful initiatives include ensuring the necessary funds and resources to implement the model; engaging with directly affected communities; developing a nonpunitive approach to matters that need additional intervention, such as the use of mental health or crisis response teams; avoiding a revenue-driven model that financially penalizes drivers; and designing city infrastructure to encourage compliance with traffic ordinances.

Initiatives should concentrate on redesigning roads and infrastructure to make it more challenging for drivers to engage in speeding and other traffic offenses. Vision Zero is a comprehensive strategy aimed at eliminating all traffic fatalities and severe injuries while promoting safe, healthy, equitable mobility for everyone. Originally implemented in Sweden in the 1990s, the approach has demonstrated success across Europe and is increasingly adopted in major US cities, integrating diverse interventions spanning policy, design, and community involvement.[55] This holistic approach to road safety has shown promising results in transforming how traffic safety is managed worldwide. Designing safer roads is a critical component of reimagining traffic safety that does not come with the dangers and harms of police and punishment-driven traffic enforcement.

As I wrote in a report for the Community Resource Hub for Safety & Accountability, an organization where I served as a senior research and policy associate, there are ways to shift from law enforcement–centered traffic safety to a new approach focused on nonpunitive, noncoercive methods of enhancing road safety.[56] This approach would ensure that traffic safety rules aren't exploited as excuses for criminal charges, surveillance, or the targeting of marginalized communities. Measures to be taken include the following.

End the criminalization of driving offenses. It's essential to establish a strong separation between the criminal-legal system and the oversight of traffic safety. This will necessitate not just a decrease in police involvement in road traffic enforcement but also a fresh approach to dealing with drivers who might pose a public risk. Initiatives focusing on sober driving, public health, and driver education, along with the development of alternative nonpunitive accountability measures, are critically important. If traffic violations occur that a community collectively deems need addressing, the response should involve an educational and reparative approach based on a framework such as transformative justice, instead of a punitive criminal-legal method. There should also be an end to pretextual or investigatory stops, in which police pull someone over for a traffic-related concern but turn the stop into an opportunity to explore whether a driver is doing something criminal.[57] Organizers have pushed to end the practice of pretextual stops, and in 2021, Philadelphia became the first city to curtail it.[58]

It is also essential to end the use of any form of immigration enforcement or surveillance during traffic stops and traffic safety accountability processes. The pipeline from traffic safety to deportation contributes to unjust detention and the forced removal of individuals. Rethought traffic safety models must establish protections to prevent any form of criminalization, surveillance, or enforcement related to immigration laws.

Several laws recently implemented in cities such as Atlanta, Philadelphia, and New York City focus on specific off-road driving activities and behaviors (for example, operating dirt bikes or ATVs, neglecting to wear helmets, performing stunts such as wheelies and donuts) that can potentially lead to criminal charges, complicating the efforts of organizers aiming to do away with these chargeable offenses. These punitive traffic enforcement tactics tend to unfairly affect Black, Latinx, underprivileged, and marginalized communities. It is important for organizers to advocate for the decriminalization of off-road driving, preferring public health and transformative systems of education, accountability, and design. One way to interrupt the criminalization of off-road driving could be to establish parks in urban areas for ATV, dirt bike, and other off-road riding activities.

Remove financial incentives from traffic safety. Across the United States, traffic enforcement is often used as a revenue source, a practice that disproportionately affects people of color. It can persist even without police involvement in traffic safety, through financial penalties aimed at revenue generation rather than public safety. Automated traffic enforcement methods, such as red-light cameras, can also contribute to this type of enforcement, pose significant surveillance risks, and burden marginalized communities. New strategies must be grounded in safety models focused on public health that prioritize accountability and education, as well as repair and transformative justice for harm caused by drivers.

Develop plans for traffic infractions that escalate into crisis or harm. A genuine reimagining of public safety models involves entities capable of providing necessary safety interventions. For this purpose, nonpolice-affiliated crisis response teams and trained violence interrupters that can be quickly dispatched can help deliver interventions that don't rely on criminal-legal mechanisms. These teams would have the training and tools to meet the scale of the crisis at hand while emphasizing violence interruption and de-escalation.

Invest in new institutions for traffic safety. We need to invest in new traffic management methods aimed at improving road safety without police. Regions where an entity capable of assuming responsibility for traffic safety already exists may need resources for their implementation. In areas where no such entity exists, new organizational bodies can be created that are separate from the police, as proposed in Berkeley, to take over the primary responsibility for traffic safety. Such bodies should include traffic safety workers who can help manage routine concerns on the road.

Redesign roads. There is an urgent need to launch and expand initiatives that focus on enhancing roadway safety through design. This includes constructing narrower streets, installing roundabouts, and reducing speed limits to diminish traffic collisions and injuries. Additionally, improving walkways and bike-friendly infrastructure, along with implementing advanced traffic signal systems, are critical measures to increase the safety of all road users. Lower speed limits also contribute to reductions in traffic-related fatalities and serious injuries. Improved traffic light and walk signal regulation systems have also proven effective.

The exploration of traffic safety management without law enforcement is still in its initial stages. It's important for reimagined traffic safety models to focus on developing noncoercive, nonpunitive approaches to managing road safety. Such approaches can improve public safety on the roads while helping mitigate the deep and historic harms of police-involved traffic enforcement.

People are far less likely to run when they don't think the people stopping them will harm or kill them. But when there is an actual driving-related threat to public safety, there are alternative ways to manage the situation — including allowing the car to run out of gas or using interventions that do not carry the danger and risk of precision immobilization technique (PIT) maneuvers, in which police attempt to use their cars to cause the driver of a fleeing car to lose control and ultimately stop, and high-speed chases. Some of those tools and strategies already exist. But police rely on the threat or use of violence as the core of their work — and it is positioned as the only answer simply because it has been the classic strategy. Transformative approaches to safety are possible, but developing them requires resources, commitment, and innovation.

Imagine a traffic safety approach that employs specialists who can have a conversation about traffic matters that focuses on safety, not punishment. Or that traffic infractions weren't used as a tool to generate revenue that doesn't seem to be improving many people's quality of life and is funding more police. Instead, drivers who engage in unsafe practices can contribute — if they are able — to a fund for families of people killed by vehicles or survivors of traffic accidents as a mechanism of accountability, or public health approaches to tackling unsafe driving that include public education and alternative interventions. And during incidents where there is a threat to safety, crisis responders are able to intervene without flipping a car or killing anyone.

COMMUNITY SAFETY HUBS

Community safety hubs* can involve a variety of safety-focused strategies, teams, methods, and tasks. People have organized for safety within their communities for as long as we know of, at various levels of effectiveness and for a range of purposes. Their efforts have included the Black Panther armed copwatch patrols and survival programs, antiviolence organizations, safe passage initiatives for youths and vulnerable community members to commute

---

*   I offer community safety hubs as a concept and framework, but local community-based safety networks and collectivities should identify with whatever specific name they decide upon.

safely, and more. All the safety intervenors mentioned in this chapter can be considered to be part of a broader constellation that forms a local safety hub.

Imagine, for example, that people had the option to call a number for a local community safety hub—say 727—that could dispatch trained response teams for support, violence interruption, and violence prevention; that all neighborhoods had such teams for various forms of violence, including interpersonal violence, domestic violence, and sexual assault; that there were dedicated conflict mediators and interrupters throughout communities capable of managing a wide range of issues that are often exacerbated or criminalized by the criminal-legal system. There would be more peace, resolution, and safety.

Municipalities can experiment with identifying certain emergencies, such as mental health emergencies and drug abuse, and deploying trained dispatch teams through the nonemergency services number 311. Communities can scale this down further by developing pilot sites within a particular neighborhood or set of blocks to experiment with emergency response alternatives at varying scales and levels.

Building beyond policing is not only about reducing police involvement in community life; it is fundamentally centered on creating the conditions in which we do not need police to begin with. To that end, high-quality schools, housing, and hospitals, work that is rooted in dignity and not profit-based exploitation, violence interruption, domestic violence support programs, drug treatment, and efficient emergency medical response—including for mental health emergencies—are all programs that help foster safety and would help to transform Black communities and all communities.

Collectives have tried a number of ideas, initiatives, and experiments to prevent, intervene, and respond to various emergencies and crises. These initiatives have often been carried out with little funding and could be scaled up with appropriate resources. Community safety hubs can help stitch together a broader tapestry of restorative and transformative justice and community accountability agencies that now operate without much interaction. Other efforts can also be developed.

The current regime of policing and criminal punishment dominates the landscape of funding for and investments in public safety, limiting reliable community-based safety approaches. These interrelated initiatives can and should be community institutions. Governments tend to co-opt and corrupt these approaches. Before they can be housed within governmental structures, we first need a significant overhaul of the current system. Any approach to organizing political life should genuinely serve the public interest, be truly democratic, and adopt participatory decision-making models. But as things stand, in order to avoid government co-optation, these initiatives should be community based, free from the private finance sector, and without influence from political structures that are not invested in community-based safety.

Community safety hubs can implement other interventions that will reduce conflict, harm, and violence within communities, such as reclaiming abandoned houses to provide housing and converting empty lots into green spaces. Community safety hubs operating in a transformative framework understand that when people don't have a safe home to sleep in, it is a form of violence and contributes to instability that can lead to other forms of harm. Thus, providing safe housing and addressing communities' range of basic needs is as much about interrupting violence as stopping someone from pulling a trigger. Organizers can also create youth after-school and summer programs; develop new community institutions that build social and communal life; and help develop intentional communities, planned residential communities that operate with a focus on social cohesion and share common goals, interests, and values, neighborhood schools, health clinics and interventions, food and water provision efforts, guaranteed basic income, and more. In other words, safety hubs can address safety not only by facilitating direct interventions but also through attending to the structural needs of communities and building, as Ruth Wilson Gilmore put it, "life-affirming institutions."

In order to move beyond policing, we must fully appreciate how broader social and communal contexts make certain outcomes more or less possible. When inequality and oppression proliferate, a range of consequences tears apart the social fabric, destroys lives, and makes outcomes such as harm and violence serious problems. With adequate resources and a capacious framework, community safety organizers can focus on different areas but share commitments to reorganizing community safety and society more broadly. Of course, many of the efforts that I mention are already being implemented to meet immediate needs, providing mutual aid and survival programming to many people across the United States and beyond. But through integrating these efforts within a broader landscape of safety organizing, we can begin to transform communities immediately and also build the conditions for new communal possibilities.

US child welfare agencies launch investigations or other interventions that affect more than 3 million children each year.[59] Between fiscal years 2018 and 2022, the foster care system in the United States processed an average of approximately 634,468 children annually, reflecting the total count of children impacted by the system each year over this five-year period.[60] Black, Latinx, and Indigenous children are investigated and removed at disproportionately high rates. Approximately 37.4 percent of all children experience a child protective services investigation by age eighteen.[61] The child welfare system, which Dorothy Roberts has rightfully called the "family policing system," produces unfathomable violence and trauma for children and families. As Roberts stated:

> Fifty-three percent of Black children in America will experience a CPS investigation at some point before their eighteenth birthday. During CPS investigations, caseworkers may inspect every corner of the home, interrogate family members about intimate details of their lives, strip-search children to look for evidence, and collect confidential information from schools, healthcare providers, and social service programs. If caseworkers detect a problem, like drug use, inadequate medical care, or insecure housing, they will coerce families into an onerous regimen of supervision that rarely addresses their needs.
>
> More disruptive still is the forcible family separation that often follows CPS investigations. Every year child welfare agencies take over 250,000 children from their parents and put them in the formal foster care system. At the same time, these agencies informally separate an estimated 250,000 more children from their parents each year based on so-called "safety plans"—arrangements parents are pressured to agree to in lieu of a formal court proceeding.[62]

I've witnessed firsthand how CPS devastates familial and communal bonds in my own family. So much trauma was endured by generations of family members because there were not adequate means of helping children and their caregivers. I have seen, very vividly, how the afterlives of foster care, group homes, and abusive caregivers continue to wreak havoc on the lives of people I care about and love. The system tears apart families and can expose children to conditions that are as or more harmful than their original ones, but in wholly unfamiliar contexts. There are certainly scenarios where children and families need interventions and support, but the family police system does not serve that function. We are in deep need of care-centered approaches to supporting families and children, especially those who are most in need of support.

While some caseworkers may have good intentions and are often over-worked and may feel pressured to comply with rigid bureaucratic guide-lines set by state agencies that they might not agree with, as a whole, child protective agencies operate with harmful policing and carceral practices. In addition to the traumatizing effects that investigations have on families, they often do not yield safety for children. The foster care system is one of the largest pipelines to sex trafficking, incarceration, homelessness, and pov-erty. Children are removed from families at the discretion of caseworkers for issues ranging from neglect to abuse. But forcible removals often lead youths into cycles of violence and harm. The current model relies on surveillance and policing of families in ways that disproportionately target Black, Latinx, Indigenous, and poor and working-class communities. In *Torn Apart: How the Child Welfare System Destroys Black Families—and How Abolition Can Build a Safer World*, Roberts and other activists, abolitionist social workers, and families affected by the system called for the abolition of child pro-tective services.[63] Moving beyond policing includes abolishing this violent institution with a history of racial violence and dispossession.

It's vital to have dedicated safety measures in place for families and children in distress. While such interventions are necessary, they must be approached with care and compassion. Cases of abuse and neglect must be investigated. The main goal should always be to supply families with the resources they need to succeed and grow together. If an immediate intervention is needed to ensure the safety of children, community safety mobilizations can deal with the specific contextual factors and provide a tailored response to the situation to ensure the safety, stability, and over-all well-being of the children and family. If the problem is being caused by poverty, addressing that and lifting families out of poverty can be a priority. If it is related to drugs or alcohol, providing the necessary help can be the focus. Importantly, because community safety hubs would be local and have strong communal ties that center on care, safety workers would be able to strategize with families to ensure that children have immediate places to stay safe with an effort to keep siblings together and ensure that the process is not carceral. Responses must address what a family needs to be healthy, if possible, and ensure long-term support if necessary.

Children are among the most vulnerable in communities, and they deserve safety and stability. Focusing on the issues that give rise to unstable dynamics and patterns of abuse, including issues surrounding poverty and housing, can lead to reductions in instances of abuse. Restorative and transformative justice approaches are essential to ensure transformative healing approaches for children and families when possible. The care-driven practices used by collectives such as the Network to Advance Abolitionist Social Work, which "strives to amplify a practice of social work aimed at dismantling the prison industrial complex (PIC) and building the life-affirming horizon to which abolition aspires,"[64] are key to dismantling the current family policing system and building safety and accountability approaches centered on children's and families' well-being.

The key question is: How can we ensure the safety and well-being of children, particularly in cases of abuse and neglect, without resorting to family separation? To foster safer environments for children, we must consider innovative solutions such as kinship programs, in which children are cared for within their extended family or community network, rather than being placed in unfamiliar environments. Neighborhood child care centers and community centers can provide accessible and reliable child care, creating a sense of belonging and stability for children.

For families dealing with specific challenges, such as addiction or mental health issues, specialized support is essential. Safe haven shelters for parents with addiction disorders, mental health hospitals with family wings for in- and outpatient care, and group homes that allow parents to stay with their children can provide the necessary support while keeping families intact.

Support mechanisms for older children who care for their younger siblings, guardian supervisors, and stable individuals in similar situations leaning on one another can also help maintain family unity. These approaches prioritize keeping the family together as the first form of intervention, addressing the underlying issues impacting the family. Additionally, developing educational opportunities on transformative approaches to child rearing, understanding children's needs, and helping manage the stressors of parenting can empower families to create nurturing home environments.

Addressing poverty and its impact on families requires the development of a comprehensive strategy involving not just providing immediate support but reconstructing societal perceptions of poverty and implementing solutions for the challenges faced by families living in poverty. A system in which law guardians advocate for children's rights and community interventions are tailored to specific needs can prevent children from being vulnerable to the harms of foster care and group homes.

Building strong, healthy communities through localized support systems and interventions can provide a viable alternative to the destructive family policing system. By focusing on keeping families together and addressing their specific needs, we can create a safer, more nurturing environment for children, free from the risks of further separation and disruption.

Ultimately, ongoing safety mobilizations within an entity such as a community safety hub can cultivate safety and serve as an off-ramp from the violent and destructive family policing system in the United States that rips families apart and often moves children from their current unsafe conditions to other unsafe conditions with unknown people. As Derecka Purnell emphasized in her book *Becoming Abolitionists: Police, Protests, and the Pursuit of Freedom*, parents and guardians should also have guaranteed access to quality child care at any time within their communities. Communities that are strong and healthy can develop specific interventions that will not leave children vulnerable to abuse and violence within foster care and group homes and separation from their parents by the family policing system.

Public housing residents experience intense policing and surveillance by housing authority officials and police. Safety mobilizations among residents can address concerns through community organizing and collaboration. As a society, there is a need to address the specific dynamics that create hardships for public housing communities. These efforts should squarely lie in ensuring adequate, safe places to live, providing safety interventions, and addressing poverty and inequality. Community safety hubs within public housing communities can help residents navigate concerns, including those related to maintenance, that housing authorities fail to address. With the proper resources and access to mechanisms for repair, safety hubs and resident councils can operate from a place of community empowerment with direct decision-making power, rather than using top-down approaches run by city officials and housing authorities that remove housing autonomy and disempower residents. Other communities can also organize community safety hubs, or larger community safety hubs can have focus areas that center on residential communities such as those in public housing and beyond. Any collective of people who see themselves as a community can have a safety hub if it seems useful, with varying focus areas and functions depending on the specific size, scope, and nature of the collective. Safety hubs can act in collaboration with other hubs of different scopes to establish shared principles and understandings, such as a shared understanding of community safety as a framework as well and concepts such as restorative and transformative justice, allowing for context specificity but preventing the development of abusive or punitive attempts to steer the efforts of the collective.

Safety hubs and efforts can—and should—address housing. Without housing, it is very difficult for people to stabilize their lives and feel safe. In the realm of housing, a crucial shift is needed from the traditional dichotomy of private versus public models to more equitable and just alternatives. Social housing is a promising solution in this context. It represents a range of models that move beyond conventional frameworks, offering a vision of housing not merely as a commodity but as a fundamental right. The national Homes Guarantee campaign is one such example, advocating for housing—including more funding for the repair and expansion of public housing—as an essential entitlement for every individual.[65]

The intersection of housing and policing is increasingly recognized, particularly in urban areas such as New York City. The federal Rental Assistance Demonstration (RAD) program, initiated during the Obama administration, is proposed as a way to revitalize and preserve public housing. The program enables public housing agencies to leverage public and private debt and equity for reinvestment in their properties. Despite these goals, the program has encountered opposition from grassroots movements such as Fight for NYCHA and Residents to Preserve Public Housing. These groups actively resist RAD conversions and the privatization of public housing, voicing concerns about the potential adverse effects on the communities they represent. These movements not only demand the preservation of public housing but also call for the redirection of funds from bureaucratic coffers and police budgets to housing. The argument is clear: the resources to sustain and improve public housing exist, yet they are often diverted to other areas, such as policing, reflecting a misalignment of societal priorities.

To transform the housing landscape, we must embrace models that break away from the conventional structures. Housing cooperatives and community land trusts (CLTs) represent such transformative models. These approaches empower residents, allowing those who live in a community to make decisions and have the resources to improve their living conditions. This concept of housing autonomy is central to creating equitable and sustainable communities.

Housing cooperatives offer a democratic approach to housing, where residents collectively own and manage their properties. This model fosters a sense of community and shared responsibility, contrasting sharply with the isolation and inequality often seen in private housing markets. CLTs take this a step further by removing land and housing from the speculative market. In CLTs, the land is owned by the community, ensuring long-term affordability and stability for residents. This model not only provides secure housing but also empowers communities to shape their development without the threat of displacement.

In conclusion, the shift toward social housing, cooperatives, and community land trusts is not just about providing shelter; it's about reimagining housing as a collaborative, community-centered endeavor. This approach aligns with the broader goals of social justice, challenging the systems that perpetuate housing inequities and are intrinsically linked to issues such as policing and the criminalization of poverty. By prioritizing housing autonomy and community empowerment, we can pave the way for more just and inclusive cities.

SAFETY MOBILIZATIONS

People like it when they see others they know who are there to keep them safe. Police patrols can have the opposite effect on vulnerable communities, and they do not provide sustainable approaches to safety and accountability. So what other safety watch systems can we imagine to manage concerns around safety? I offer safety mobilizations as a framework for community-based safety efforts that center on active presence and mobilizing in communities to cultivate a sense of safety. Rather than being centered on policing, surveillance, and exerting coercive control, safety mobilizations are centered on community and care. Organizers must not attempt to surveil, alienate, or criminalize members of the community but attempt to foster a safer community for all. Such efforts have targeted street harassment, community conflicts, police violence, and more.

Safety mobilizations are efforts that engage a range of community members with an aim to address particular safety concerns. They can be long term or temporary. They are guided by frameworks such as transformative justice, de-escalation, restorative justice, and community-based safety. The aim is not to surveil, police, or control through violence or the threat of it. Safety mobilizations can center on the community mobilizing with care, concern, and compassion. Importantly, these efforts do not need to mobilize with weapons as a default to addressing safety concerns.

There are endless possibilities for unarmed, community-based safety mobilizations. One example comes from Australia, where Aboriginal communities have set up night patrols to ensure that people are safe, such as the Julalikari Night Patrol[66] in northern Australia and the Nyoongar Patrol.[67] These patrols create distance between Indigenous communities and police, which have a long history of abuse and violence, and police typically do not have a full-time presence in areas with night patrols. In a study, the night patrols seemed to reduce arrests by up to 30 percent.[68] Without having formal policing powers, the patrols gain legitimacy, and trust comes from their having the support of elders, being established by community councils, and relying on Indigenous cultural traditions and practices.

As the sociologist Patrick Sharkey wrote in *Uneasy Peace: The Great Crime Decline, the Renewal of City Life, and the Next War on Violence*:

The challenges that emerge over the course of a shift change on a nightly basis, but the overarching goal of the patrol teams is to maintain a presence in the public spaces where young people hang out, to search for Aboriginal people who look as if they could use some help, and to give anyone who is causing trouble the chance to cool off or to go home before the police get involved. At times the patrol team's intervention comes with a stern warning, but usually it comes with a warm smile.[69]

Communities can activate a range of different patrols for different issues that center on preventions and intervention without policing, violence, or coercion. Through these patrols centered on communal safety and accountability, people can disrupt problems before they come up and manage those that do emerge. The public presence of safety workers and organizers can be relieving and supportive to community members.

Community safety mobilizations, which differ from neighborhood watch groups that are organized around racial, class, and gender-based discriminatory logics, can focus on any safety concern within a community. In my conception, safety mobilizations focus primarily on communities and active community organizing and building to produce a desired result. But community safety mobilization efforts specifically focus on being visible and present in community life and providing prevention and intervention. Safety mobilizations are not an individual category but rather a strategy for any kind of safety initiative. Proactive solutions can center on community-based teams engaging in community mobilizations around particular issues. This can make people feel safe by the direct presence of someone or an entity that has ties in a community, is safe, and does not use threats of police power that alienate people.

An array of organizations has been engaging in this work on various scales both historically and in the present day. These models collectively offer us different pieces of a broader tapestry of community resolution. Transnationally, there are community mediators who engage with communities and rely on community bonds to engage in mediation and outreach. There are community safety workers in South Africa, Great Britain, Belgium, France, Australia, and the Netherlands.[70] They are unarmed and do not have police power. They engage in efforts such as youth outreach, conflict resolution, and safety interventions. Given that these efforts don't involve the violence of policing and are focused on safety and not punishment, they can prompt different responses among communities. The workers also try to prevent and manage minor incidents as they emerge. These efforts seem to have had promising results.[71] One important consideration, though, is that communities distrustful of governments more broadly may feel alienated if these initiatives are government sponsored and feature collaboration with police. It's also important to be wary of professionalization and expectations of funding—whether by foundations or government entities—that steer these approaches away from being rooted in and guided directly by communities.

MASK (Mothers/Men Against Senseless Killings), established in 2015, set out to make a difference by actively being present on the streets, disrupting violence, and fostering a sense of unity among children. Composed of community-minded people, the group began by spending time on the streets, preparing meals, and spreading love and positivity. MASK also collaborates with partners to ensure access to necessary city services, educational and professional growth opportunities, and economic development. MASK started when Tamar Manasseh, in June 2015, decided to take a stand at an Englewood, Chicago, corner where three women had recently been victims of a shooting. Accompanied by a dozen other women wearing striking "Moms on Patrol" shirts, she began to engage the local community through food and conversation. That act marked the beginning of a persistent presence.

MASK focuses primarily on fostering stronger communities by addressing violence, food insecurity, and inadequate housing. In a 2017 *New York Times* op-ed, Manasseh described MASK's work, emphasizing how the group had reclaimed a violent corner in Englewood, turning it into a space for community and care. She stated that the group provided meals for local children, fostering a sense of extended family. In her powerful op-ed, she shared the following about MASK's work:

> After just three summers on the block, violent crime and gun-related incidents in that census tract have declined dramatically. We also listened to the people there. They told us how to stop gun violence in their neighborhood.... They told us they needed resources, jobs

and skills training. . . . They need a share of that $95 million planned for a new police and firefighter training center.[72]

The positive impacts of MASK went beyond violence reduction, impacting the broader community. Manasseh notes that the effects were felt up to a mile away. The local elementary school that many of the children from the neighborhood attend also experienced a notable increase in academic performance. As the author notes, all of this occurred without the infusion of new resources, job opportunities, or direct governmental intervention. The approach of MASK can be attributed to a simple, yet powerful approach: caring and presence. Residents wore bright pink T-shirts, gathered with lawn chairs and hot dogs, and established a visible, positive presence in their neighborhood. This grassroots initiative expanded to MASK committing to developing community centers in vacant lots to provide safe spaces for children to play, study, and eat. The organization focused on listening to residents' needs around how to increase feelings of safety and well-being in their neighborhood. The residents emphasized the need for resources, job opportunities, and skill training, especially in an increasingly computer-driven world. They also called for better-equipped schools to prepare children for future challenges. This grassroots effort starkly contrasts with the planned investment in a new police and firefighter training center, highlighting the need for community-based approaches to violence reduction and overall safety.

MASK's work was built on the simple but effective idea of maintaining adult presence to promote different behavior among young people. This idea draws from a long-standing tradition of community motherhood, and MASK embodies the adage that "it takes a village to raise a child." By reviving this spirit, MASK aims to restore carefree childhoods to children in underresourced neighborhoods. MASK showcases an approach that addresses the underlying causes of violence, relies on community care, and understands the multidimensional nature of violence. Moreover, MASK is a model example of a safety mobilization initiative that emphasizes community presence as an intervention.

There is a range of safety mobilization possibilities, and communities are already engaging in various forms of mobilization. The Safe Passage initiative, implemented by Chicago Public Schools in 2009, enables certain schools to ensure a comforting and reliable adult presence for pupils during their commute to and from school.[73] Workers associated with the Safe Passage initiative are stationed along designated Safe Passage routes to ensure children a safe commute both before and after school. These workers can be identified by their bright-colored Safe Passage vests. They are employed by community-based organizations located in the school communities they serve. Importantly, in all the listed examples of safety mobilizations, communities are repurposing the traditional understanding of patrols, changing them from law enforcement entities centered on surveillance, dominance, and control to community-driven groups rooted in care, belonging, and the understanding that safety stewardship is a collective, community-driven endeavor. The armed copwatch patrols that the Black Panthers began in Oakland to disrupt patterns of police violence were a form of community safety organizing. Mutual aid organizing is another, as it disrupts harm caused by state violence and abandonment. Safety mobilizations can also look like cultivating safety for sex workers; creating safe passage for the elderly; ensuring accessibility and transportation for people with disabilities; creating safety and security mechanisms against racial violence; and interrupting street harassment.

I believe that specialized response teams need training and tools to respond to heightened levels of violence that mediation and de-escalation are not able to address. These safety mobilizations would need to be developed from square one. The central task of safety mobilizations in response to extreme forms of harm and violence is not to replicate the logic, culture, or functions of policing. We have to ensure that these teams do not become police by another name but remain focused on providing safety interventions while doing as little harm as possible. Relying on known, trusted community members to de-escalate when appropriate is one strategy. Severe situations are rare, but there should be interventions to meet and de-escalate the harm people are facing. Safety mobilizations in response to severe cases need to be used sparingly and only when they are the only option, with the ultimate aim of minimizing harm for all people involved and providing trauma support and resources to affected communities in the aftermath.

Ideally, we would live in a world without guns, violence, harm, and oppression. But given that we do not, we need to develop responses to the full gamut of possible safety concerns while we look to weaken and end cycles of conflict, violence, and harm. Such responses include immediate interventions to severe cases of harm and violence as well as strategies to manage people who refuse to enter processes such as restorative and transformative justice and are committed to continuing patterns of abuse and harm. Again, while these situations will be much less likely, they may occur. Thus, it is important to develop responses that still center on compassion and the potential for growth in ways that do not replicate policing and prisons in the United States and that still acknowledge the humanity and needs of the people engaging in acts of harm. By using all the creativity and imagination in the world, we can find ways to respond to even severe incidents that do not rely on police or cages. Police fail to address the most serious problems within communities. Community safety hubs and mobilizations can work to prevent and disrupt human trafficking, find missing people, and address all the concerns that affect communities that police are unable to respond to.

A larger container, such as a community safety hub, to support a range of work can help bring various teams and interventions together. Concerns about safety are often intertwined. As a result, holistic safety is cultivated through addressing the range of concerns a community has. The aforementioned examples are only a subset of possibilities for community safety organizing. Concerns will vary by community, and people should have the ability to discard safety approaches that don't work or that produce undesirable results and do not seem capable of creating real change. It's hard work. But it is meaningful. And people can engage in it when they can as members of their community or focus on it full-time. Safety workers can be funded through guaranteed employment and universal basic income programs; income-sharing approaches to communities in which residents pool and distribute financial resources to ensure equitable economic support; resources diverted from policing, punishment, and extractive institutions; or community pooled resources. It is important for a community—regardless of how big or small—to have approaches to manage safety and harm. For safety to truly flourish, people must be committed to caring for one another and being accountable when someone is wronged. Any time conflict outgrows the capacities of the members of a group, safety organizers must be able to create and manage community safety.

But how can we transition from what currently exists to a world in which a tapestry of safety approaches is available? There isn't one answer. Some solutions, as a result of political climates and cultural contexts, will take a very long time to pilot, experiment with, and implement. For violence and harm there are steps we can take right away, such as using violence interrupters. Other solutions can be implemented quickly, such as crisis intervention models like CAHOOTS and MH First. But transitioning away from a police- and prison-based society will require study, pilots, analysis, and adaptation. In the end, societies can change very rapidly given social movements or environmental shifts. All of these interventions and approaches can be implemented in a society either with or without government participation, those that look similar to society today and those that are wholly unfamiliar. The driving concept is that safety is central to human life, and harm and conflict are embedded in human relationships. If we begin from that place and underpin all our approaches with transformative, safety-driven approaches, we will never produce a society that is organized and managed through police violence and carceral machinery.

Our society places a high value on punishment. It structures a shared cultural frame of understanding how criminalized actions should be responded to. Many of us, from a young age, are taught that punishment is the best way to deal with breaches of the social order. But punishment is not the only way to deal with wrongdoing and harm. In the end, if we shift away from the ideas we collectively hold about punishment, we'll realize that we need to move beyond policing in order for alternative systems and approaches to flourish.

INTERLUDE IV

(PART A) FOR BLACK FUTURES, CHICAGO

It was October 24, 2015, an autumn morning in Chicago, the kind when the air is crisp and change seems imminent. As the city awoke, I felt anxious but committed to the plan. Unbeknown to the city, a plan was unfurling, one that would bring attention to the need to invest in Chicago's community and urge a shift in resources from policing to community support. A group of us from the New York City chapter of BYP100 had traveled to Chicago to join a broader united front of protestors looking to disrupt the International Association of Chiefs of Police conference. It was taking place after the city had closed fifty public schools and half the mental health centers in Chicago.[1]

The conference was in full swing. A professor of mine had recommended that I attend to observe the myriad tools and strategies on display that might inform my research, which at the time was focused on police militarization. But I had already planned to go for other reasons. As I navigated my dual roles that day, I felt the tension.

Our group had been coordinating for weeks. Our goal was to create a barrier near one of the bridgeways to the conference. Once we got to the area, trying to be unassuming, we quickly sprang into the plans. Some of us locked arms as others secured the locks and chains that fortified the barrier of those joined by arms. The bridge blockade established a front line of the day of protest. Those of us in the supporting roles ensured that those in the blockade had everything they required, standing as a buffer between the protestors and the police, providing the immediate necessities, and acting as intermediaries when tensions heightened.

Word of our actions spread swiftly. As the bridge was blocked off by the chained-in protestors, other actions sprang up from BYP100 members and other collectives such as Assata's Daughters, We Charge Genocide, Lifted Voices, #Not1More, and Organized Communities against Deportations to shut down the conference in other areas and on the main streets. Masses gathered on the streets, and the air was thick with determination. Other activists locked themselves to one another, to ladders, and to objects that named their demands and listed people murdered by the police. It was a decentralized movement with organizers across Chicago and elsewhere. The decentralized nature of the day of action freed any one person from being the sole target.

Lawyers, point people, and keen-eyed legal observers mobilized. On the bridge, people started to realize the act of resistance. Aware of what lay ahead, we all memorized important phone numbers or scribbled them on our bodies. The police, caught off guard, eventually found ways to cut the chains, arresting those who had been linked together. News agencies caught wind of our message and magnified our cause.

The hours turned into a blur. As night enveloped the city, our unified stance didn't waver. Everyone who hadn't been arrested went to the jail to await the release of our friends. The atmosphere was fraught with anticipation, but we were resolute. We wanted to wait until everyone was released. The police released almost everyone that night, holding only a few people because of prior offenses or for other reasons.

Each release was celebrated with tight hugs, relief evident in our eyes. The support was overwhelming. Professors, friends, family all congregated, bearing witness to a day that epitomized the spirit of community and activism. The following day, many of us gathered, talked, reflected, and shared community. Those of us not from Chicago returned home in the coming days.

BYP100 released a list of demands that day:

We demand all local, state and federal budgets to defund the police and invest those dollars and resources in Black futures. We want reparations for chattel slavery, Jim Crow and mass incarceration. We want to end all profit from so-called "criminal justice" punishment—both public and private. We want a guaranteed income for all, living wages, a federal jobs program, and freedom from discrimination for all workers. We want the labor of Black transgender and cisgender women (unseen and seen, unpaid and paid) to be valued and supported, not criminalized and marginalized. We want investments in Black communities that promote economic sustainability and eliminate the displacement of our people.[2]

(PART B) BUTTERFLIES IN CLEVELAND

"We gon' be alright."

The summer air in Cleveland was thick with purpose as the Movement for Black Lives convening commenced at the tail end of July 2015. The city was filled with more than a thousand Black organizers and activists from across the country, as well as activists from abroad. Cleveland State University's campus glowed with the energy of nearly two thousand individuals, including members from a number of organizations affiliated with the Movement for Black Lives umbrella, student organizers, and more. It was a powerful convening of organizers and communities, including the families of people murdered by the police. One of my duties was to pick up some of the family members from the airport and drive them to the convening location. Throughout the weekend, I was forced to reflect on the pain caused by the loss of a loved one at the hands of police.

The movement was uplifting, and organizers strategized ways to transform Black communities, including ways to address the violence of policing. But what happened as the convening ended soon turned into the same issues we'd discussed at Cleveland State.

Outside the walls of the campus, people anxiously talked about a young boy, only fourteen years old, who had been taken into custody by Cleveland police officers. The allegation? Intoxication on a bus. I was with a close friend, Karl, taking a walk outside as the convening was ending, and we hurried to the scene where the teen was in the police car.

Within moments, hundreds of us from the Movement for Black Lives convening mobilized, forming a human barrier around the officers and their vehicles. Our demands were clear: the boy needed medical attention, and he belonged with his mother, not in a cell.

Media accounts would later highlight the pepper spray, the growing crowd, and the police's justification for their actions. But those present experienced something far deeper: a moment of raw emotion, community solidarity, and the visceral power of collective action.

For me, the scene was a blur of adrenaline and purpose. As pepper spray filled the air, many of us already knew of one solution shared by Palestinian organizers on social media during unrest in Ferguson: the use of milk to help treat the burn of pepper spray and tear gas. I, along with some others, sprinted to nearby stores, buying whatever milk we could find to aid those affected. Most of us didn't know each other, but we were united in our commitment: the freedom of this teenager.

As the boy's mother arrived and the negotiations, led by Rukia Lumumba and Beatriz Beckford from the Malcolm X Grassroots Movement, reached an end, the volume of our chants rose: "WE-LOVE-YOU! WE-LOVE-YOU! WE-LOVE-YOU!" We didn't know his name, but it didn't matter. He mattered.

Experiencing police violence at a convening sparked by an uprising against police violence. Ironic. But this is the violence of policing.

Celebrating, we chanted, "We gon' be alright," lyrics from Kendrick Lamar's "Alright" from his album *To Pimp a Butterfly*. The police eventually retreated. At one point, a butterfly flew overhead. It gave me chills as those of us in the area pointed, elated, at the butterfly. It was surreal.

That day in Cleveland was not just about a single arrest. It was about the spirit of a movement that refuses to be silenced. It was a demonstration that, with unity and perseverance, change is within our grasp. Our demand remains steadfast: a world that transcends the need for policing; a world in which every life is cherished and protected.

On a large scale, the kind of collective solidarity and commitment I witnessed in Cleveland has the power to free us all. The reality is that most people don't have community defense mobilizations when they face harm from police. But how can we build the capacity to create shields that disrupt policing? How can we engage in practices of community defense? It required putting our bodies on the line to demand that a teenager be free. Getting pepper-sprayed was worth it. The boy got to go home with his mother, not to a police station. That was community defense in action.

PART III

FUTURES

CHAPTER 5

THE TRANSFORMATION
OF JUSTICE

Justice demands integrity. It's to have a moral universe—not only know what is right or wrong but to put things in perspective, weigh things. Justice is different from violence and retribution; it requires complex accounting.

—bell hooks

Without new visions we don't know what to build, only what to knock down. We not only end up confused, rudderless, and cynical, but we forget that making revolution is not a series of clever maneuvers and tactics but a process that can and must transform us.

—Robin D. G. Kelley, *Freedom Dreams: The Black Radical Imagination*

IMAGINE A PLACE THAT FEELS SAFE TO YOU. WHAT DOES IT LOOK LIKE? HOW does it smell? Is it cold? Warm? What do you see? What do you hear? What do you *feel*?

When people do this exercise, they typically don't imagine police, prisons, or surveillance. The answers range widely, but similar themes emerge: family, community, love, freedom, art, beauty, culture, food, care. Some may feel safe in a particular place around certain people such as family, others feel safe at home in bed, still others may attach safety to an object. Some may describe being home with family and loved ones, the smell of their favorite childhood dishes being cooked, or laughing and having a good time with friends.

In the United States, as well as other punitive societies, policing is framed as the solution to threats to safety. Building strong, accountable, transformative communities is the way we get to safety. It's also the way to stop police violence. In order to do this, we have to transform our approach to justice—and society overall. Some people may ask: Why is abolition—rather than reform—necessary for developing safer communities? Why are "nicer," more professional cops still not the answer? Would prosecuting the police end police violence and harm? How do the police create violence far beyond individual cases of brutality and murder? Why does police violence in particular spark rebellion? What are the steps we need to take on the road to abolition? And most important: What would it mean to live in a world free of police violence and terror? These questions led me to the conclusion that to create a new paradigm of safety, it is necessary to abolish all systems of policing, the entire criminal punishment system more broadly. Even more, we can contribute to a cultural transformation that does not reproduce and market fear, punishment, and violence.

There isn't one vision for a police- and prison-free world. There are many, and it's important not to conflate them. Collectively, they can serve as seeds to help communities forge safety free of police and cages. Abolition is, at its core, a process. In my estimation, it's important not to replicate the forms of policing, surveillance, and imprisonment that have come to mark contemporary society. I learn from, and hope to contribute to, the work of the abolitionists who have come before me, those who think alongside me, and those yet to come. There are many visions; this book represents my analysis of the problems of policing and visions for ways forward.

What we need to escape the cycles of police and carceral harm and violence is a break with the paradigms of policing and punishment altogether. This requires decriminalization, decarceration, and the defunding of the punitive policies and institutions that created the current police and carceral state; more pointedly, a departure from the current model and a turn toward transformative visions of safety and accountability intended to prevent conflict, violence, and harm before it happens; toward mechanisms to provide safety interventions that *actually* provide safety; and toward strategies for responding to conflict and harm in ways that transform the conditions that gave rise to the harm in the first place.

Addressing the root causes of harm and violence is essential for building safer communities. Investing in resources such as education, mental health support, and economic opportunities can create environments where people thrive and conflicts are less likely to escalate into violence. Additionally, fostering strong social ties and community engagement helps build trust and mutual support. Implementing restorative and transformative justice practices allows communities to address harm through dialogue and healing rather than punishment and retribution. By focusing on prevention and community empowerment, we can create a society where safety is achieved through collective care and responsibility, rather than defaulting to policing and incarceration. Ultimately, building a police-free world is a community endeavor.

WHO DEFINES JUSTICE?

What is justice when someone is hurt or harmed? Is it vengeance? Punishment? Some people believe so. That model of justice has become the leading paradigm in the United States and other places around the world. That is why the United States became the incarceration capital of the world; its culture produces a climate in which such political decisions are justified. Punitive justice also justifies other forms of violence in response to conflict and harm. The state proposes a model that centers on vengeance and punishment as a response to make people "pay" for their wrongdoings. And it has become deeply embedded in the culture and people's own emotions. In many environments, when someone feels violated, they respond with violence. In communities where the state is not seen as a reliable provider of safety, a model of punitive justice will lead people to replicate the logics of punitive justice in their own communities. If the members of a community don't believe in calling law enforcement but still believe in punitive justice, it will lead to cycles of violence. While the roots of violence are complex, emotional and ideological attachments to cultures of violence will continue to beget more violence.

In the previous chapter, I mentioned the use of restorative justice as a strategy to mediate conflict as well as harm within communities. Restorative justice practices center on the direct harm or conflict that has occurred between individuals or groups and aim to repair the damage caused. Restorative justice involves both those who practice and those who experience harmful behaviors—and often others—to engage in a peacemaking dialogue about the harm and how it might be repaired, centering on those who experienced the harm throughout the process. Restorative justice, like transformative justice, encourages the person who caused the harm to accept responsibility for their actions and for all involved to work together toward a resolution. Restorative justice processes can include restitution or reconciliation, the aim being to restore relationships to the state they were in prior to the fracture.

As discussed, restorative justice is a useful framework for building community capacity to manage conflict and relational challenges. The strategy focuses on bringing involved parties together to discuss, learn, and restore the bonds that may have been broken through the action that led to the need for mediation and intervention. Centrally, the strategy doesn't focus on punishment or vengeance as a way to engage justice; it gives people the space to share their sentiments when appropriate and a context in which they can find healing and growth. Thousands of restorative justice practitioners and initiatives exist in schools, communities, and organizations. As sujatha baliga wrote, restorative justice has been used to respond to all forms of harm and wrongdoing, including assault, robbery, sexual violence, intimate partner violence, and murder.[1]

Many resources are dedicated to restorative justice training. Rather than investing in police and prisons, one way to fund community capacity to deal with harm is by increasing the amount of resources and training and the number of practitioners dedicated to engaging in healing and restorative work in response to cases of conflict, as well as harm and more serious disputes. In addressing individual cases, restorative justice can help prevent issues from escalating and cycles of conflict from continuing. In addition, from a structural perspective, these practices can help to reshape cultures, make patterns of harm and conflict less likely, and build a framework for navigating these issues when they do happen. This can be central in building communities that are safe and accountable.

As baliga noted, the concept and implementation of restorative justice has roots in Indigenous societies worldwide and is effective in many areas. In a recent examination of the first one hundred felony incidents referred to restorative justice in Alameda County, California, which included some cases of sexual violence, there were promising outcomes. The restorative justice processes centered on resolving harm "through an organized, facilitated dialogue in which young people, with the support of family and community members, meet with their crime victims to create a plan to repair the harm caused by their offense."[2] Ninety-one percent of the survivors involved indicated that they would participate in another process, with the same percentage of people saying that they would advise a friend to consider participating in one. The program saw a 44 percent decrease in the likelihood of youths reengaging in the harmful behavior, compared to those handled by the county's juvenile justice system.[3]

The Restorative Justice Project, which began in 2015 at the organization Impact Justice, stands as the only national initiative providing technical support and training on such processes to communities throughout the nation, partnering with them to address harms via precharge restorative justice diversion programs that allow individuals to avoid traditional court processes and sentencing.[4] Amid ongoing societal changes and advocacy efforts pushing the national dialogue away from punitive responses and toward healing and well-being, the need for community-based alternatives has never been more significant. Since November 2023, the Restorative Justice Project has been housed at Equal Justice USA.

This project aims to transcend the traditional crime-and-punishment framework, adopting a more comprehensive view that recognizes harm as a multifaceted issue requiring accountability and healing across individual, interpersonal, community, and system levels. By employing restorative justice diversion, the project enables survivors to take a healing journey and those who have caused harm to be accountable without the coercive and carceral focus of the criminal-legal system. Made up of a diverse team of experienced restorative justice facilitators and advocates for criminal-legal system reform, the project strives to construct avenues for healing, safety, and well-being, particularly in communities of color, which are disproportionately affected by the criminal-legal system.

Community justice processes impart valuable skills in listening, conflict resolution, and accountability that people can use in their daily lives. This extends beyond immediate disputes and can improve family, school, and workplace dynamics. Through these approaches, community members can reinforce their agency and strengthen their bonds to encourage safety and justice.

What if we were to steer our conceptions of justice away from violence, punishment, and vengeance and toward accountability? We could also approach justice in ways that reduce the likelihood that similar events will happen in the future. We can do this by allowing those responsible for harm to engage in a process in which they are able to understand and account for their actions. But we can also accomplish this by seeking to understand the broader conditions that produced the incidents in the first place and transforming those conditions. This is what transformative justice does.

Research shows that many people who have been harmed report not being satisfied by criminal court processes and not making an emotional recovery through the process,[5] even when the people who harmed them are convicted. Often, people want to share their feelings, to have someone who harmed them understand and recognize what they did, and to know that that person will not engage in such actions again. Of course, in moments of anger in response to being harmed, some people may want the person who harmed them or someone they love to suffer. This anger and desire for vengeance are completely understandable. It can be instinctual—albeit largely shaped by a culture that socializes us—to feel a desire for vengeance and punishment. But feelings of anger in response to harmful moments should not be allowed to steer policy and the way we approach matters of safety and justice. As Mariame Kaba has emphasized, intense anger in response to harm, while understandable, is not what should drive an entire social, political, and cultural paradigm toward punishment and vengeance.[6]

Transformative justice is meant to address the root causes of harm and violence within society and to promote healing, accountability, and community-based solutions rather than punitive responses. Transformative justice is a paradigm shift away from punitive justice to a more holistic approach that acknowledges how systemic issues contribute to harmful behavior.

A central underlying tenet of transformative justice is that harm, such as violence and abuse, occurs not within a vacuum but in a broader social context. Practitioners recognize that structures and institutions within society play a significant role in reproducing patterns of harm. Thus, rather than just punishing an individual for causing harm, transformative justice looks at the societal conditions that enabled the harm and aims to change them. A range of people embrace transformative justice, and there are different ways to practice it. But they tend to have several key principles in common.

During transformative justice processes, there is a focus on the needs and experiences of those harmed. The individual or group that has experienced harmful behavior is given a central role in the development of responses to harm. The needs, emotions, and perspectives of those who were harmed are prioritized. This stage involves creating an environment that is safe and supportive for those people to express what they are feeling and their needs. In centering on those who experienced the harm, this stage is meant to restore a sense of control and autonomy, which can feel taken away during violent and harmful experiences. Importantly, transformative and restorative justice processes can include consequences for harmful behavior. For example, if someone is abusing a role in an employment setting, an intervention can be their being fired. Reparations can be another approach to accountability and transformative justice. This can take place between individuals as well as between institutions.

On May 6, 2015, after decades of organizing and struggle by individuals and collectives, the Chicago City Council passed legislation that provided reparations for police torture committed by former Chicago police commander Jon Burge, who served in the Vietnam War, as well as detectives under his command. Burge tortured his first known victim in 1973 and more than 125 people, mostly Black, over two decades. Detainees were subjected to abuse that included electric shocks to the genitals and other parts of the body, suffocation, mock execution, and brutal beatings, paired with racist comments and slurs.[7]

The reparations resolution provided compensation, restitution, and rehabilitation resources to survivors. It was the first time that survivors of racist and classist police torture were provided with the reparations they are entitled to under international law. Reparations was the demand, rather than punishment under the criminal-legal system, which was not available given statutes of limitations and was not a route that abolitionist organizers—many of whom were involved in the campaign efforts—would have supported. The approach represents a future pathway for survivors of police violence and their communities. The campaign was driven by survivors and collectives, including Project NIA, Chicago Torture Justice Memorials, We Charge Genocide, and Amnesty International. Attorney Joey Mogul, who is a partner at the People's Law Office, drafted the original City Council ordinance outlining reparations for the Chicago police torture survivors in 2013 on behalf of Chicago Torture Justice Memorials, which Mogul helped cofound. Those who had directly experienced the violence were central to the effort. Many of the individuals and collectives involved were abolitionist and transformative justice organizers.

The package included a formal apology by the city of Chicago, specialized counseling resources for survivors and their families at a dedicated center, free enrollment and job training for survivors and their families at City Colleges of Chicago, and a mandate requiring that the history of the Burge torture cases and police violence be taught in Chicago public schools.[8] The ordinance also created a $5.5 million fund for survivors. There was also a mandate to create a permanent public memorial to torture survivors, though the memorial remains an unfulfilled promise.

For people in community with one another, promoting accountability and transformation in a noncoercive way for those who cause harm is an important step. If we change our culture and understanding of harm, and if there is not an intense focus on punishment, people may be more willing to engage in accountability processes. As Mia Mingus wrote, in cases that need immediate intervention or involve strangers, removing the immediate danger and ensuring the safety of those affected can be the focus of a transformative justice approach.[9] Importantly, rather than focusing on punitive responses, transformative justice encourages those who have caused harm to accept responsibility for their actions, understand the impact of their behavior, and stop engaging in harm. The process is not rooted in shaming or blaming someone but in fostering empathy, self-awareness, accountability, and personal growth so they cannot continue perpetuating cycles of harmful behavior.

Accountability is practiced by those in community with one another. Ideally, society can be organized such that everyone sees themselves in community with and mutual connection to others, regardless of their identity and background. But we do not yet live in that world. Thus, mechanisms that will ensure the safety of communities—especially those who experience the brunt of unjust systems—and forms of self- and community defense are critical in building safety in the here and now.

Understanding the broader community context in transformative justice is central. Transformative justice acknowledges that harm affects not only individuals but also interpersonal relationships and broader communities. Therefore, transformative justice processes involve communities in order to encourage social cohesion, collective understanding, and healing. The community's role in a process might include supporting the person harmed, participating in processes of accountability, and collectively addressing harmful norms, cultures, and behaviors.

Transforming the structural conditions that perpetuate harm is a critical component of transformative justice. Addressing structural conditions includes identifying and challenging social structures and cultural norms that contribute to harm. This might include dismantling social policies that reproduce problematic behaviors and abolishing belief systems and structures of oppression, such as patriarchy, racism, LGBTQ+ antagonism, ableism, and capitalism. These institutions create a culture that makes harmful behaviors more likely through socialization and their impact on relationships between people.

Also central is refusing to reproduce cycles of violence, such as by responding to violence and harm with punishment, vengeance, and vigilantism. An emphasis on healing, safety, and transformation collectively makes up transformative justice. The ultimate goal is to tend the wounds caused by harm, strengthen the ability of individuals and communities to manage their concerns independently of the state and criminal-legal system, and create social transformation that will prevent future cycles of harm.

Transformative justice is often associated with social justice movements, including abolitionist movements. Transformative justice is already being carried out by a number of organizations and communities in response to various areas of harm. It presents a pathway for a far more compassionate, accountable, and just society, one in which harm and violence are addressed not through punishment but through healing, accountability, and social transformation. Transformative justice can be applied in all kinds of settings: within families, schools, neighborhoods, places of employment, and more.

Transformative justice and restorative justice are frameworks for addressing conflict and harm that emphasize healing and repair over punishment. However, there are some key areas where they differ in focus. Transformative justice can be compatible with restorative justice. But the former broadens its focus by seeking to address the systemic and social root causes of harm. Transformative justice acknowledges that harm and violence are often rooted in underlying social structures and systems of domination. A transformative justice approach seeks not just to restore relationships between people to their prior state but also to transform relationships and social conditions that enable harm. The aim is to engage in social transformation in addition to addressing individual instances of harm, for which restorative justice practices, inspired by Indigenous peacemaking processes, have long been used.

Restorative justice processes, in some contexts, are administered and managed by court and criminal-legal systems, which threatens the processes, given the punitive nature of criminal courts and legal agencies. Even when implemented by well-meaning actors, restorative justice can be steered away from its peacemaking and restorative origins when it is intertwined with the criminal-legal system. If courts and criminal-legal systems became the administrators of restorative justice processes, that can also remove the role communities play in restorative approaches, reproducing criminal-legal logics that focus on punishment, albeit under the guise of a restorative process.

While restorative justice focuses on repairing relationships once they are fractured, transformative justice focuses on preventing the social realities that give rise to these events in the first place. In building non-criminal-legal responses to harm and violence, transformative justice also addresses prevention and intervention during cases of harm. A transformative justice approach can inform safety mobilizations and hubs, incorporating an emphasis on transforming safety in its entirety. Restorative justice provides invaluable sets of tools for addressing harm. Transformative justice allows us to move toward safety from individual actions to structural conditions. A model put forth by the Bay Area Transformative Justice Collective, for example, focuses on addressing childhood sexual abuse once it has occurred but also sees the formation of pods as a strategy to prevent and intervene in patterns of abuse at earlier stages.

The best way to make the case for a police-free world is not just to detail the ways policing today is devastating and to share suggestions for change but to show a world where it is possible. A number of initiatives center on transformative justice. The Oakland Power Projects has documented its work on alternatives to policing and emergency preparedness and decoupling health care from policing. Don't Call the Police is an online resource that enables people to search by city for community alternatives to policing.[10] Ahimsa Collective, a California-based organization, focuses on restorative justice and transformative justice programming, providing resources for community-based safety, practicing mutual aid, implementing housing and transportation initiatives, and working with incarcerated people and those affected by harm.[11] Common Justice develops and advances solutions to violence that transform the lives of those harmed and foster racial equity without relying on incarceration.

As for feminist abolitionist organizing, INCITE! Women, Gender Non-conforming, and Trans People of Color against Violence is a network of radical feminists of color who reject carceral feminism, working to end violence against women, gender-nonconforming people, and trans people of color and their communities. A number of other feminist collectives and organizations have proposed models of safety and justice.[12] Sista 2 Sista is a Brooklyn-based, women-led collective that engages in transformative models of support and intervention in response to gender violence. Just Practice is a training and mentoring group for individuals and organizations seeking to grow their skills in transformative justice and community accountability responses to harm. The Audre Lorde Project is a center for LGBTSTGNC (lesbian, gay, bisexual, two-spirit, trans, and gender-nonconforming) people of color and their communities. The Safe OUTside the System (SOS) Collective, an initiative of the Audre Lorde Project, works on creating safety models against hate and police violence within LGBTQ+ communities of color by identifying public spaces where people can go to escape violence, and training individuals and organizations how to respond to violence without calling the police. The 2023 book *Healing Justice Lineages: Dreaming at the Crossroads of Liberation, Collective Care, and Safety* by Cara Page and Erica Woodland also

showcased transformative collective care and safety work rooted in legacies of healing justice.

A number of other initiatives focus on violence in various forms. They
provide education about strategies to create safety and address harm outside
punitive systems. Generation FIVE is an organization aiming to end child
sexual abuse within five generations through survivor leadership, community organizing, and transformative justice approaches. The Bay Area Transformative Justice Collective is a community collective working to build and
support transformative justice responses to child sexual abuse. Creative
Interventions has developed a tool kit for transformative justice aimed at
addressing interpersonal violence. Survived and Punished is an organization
that advocates for the abolition of all forms of punishment and seeks to
eliminate the criminalization of survivors of domestic and sexual violence.

The Harm Free Zone Project was created by Critical Resistance to
develop practices that communities can use to autonomously manage
conflict, harm, and violence. Critical Resistance has also published a
range of reports and resources, including *Toward Transformative Justice:
A Liberatory Approach to Child Sexual Abuse and Other Forms of Intimate
and Community Violence*, which charts transformative pathways forward
for responses to child sexual abuse and other forms of violence and harm.

REIMAGINING GLOBAL SAFETY

Around the globe, police and military forces reinforce deeply entrenched
societal inequalities. From Hong Kong to France, Brazil, Palestine, London, South Africa, and beyond, uprisings have erupted in response to the
violence of policing. Though the uniforms may differ and the badges vary,
the underpinning ethos remains strikingly consistent: preservation of the
status quo. The United States, interestingly, has been both a student and a
teacher in the realm of policing. While it borrows from global practices, it
simultaneously exports its enforcement strategies, furthering the reach of
its control. International exchanges between policing entities, such as US
police training with Israeli forces,[13] illustrate a web of control that transcends borders. This is not merely an American issue; it's a global narrative
that has roots in colonization and imperialism. At the heart of it, police

universally serve as guardians of inequality, propping up systems that privilege a select few.

In an example highlighting the expanding use of surveillance technology within law enforcement, Eric Adams, the mayor of New York City, returned from a visit to Israel in August 2023, having observed the integration of drones and motorcycles by Israeli law enforcement at its National Police Academy.[14] Inspired by these tactics, the New York Police Department utilized drones to oversee the crowd during the 2023 West Indian American Day Carnival over Labor Day weekend, an event attracting more than 2 million attendees.

This is part of a broader trend in which technological advancements are increasingly shared by law enforcement agencies around the globe. The mayor's endorsement of advanced technologies in policing is further exemplified by his support for Digidog, a robotic canine used in emergency situations, such as building collapses. The adoption of such technologies by the NYPD reflects a growing inclination toward sophisticated surveillance and intervention tools in urban law enforcement, signaling a shift toward a more technologically advanced and interconnected police state.

These developments not only raise questions about privacy and civil liberties but also underscore the international dimensions of policing strategies. The exchange of tactics and technologies between countries such as the United States and Israel illustrates a global trend in the increasing militarization and technological sophistication of police forces. This trend points to a broader pattern of escalating surveillance and control, blurring the lines between domestic law enforcement and military operations, and raises critical concerns about the future of public policing and community safety.

But we stand at a pivotal moment. It's time for a collective reimagining of safety. The global economy is buttressed by what can only be termed violence work. Under this framework, the police are not just enforcers but crucial cogs, ensuring that existing imbalances remain undisturbed. Yet there are pockets of the world in which police presence is minimal, where safety doesn't mean armed patrols. Such communities often lack what mainstream society would label "the other." In other communities, people experience harm, violence, and precarity that require transformative solutions. These examples underscore the need for expansive dialogues on safety.

Our challenge is to ask ourselves and our communities: What does genuine safety look like? How do we cultivate environments in which everyone can thrive, free from the shadows of exploitation and resource extraction? The answer may well lie in embracing Huey P. Newton's vision of intercommunalism, unshackling ourselves from the chains of capitalism and oppressive politics that necessitate policing in the first place, and finding ways to peacefully coexist through difference.

For organizers globally, it is essential to ask: What does our community need right now? What will it take to prioritize safety rather than managing inequality? All people deserve the resources they need to thrive, and the key to providing them is disrupting the unjust global economy that favors the wealthy and challenging resource extraction, imperialism, and exploitation. There's an urgent call to challenge the roles of police and military as violence workers, gatekeepers of a status quo that benefits those with power and privilege. A growing number of voices have rightfully critiqued the existence of borders and the violent measures employed by police and military forces to uphold them, all of which originate from the roots of settler colonialism.[15] Abolition is not confined by national borders; it's a universal aspiration. By striving for it, we can collectively evolve, fostering relationships founded on equity and mutual respect. Abolition is a global movement, a journey to redefine humanity's commitments and future.

TRANSFORMATIVE JUSTICE IN ACTION: SUCCESS STORIES

Transformative justice initiatives and experiments can appear in a wide array of ways. One notable model is the work of the abolitionist organizer and artist Richie Reseda through feminist organizing in prison. While incarcerated in Soledad, California, Reseda began organizing other incarcerated people to engage in conversations and learning sessions that centered on male dominance, patriarchy, and violence. Reseda's work was showcased in a 2018 CNN documentary, *The Feminist on Cell Block Y.*[16]

Reseda was serving a ten-year sentence. The documentary centers on his journey of self-transformation as he discovers feminist literature, comes to identify as a feminist, and starts a group called Success Stories with the aim of challenging toxic masculinity among the people he is incarcerated with. Toxic masculinity manifests as aggression, dominance over others, and a broad lack of emotional expression. Having realized the harm caused by these expectations both inside prisons and out, Reseda deconstructs these norms with his community in a setting that is usually associated with toxic hypermasculinity and violence—which the criminal-legal system sets the stage for. The documentary chronicles how Reseda's submersion in feminism provided him with new insight into gender, power, and privilege. He realized the harm caused by patriarchal norms and toxic masculinity, which encouraged him to share his learnings with others as a strategy to change lives, relationships, and broader communities.

The group engages in open dialogue about the far-reaching negative effects of toxic masculinity on men, women, and other people of all genders while showing the peacemaking value of an abolitionist feminist. Male dominance drives aggression and violence in a number of ways, and engaging in deconstructive initiatives to unpack lessons that many are socialized to accept and perform is a novel and promising approach to antiviolence work and transformative justice.

Success Stories continues as an innovative thirteen-week workshop series that employs feminist theory to fundamentally change how participants, especially those who have caused harm, perceive themselves, their aspirations, and their interactions with others.[17] This transformative program is offered primarily in eleven California prisons, targeting men between eighteen and thirty-five years of age, the demographic with the highest rates of recidivism. The program offers programming and workshop series outside prisons as well.[18]

What sets this program apart is its peer-led model. All workshops are facilitated by people who are currently or were formerly incarcerated, creating an environment of empathy and shared experience. The program operates under the "Relate—Investigate—Recreate" model, in which facilitators share their experiences to relate to participants, encouraging introspection and personal transformation. Upon completion, graduates become part of the Alumni Network, which provides resources, ongoing programming, and accountability. This network supports their continued personal and collective growth, with many graduates becoming facilitators themselves.

Originally focused on prisons, Success Stories expanded in 2020 to include settings outside the correctional system. It now offers workshops in schools, reentry programs, and other nonprofit organizations, reaching out to cis men who either were formerly incarcerated, have had interactions with the criminal-legal system, or are at risk of being criminalized.

The program's mission is to provide an alternative to the prison system by delivering feminist programming to individuals who have done harm. This mission is grounded in the vision of a world free from prisons and the dominance of patriarchal culture, in which harmful behaviors are seen as symptoms of systemic issues to be addressed through community-based programs.

Core to its values is intersectional feminism, which recognizes the compound impact of multiple identities on lived experiences. The program advocates for the abolition of prisons and the criminal-legal system and firmly believes in transformative justice. This concept is seen as a liberatory approach to violence that seeks accountability and safety without resorting to punitive or state violence.

Success Stories emphasizes the importance of love, community, and nonhierarchical structures in healing and transformation. Rooted in love and community, the program believes in continual healing and decolonization through communal experiences. Although not a healing justice organization, it acknowledges the impact of trauma on individuals and incorporates this understanding into its work.

The feminist organizing work of Reseda and his incarcerated community illustrates the power of feminism and antiviolence as a way to transform people and their conceptions of society. In connecting the dots between male dominance and violence toward those of all gender backgrounds, it provides a powerful exploration of transformative justice, showing how people can transform themselves and their relationships with other people through understanding and acknowledging how broader systems—in this case patriarchy—produce harm and violence. Reseda has since returned home and is engaging in a number of abolitionist endeavors through Question Culture and its political education work.

Toxic masculinity, a concept characterized by the enforcement of traditional male gender roles that restrict the kinds of emotions allowable for boys and men to express, including the social expectation that men should seek to dominate and control others, contributes significantly to the prevalence of domestic and intimate partner violence. Programs that focus on addressing and dismantling these harmful norms are essential to efforts to reduce such forms of violence. Initiatives such as Success Stories and others dedicated to uprooting gender violence and toxic masculinity are key to building a safe, accountable world.

These programs not only work toward preventing violence but also encourage individuals, particularly men, to engage in conflict resolution in a less aggressive and more empathetic manner. This approach aligns with broader efforts to promote nonviolent communication and conflict resolution skills, which are essential to building safer and more cohesive communities.

Addressing toxic masculinity is vital for developing comprehensive strategies that will go beyond policing and law enforcement to address domestic and intimate partner violence, as well as other conflict-related aggression. A greater focus on toxic masculinity and its associated programs provides a crucial perspective in the quest to reduce violence and promote healthier, nonviolent forms of conflict resolution. Such an examination is relevant not only for understanding the roots of certain types of violence but also for envisioning alternative approaches to community safety and well-being.

PROJECT NIA

Mariame Kaba is perhaps the best-known transformative justice and antiviolence abolitionist organizer. Born and raised in New York City, she became involved in social justice at a young age. She has dedicated decades to working to abolish the prison-industrial complex and centering on community-based approaches to addressing harm and violence within communities. Her political education and cultural work have been pivotal in bringing prison-industrial complex abolitionist efforts to the forefront, and she wrote *We Do This 'til We Free Us* and cowrote *No More Police* with Andrea J. Ritchie.

Kaba has emphasized the importance of community, transformative justice, and mutual aid. She has been a leading force in advocating for meaningful social change by building power within communities and creating community approaches to harm. Kaba emphasizes the multidimensional violence that people experience in their communities interpersonally, from the state, and within their communities, and the need for holistic solutions.

One of her organizations, Project NIA, is a grassroots organization she founded in 2009. Based in Chicago, it aims to end the incarceration of children and young adults by promoting restorative and transformative justice practices. Project NIA organizes community-based responses and interventions that focus on healing, accountability, and transformation without punishment. The organization employs various programming efforts to achieve its goal. Project NIA develops and distributes educational resources to raise awareness and understanding of the juvenile justice system. It hosts public events, workshops, and training aimed at cultivating a community invested in accountability and safety. The organization also carries out participatory actions, working with young people and community members to document and showcase the impact of the juvenile justice system.

Project NIA emphasizes supporting and facilitating community-based transformative justice practices. These practices provide a framework for responding to harm and violence in ways that move beyond policing and incarceration toward healing, accountability, and community justice. Project NIA works to build a future in which we will rely less on policing and imprisonment, fostering a more compassionate and equitable society through the principles of transformative justice. Project NIA has produced a range of research and reports, educational resources, and the Building Accountable Communities Toolkit, and has developed the NYC Transformative Justice Hub, "a pilot program that aims to support transformative justice (TJ) and community accountability (CA) work in New York City. The Hub provides political education, consultations, and support from experienced practitioners, and increases connectivity and visibility across groups doing TJ and CA work."[19]

Other Project NIA programs have included[20] Circles & Ciphers, an organization blending hip-hop with restorative justice principles, led by young individuals impacted by violence. Other Project NIA initiatives include a movement dedicated to the closure of youth prisons in Illinois, aiming to revamp and minimize the state's youth correctional system, as well as the Chicago Student Safety Act Coalition, which strives for enhanced transparency in school discipline and safety within Chicago public schools. It also produced *Black & Blue: Art about Policing, Resistance and Violence*, an exhibit showcasing art by both children and adults focusing on policing, violence, and resistance, and *A World Without Prisons*, an art exhibit that amalgamated the visions of incarcerated youths and external contributors of a world free of prisons. The project also produces a blog, Community Safety Looks Like, that displays photographs of Chicago residents answering the question "What does community safety look like?"

Kaba has also been instrumental in founding other organizations, such as the Chicago Freedom School, the Chicago Taskforce on Violence against Girls & Young Women, and We Charge Genocide. She also founded TransformHarm.org, a platform that provides resources about transformative justice; restorative justice; community accountability; abolition; carceral feminism, a term for a branch of feminism that embraces prisons, policing, and punishment for addressing gender issues; and healing justice, which provides those who experience harm with the tools and resources to heal. Kaba also is a cofounder of One Million Experiments, which presents a curated collection of community-based safety approaches.[21]

As Kaba and Ritchie discussed in their book *No More Police*, one way to transition to a police-free world is to create ways for cops to be accountable for abusive behaviors they are involved with or complicit in while giving them opportunities to transition into work that is not centered on violence.[22] If they have the desire to help people, there is a range of ways they can do so. Policing has become a tool of economic mobility in Black communities. In a police-free world people will not see being a cop as one of the only viable options for stability because there will be, in the visions of many abolitionists, a society that guarantees that everyone has their basic needs, including food, housing, education, health care, and dignified work, met.

CHANGING THE NARRATIVE: MPD150, BLACK VISIONS, AND RECLAIM THE BLOCK

In early June 2020, the Minneapolis City Council voted to disband the Minneapolis Police Department (MPD) and introduce a novel approach to public safety in the city: the Department of Community Safety and Violence Prevention. The new department was meant to focus on efforts such as community-led solutions, crisis response, and restorative justice, and to greatly reduce police power and scope. The move followed the tragic murder of George Floyd by the Minneapolis police on May 25, 2020, which sparked an uprising in Minneapolis and widespread protests across the nation and beyond, with many calling for defunding and abolishing US policing. As the days went on, the nation held its breath as the Minneapolis Police Department's Third Precinct went up in flames—something never before seen in generations of responses to police violence. Minneapolis became the first city to develop a plan to disband its police department, while other cities made commitments to divert funds from policing into community-based approaches to safety. The demands that emerged out of Minneapolis were a part of a longer legacy of abolitionist and invest-divest campaign organizing by three collectives: MPD150, Reclaim the Block, and the Black Visions Collective.

MPD150, founded in 2016, is composed of organizers, researchers, and activists committed to researching and documenting the 150-year history of the Minneapolis Police Department. In a report titled *Enough Is Enough: A 150-Year Performance Review of the Minneapolis Police Department*, it exposed the long history of violently racist practices within the police force that had led it to advocate for the abolition of the police and the implementation of community-based safety approaches. While MPD150 initially planned to disband in 2020, the group's work gained renewed momentum due to the uprising against police brutality following the murder of George Floyd. MPD150 committed to continue advocating for abolition, supporting other organizations and individuals engaged in similar work, and providing resources and tool kits to help the broader public understand community safety. It also engaged with city council members and Minneapolis residents to envision the disbanding of the city's police department. The collective ultimately sunsetted in November 2022, but its website continues to host a range of digital resources and reflections developed during its six years of work.[23]

In January 2020, months before George Floyd was murdered, I wrote an article about a city that refused to divest from policing despite years of campaigns. The piece centered on a collective of organizers engaged in invest-divest campaigns to channel resources from police to community resources and institutions in Minneapolis. I pitched the piece to editor after editor. They all said no—that the story was too local and not a national news hook. Eventually it was published under the title "Increases in Police Funding Will Not Make Black People Safe, It's Time City Leaders Listened."[24] In the days following the murder of George Floyd, I realized that the coalition I'd focused on in the piece I had written in

January—Reclaim the Block—was at the center of national demands to defund and abolish policing.

Reclaim the Block is a multiracial organization founded in 2018 to advocate for redirecting funds away from police and toward social services such as housing and public education and community-based safety approaches. As Tony Williams, a member of the collective, told *Teen Vogue* in 2020:

> Our work has always been about divesting funds from the police department and investing in community-led alternatives, and we feel it has particular importance in our current moment. In 2018, we approached the city council asking for 5% of the Minneapolis police budget to be reduced. Instead, we were able to negotiate that $1.1 million that was originally meant to hire eight new police officers could be used to create the Office of Violence Prevention in Minneapolis.[25]

Reclaim the Block centered its work on efforts targeting Minneapolis's city council with invest-divest campaigning, including a campaign to divert $2 million from the MPD's public relations fund to violence prevention. The mayor and city council resisted its calls for years, but in 2020, after the murder of George Floyd, the council voted to disband the MPD.

The organizing momentum and vision of a new approach to safety was also driven by the Black Visions Collective and MPD150. Speaking with *Teen Vogue*, Molly Glasgow, a member of MPD150, described the on-the-ground work of MPD150 throughout the protests, which included delivering essential supplies and engaging in community protection and mutual aid efforts. The collective also developed posters, study guides, and lists of books that put abolition and community safety visions into context. MPD150 gave out these resources alongside Black Visions and Reclaim the Block to people in the community as well as to teachers and schools and made them available online to help people understand the promises of community-based safety.

Black Visions Collective, an organization led by Black, queer, and trans activists dedicated to dismantling systems of violence and environmental injustice, was also at the forefront of the Minneapolis uprising. Founded in 2017, Black Visions is focused on building community safety without any reliance on the police and fostering a sense of community. During the uprisings, Black Visions Collective worked with residents to increase understanding of community safety, collected donations, and provided resources and support to activists and residents protesting. The collective also orchestrated mobilizations in which members of the community visited city council members to emphasize the importance of disbanding the police department and investing in a community-led vision of safety. Those direct, unapologetic efforts helped create an environment that made city council members more open to reimagining safety in ways that had never been done before by a legislastive body, despite pushback from the mayor. The collective focused on raising the conversation beyond reform in Minneapolis and helped spark a broader conversation around abolition across the United States and beyond.[26]

While the movement gained momentum and support, the disbanding of the police, approved by a veto-proof council majority, was thwarted. The city council initially proposed a measure to replace the police force with a Department of Community Safety and Violence Prevention and intended to put it onto the November 2020 ballot. But in the months that followed, some city council members withdrew their support.[27] Then, in August 2020, the Charter Commission, an obscure oversight body affiliated with the state government, blocked the measure from appearing on the ballot, effectively ending the plan.

In place of the initially transformative vision, the city council voted to reduce the MPD police budget by 4.5 percent, which would not change the number of police.[28] The $8 million taken from the $179 million MPD budget was directed to mental health training for emergency call centers, mobile crisis teams to respond to certain 911 calls, and funding for community-based violence prevention initiatives.[29]

By engaging in research, protest, political education, and community building, MPD150, Black Visions, and Reclaim the Block collectively challenged the notion that police reform is the only option. In fact, they were able to make gains in promoting abolitionist visions and community-led safety efforts along with organizers across the United States. Thus the uprising was not simply met with the traditional cycle of responses; an intervention forced the conversation to change. The efforts led to the development of community patrols, medical treatment facilities, mutual aid initiatives, and donation centers, all without police involvement. The cycle of conversations that would typically take place after a high-profile case of police violence changed as a result of abolitionist organizing—and interconnected conversations—in Minneapolis and across the United States. The injection of abolitionist language into popular discourse changed history.

4FRONT: COMMUNITY SAFETY FROM ACROSS THE ATLANTIC

4FRONT, established in 2012 in London, is an innovative organization dedicated to empowering young people who have been impacted by violence and the criminal-legal system, which disproportionately affect Black communities.[30] Its approach includes violence reduction by building peace through healing and transformative justice. This involves directly challenging the United Kingdom's reliance on criminalization, policing, and prisons, guided by best practices from around the world.

At the heart of 4FRONT's work is the creation of safe therapeutic spaces where members can heal from trauma, cope with loss and grief, and confront mental health crises or encounters with the legal system.[31] It provides crucial emergency harm reduction and aftercare in response to serious violence, creating a culture of immediate support and nurturing resilience. Alongside these, it offers specialized advocacy support, help to members navigate and overcome systemic barriers, and the facilitation of personal development journeys that strengthen their sense of identity.

Education and knowledge building are central to 4FRONT's mission. The initiative creates opportunities for people to reimagine concepts of peace and justice, focusing on community healing, transformative justice, and youth leadership. This involves educating people about the nature of harm and effective responses and fostering a community that is both informed and empathetic. 4FRONT also emphasizes building collective power. By mobilizing youths, communities, collectives, and movements, it aims to move from harm to healing. This collective action is pivotal in documenting the impact of criminalization on racialized youths and developing frameworks to repair this harm. In doing so, 4FRONT contributes to a broader understanding of and response to systemic challenges.

Its work, deeply rooted in racial justice, is tailored to meet the needs of those with experiences of violence and the criminal-legal system, with a particular focus on the Black community, including Black British, African, Caribbean, and mixed-heritage individuals. It actively works to dismantle the systemic racism and discrimination that their members face.

4FRONT is a response to the inadequate support structures for young people exposed to serious violence in the United Kingdom. By highlighting the failures of successive governments to address the root causes of youth violence and the disproportionate impact of that violence on the Black community, it challenges the preference for punitive measures over healing-centered approaches. Its advocacy for more love, care, and support for Black communities responds to the overexposure of these communities to both community and state violence.

BEYOND POLICING

Safety is much more expansive than the criminal-legal frame allows space for. A society truly invested in safety ensures that everyone has access to health care; guarantees resources; provides safe housing; prioritizes social, political, and economic systems that center on people, not profit; and takes transformative approaches to managing interpersonal and communal conflict, violence, and harm. From the very onset of the United States as a settler colonial state, that has not been the society we have found ourselves in. Prevailing narratives about safety are often used to justify increasing punishment and control. These measures usually benefit those in power.

Police and the criminal-legal system harm and punish. The system is not organized to center on accountability or repair. The extent to which it *seems* that it remedies harm stems from a thirst for vengeance, which justifies the existence of the system and the commitments to punishment that the system cultivates in our broader culture. We learn about justice through learning about the systems that we're told are responsible for ensuring it. But in the United States, and in many other places around the world, people are taught only about containment, punishment, and control.

No one should have the power to take a life, to seize and cage a body, in the way that the state has empowered police to do, largely because of the desire to control labor, race, and class concerns. Police have increasingly played a role in managing and maintaining inequality, especially in the wake of the neoliberal shift and punitive approaches in governance beginning in the 1970s.[32] Neoliberalism, an economic paradigm that is often characterized by its emphasis on free-market capitalism, privatization, and reduced government intervention in the economy, has led to greater community fragmentation and deepened crises. In this context, it's imperative to dismantle our culture of punishment. But we also have to dismantle the foundation upon which this culture rests: white supremacy, capitalism, borders, ableism, and heteropatriarchy.

We need to ask questions about society: Why is anyone in the world houseless, without food, with little access to health care, or unable to meet basic needs when the world has more than enough to ensure that none of these conditions exists? Why do we invest more in making sure that people are not able to access what they need to thrive than in ensuring that they do? Why do policing and punishment expand as precarity grows? Why do a few people make the majority of decisions that impact so much of the world?

As Ruth Wilson Gilmore has stated, "Abolition requires that we change one thing, which is everything. Contemporary prison abolitionists have made this argument for more than two decades. Abolition is not *absence*, it is *presence*. What the world will become already exists in fragments and pieces, experiments and possibilities. So those who feel in their gut deep anxiety that abolition means knock it all down, scorch the earth and start something new, let that go. Abolition is building the future from the present, in all of the ways we can."[33] Abolition is everywhere, often in the places we least expect to find it. It exists in people, communities, experiments, and imaginations. Throughout history and in places we often don't expect, abolition is being practiced. Abolition is centered on creating a world where safety and accountability are cultivated through community care, intentional practices, and ensuring that people have what they need to thrive. Many Black communities build systems of safety outside of police. In some affluent suburbs, some experience alternate realities where residents' basic needs are met and policing is not a primary response to social issues — though policing serves a powerful function in structuring suburban realities through maintaining segregation and controlling bodies seen as threatening to the suburbs' apparent (but not real) stability. As Tamara K. Nopper argued, this is why models of abolition need to go beyond attempting to replicate conditions in white, well-off, privileged communities.[34] Police and prisons were largely established to protect those populations from those seen as racially and economically threatening. And even for those populations, police do not guarantee safety—whether from patriarchal violence, economic violence, or familial and interpersonal harm. What's required is something new and imaginative that will counteract trauma and harm in ways that center on accountability, healing, and transformative justice—and address the conditions that produce the trauma and harm.

Building beyond policing is not only about reducing police involvement in community life; it is fundamentally concerned with creating conditions in which we do not need police to begin with. High-quality schools, housing, and hospitals, work that is rooted in dignity and not profit-based exploitation, violence interruption, domestic violence support programs, drug treatment, and efficient emergency medical response, including for mental health emergencies, are all factors that foster safety and would help transform Black communities, as well as the nation.

In order to build a world that provides more avenues for safety, free of the policing and surveillance of whole communities, we need to do more than just dismantle unjust and oppressive institutions. In order for us to build a world without policing, everything has to change. It is for this reason that you'll notice that much of this book is not centered just on policing but on so much more; it is more focused on the conditions needed to move away from a global society that relies on policing. People need the conditions to thrive and transform. So much of this involves freedom from systems of oppression and cycles of harm at all levels. It also means having the resources to build, grow, and affirm all the complex realities and contradictions of life. It means having access to health care, housing, education, food, community, meaning, dignified labor, care, safety, and more in a way that affirms *life* and not punishment or profit. Moving beyond policing is not just taking money from police but taking resources—financial, sociocultural, and mental—from *policing*. It requires divesting ideologically and materially from policing and punishment as a paradigm of safety and from adjacent tools of racialized social control.

TRANSFORMING SOCIETY

We're in the midst of a national reckoning. Since the founding of this country, racially subjugated, poor, and working-class people have been systematically exploited and dispossessed, and prisons and policing have long been part of that tradition. As I have described in previous chapters, prisons and policing were never designed to maintain public safety; they were designed as tools of racial/class control. After every period of gains from freedom movements comes a reactionary movement of rollback and retrenchment. The current Movement for Black Lives and uprisings in response to police violence have been exactly that. At the city, state, and federal levels, there have been initiatives to limit and prevent divestment from policing. In August 2021, every Democrat in the US Senate voted on an infrastructure bill that would allow the federal government to embargo funds for municipalities that divest from policing. The implications of this consensus among Democratic politicians are clear. Political elites and legislative bodies will likely respond adversely to divestment and abolition efforts and continue to be a roadblock to a transformative society free of police violence—and police. Organizers and communities will have to grapple with these political realities in their defunding and abolitionist efforts.

The emergence of defunding as a framework shows that communities are asking for reliable, nonpunitive models of public safety that do not lead to police violence and carceral harm. Those invested in abolition are skeptical of minor, symbolic divestments that do not lead to deep cuts or reductions in the size and scope of policing. The core of invest-divest approaches lies in deep and substantial cuts to police funding and investments in community resources and alternative emergency responses.

Defunding and abolishing policing is not just about removing the harmful presence of these institutions but also about developing new systems and institutions that can end cycles of violence and harm. They're about creating conditions that will make us all safer and give us access to help we need when we need it. There has been no shortage of community policing and diversity programs since the 1970s, yet police violence continues. Since 2014, even though the initiatives have expanded, police violence (and resistance to it) have continued.

Instead of enacting performative reforms and the illusory promises of community policing, we could fund organizations such as Mothers/Men Against Senseless Killings, which focuses on violence prevention, food security, and housing through community building and caring engagement.[35] Or initiatives by One Million Experiments, which presents a range of community-based safety approaches and invests in the whole scope of transformation-oriented work.[36] We could fund organizations such as Designing Justice + Designing Spaces to design community parks and other public spaces, which has been shown to reduce violence.[37] We could invest in safe, comfortable housing. We could pilot a new system that will channel resources and social support to communities impacted by conflict and violence, while pulling back police presence, as was done in a limited way in Brownsville, New York, in 2020.[38]

WHAT IS OUR WAY OUT?

We need new systems that will keep us safe and transformative ways to deal with conflict, violence, and harm within our communities. Divesting from policing, prisons, and systems of control and reinvesting in communities is a step in that direction. Invest-divest campaigns and efforts have been under way for years, though many people are unfamiliar with them. We need housing, health care, schools, hospitals, community programs, universal basic income, alternative emergency response models, mental health responders, conflict resolution teams, domestic violence intervention, trauma-informed responses to violence, violence interruption initiatives that do not have ties with law enforcement, and more.

In the summer of 2020, after the wave of protest and rebellion, defunding and invest-divest frameworks became a part of mainstream conversations. Many of those who brought defunding into the national conversations are engaged in abolitionist work and saw defunding as an abolitionist strategy. For others, the invest-divest demands that were proposed by the calls to defund the police were a rational option to reduce police contact and provide communities with the resources they need. While some media outlets and politicians argued that the rhetoric was divisive, the main issue was clear: those invested in police power are not in favor of the strategy of the transformative demands.

When activists began to demand to defund the police it was seen as unrealistic and politically impossible. Then cities started to reallocate funding, albeit only marginally in many places. Despite these smaller efforts, police violence will continue to happen again and again. And time will continue to show that the current system of public safety is long overdue for a complete overhaul. It will require our whole society to change in the process — but, as abolitionists argue, that is entirely the point.

A large piece of divesting and abolitionist projects is removing police from areas of everyday life where police saturation has become routine. The police-free school movement has been gaining momentum.[39] Black Oaklanders in California were successful with their campaign to remove police from schools in 2020.[40] Ensuring that students have safe spaces in which to learn and grow that are free of police and carceral environments is a key area of abolition. Many colleges and universities across the United States maintain armed police on their campuses. Campaigns to remove police from college and university campuses are also central in building abolitionist futures in which educational spaces remain centered on education, not policing and punishment.[41] The Cops off Campus Coalition, along with the #PoliceFreeCampus campaign, which is organized by Scholars for Black Lives and the Campus Abolition Research Lab, are two collective efforts organizing for police-free campuses.[42]

Removing police from traffic safety, which is gaining momentum in places such as Berkeley, California, and Brooklyn Center, Minnesota — which has committed to removing police from traffic safety — is essential. One of the most effective ways to enhance traffic safety is instead through strategic design, public education, and community engagement and accountability.

As reported by the organization Interrupting Criminalization, organizers in more than twenty cities secured the divestment of more than $840 million from police departments and at least $160 million of investments in communities, as well as the cancellation of twenty-five city contracts with police that operate in schools, bans on chemical and military-grade equipment, and bans on facial recognition technology.[43] While this is only a small fraction of the more than $100 billion spent on police each year, the cuts reveal an interruption in the continued investments in policing, prisons, and systems of punishment.

Central to the efficacy of these experiments will be developing interventions that do not rely on punishment and carceral control. Focused deterrence, which has become a major inflection point for police reform, remains an intervention that relies on extreme punishment disguised by front-facing social services and community voices. Even more, in many places, community support, which proponents of the approach argue is essential, is lost as a program begins and communities realize the punishment focus of the initiatives. There are a number of ways to manage safety. This model of policing, the resources it siphons off, and the ideological stranglehold it maintains on many people is standing in the way of developing alternative systems of safety and accountability.

There are many different abolitionist visions, as there were different visions of the abolition of slavery. Abolitionists differ on what abolition will entail and the steps necessary to ensure that another system of domination does not take the place of the previous unjust system. We believe that policing and the criminal punishment system should end, as it is beyond reform and reform itself is a violence that preserves the current system; what will come after is open to envisioning. Some visions of abolition, including my own, center on transforming the entire political economy away from capitalism toward the life-affirming realities embraced by socialism, Black feminism, and anticolonial thought. More and more people believe that traditional legislation and political processes will be insufficient to bring us to transformative systems of safety and accountability—especially after the bureaucratic negation of the gains made by abolitionists in Minneapolis. Certainly, abolition will require political education, strategy, and mobilized power. It will almost certainly involve direct encounters with police and carceral violence along the way.

It's critical to address the underlying logics and structures of policing when building alternatives. If an intervention is centered on patriarchal power, ableism, coercive control, and marginalization, it reestablishes police and punitive logic in an intervention that is framed as an alternative. Social workers who rely on coercive control and pathologizing, entities that police without formal law enforcement, surveillance-driven strategies, and community self-policing can seem like alluring interventions, but we have to abolish the culture of not only formal policing but also third-party and ancillary policing that can be carried out by anyone. This requires political development and the ability to discern between problematic interventions and ones rooted in repair and transformative justice.

It's important to remember this: many things now considered normal were once seen as impossible or politically impractical. In coming years, more people will embrace the idea of reallocating funds, and more people will come to understand and advocate for the abolition of police and the reimagination of public safety in its entirety. Even more, many will see how defunding can be used as an avenue toward abolition. As more people understand the need to defund the police, as moments of police violence continue to happen and organizers and communities continue to engage in political development and strategic efforts centered on abolition, abolition will continue to grow as a viable pathway forward. The path to abolition requires a fully transformed society. Intercommunalism, as theorized by Huey P. Newton,[44] anticapitalism, feminism, environmental justice, transformative models of safety, mutual aid, and direct democracy can pave the way forward. The free breakfast programs, health clinics, educational initiatives, and youth programs launched by the Black Panther Party also provide a blueprint for practicing community care while simultaneously seeking to change broader social, political, and economic paradigms.

Police and prison abolition requires us to respond differently to those we deem in need of punishment. The truth is that even if all nonviolent drug offenders (for example) are released from jail, mass incarceration will still exist, because its aim is to feed the appetite of racial capitalism. If anything, shifting how we understand and feel about how we should respond to certain offenses is the meat and potatoes of transforming our culture of punishment. There is a need to divest not only from police resources, but also from the idea that the police keep us safe. In the words of Martin Luther King Jr. "Now is the time," more than ever. Police will be violent as long as they have the power and opportunity to be.

STRATEGIES OF TRANSFORMATION

We need to change the conditions that produce cycles of harm, conflict, and violence with community-based emergency response systems and conflict resolution. Prosecuting individual police, or the usual reforms such as body cameras, community policing, training, and use-of-force restrictions, have all proven ineffective in stopping police violence. And they will certainly not change the outcome of everyday police violence and harm outside of highly sensationalized moments that garner national attention.

Prosecuting police will not stop them from harming and murdering people. We saw this with the murder of sixteen-year-old Ma'Khia Bryant in Columbus, Ohio, on the same day the Derek Chauvin verdict was delivered. The case of George Floyd took the largest protest movement in history to deliver *one* conviction. The only way to guarantee that police violence does not occur is to remove police encounters altogether, in favor of alternatives. The vast majority of calls to 911 are not made for incidents involving violence;[45] fewer than 5 percent of arrests are made during violent incidents.[46] Even then, there can be alternative approaches to addressing serious incidents and concerns in addition to the wide range of incidents that police respond to which do not involve violence.

Divesting from policing is also connected to divesting from other systems of punishment, such as prisons, and investing in nonpunitive approaches to accountability such as transformative justice and community safety. More than anything, we need a world in which everyone has their basic needs met and the resources to thrive. Guaranteed housing, good-quality health care and education, a universal basic income, climate justice, food, and clean water are all in the realm of possibility. But capitalism has created a world of unnecessary suffering and inequality. It's fundamentally a question of prioritizing lives and people over property and capital. Participatory budgeting, income-sharing communities, community safety hubs, worker co-ops, community stewardship of land rather than private ownership, and state welfare housing are all concrete approaches to building sustainable, autonomous communities that are able to manage conflict, harm, and violence while aiming to end patterns of harm altogether.

The criminal-legal system has moved us further away from creating accountable communities. Police manage inequality. If you can't feed yourself and end up stealing from a grocery store, who shows up? If you can't pay your rent (despite the fact that there are enough resources to ensure adequate housing for all), who shows up? If you steal water because you have lead in your pipes, who shows up? If, after all this deprivation, you stage a protest against poverty and racism, who shows up? Police are used as the bodyguards of unjust racial, class, and gendered social orders.

We need to begin asking big questions about the economy, politics, education, environment, culture, war, public safety, and more. We need ways to ensure direct democracy—as representative, neoliberal democracy is locked into an inextricable relationship with right-wing conservatism.

Capitalism creates instability. Capitalism transcends mere market fluctuations, becoming a catalyst of national and global crises. It engenders a spectrum of adversities, from everyday suffering to systemic subjugation. The issue with capitalism is not just its inherent crises; it's its propensity to spawn crises. This phenomenon has precipitated a crisis of political legitimacy wherein the public's faith is shaken not only in its leaders but in the very framework of governance. Amid this tumult, far-right and fascist ideologies find fertile ground, exploiting the disarray wrought by capitalism to fuel a resurgence in populism, potentially paving a path toward fascism. Moreover, it's arguable that the seeds of fascism have long existed within our own borders, particularly evident in our carceral systems. These systems, with their inherent tendencies toward control and suppression, often mirror facets of fascist ideology, especially in their treatment of marginalized communities. This reflection is not just in overt actions but in the underlying ethos that governs these institutions, revealing a disturbing parallel with the authoritarian aspects of fascism.

The way out is to reimagine society as we know it. Our understanding of the economy, culture, politics—the Constitution itself—all of what we assumed to be true and our beliefs about the best ways to design systems of governance have led us to the current crisis.

Modern policing is a product of racial capitalism and the culture of punishment that emerged in service of it. Policing is also fundamentally centered on violence work.[47] Police aren't limited to municipal law enforcement; correctional officers, prosecutors, private security guards, sheriffs, state troopers, the military, and probation and parole officers all perform policing functions. Many entities, including welfare agencies, child protective services, schools, job training programs, mandated drug treatment programs, hospitals, social workers, social services, and more, engage in policing, operate as third-party police, often call on formal police and the criminal-legal system in their day-to-day work, and are often mandated to do so.

One might rightfully argue that harm is embedded in human relations.

A more transformative approach would consist of teaching people how to care for one another better, how to be accountable, how to apologize and make amends, and how to restore safety in moments when harm is committed. This would create safer, more accountable communities rather than caging, policing, and surveilling people.

Moving beyond the punishment paradigm requires freeing people from jails and prisons through mass release (which we saw is possible during the COVID-19 pandemic); ending three-strikes laws, life sentences, and mandatory minimum laws; creating community-based systems that are separate from the criminal-legal system and do not embrace "e-incarceration" through mechanisms such as electronic monitoring; decriminalization; and clemency, compassionate release, and expungement.

Local officials with progressive leanings are being elected around the country. At the same time, increasing attention is being given to building alternatives for safety outside of policing. The wave of newly elected leaders and the political shift toward safety beyond policing create possibilities for experimenting with new models. This includes creating alternatives to how we understand emergency and crisis response.

Police and police unions often have significant political clout in elections, and being "tough on crime" can win political support for candidates. But progressive candidates can also run on a commitment to finding alternatives to police contact, arrest, and imprisonment if there is enough backing and support, which third-party political parties, such as the Working Families Party, may be able to marshal.

Legislators should be looking into any and every way to repeal and decriminalize criminal codes that pave the way for police contact; in the meantime, localities should usher in nonenforcement policies whereby police do not enforce unjust laws.

There should be a continued push to ban no-knock warrants, whereby police enter homes without announcing themselves; dissolve police unions; make it easier to fire officers through ending collective bargaining agreements with police unions; end qualified immunity, which protects police from legal action aside from very specific cases; repeal the 1994 crime act; and start decriminalizing entire classes of offenses.

Activists and organizers in the Movement for Black Lives, such as

BYP100, have begun to offer viable policy alternatives that would dismantle mass policing and generate safety in Black communities that center on the defunding of police, reinvestment in communities, and a move toward community-based accountability mechanisms. As organizers continue to make this push, we are reminded that the very existence of mass policing, and systems of control and punishment more generally, are at the root of the issue. Attempting to tweak or reform mass policing or mass incarceration will continue to result in similar systems of punishment and control in different iterations. To truly address the issues and not simply marginally improve them in ways that render the systems more entrenched, we must provide new systems and ways of relating.

The Movement for Black Lives has put forth the Vision for Black Lives, a blueprint for moving closer to freedom and liberation. And given the range of identities that exist within Blackness, true liberation from the ways in which heteropatriarchy, racial capitalism, and white supremacy intersect will not only transform the lives of Black people in the United States, it will transform the world. The policy demands put forth by M4BL and abolitionist organizations are expansive, which is what a transformation of this magnitude requires. Some people who are new to abolitionist principles and organizing may see the visions and demands as politically out of reach, or unrealistic, but the Black radical imagination and Black dreams of freedom have always centered on suspending disbelief and our assumptions concerning the impossible.

We have to be attentive to material conditions in the present, while also acknowledging that there is a need to strategize and organize for the years to come. It is a fundamental problem when a small percentage of the population owns the vast majority of wealth produced by, and at the expense of, the many. Guaranteed jobs and universal income are essential, but we need a fundamental reconfiguration of the economy that will place people over profit. True transformation includes a reconfiguration of the current economic system away from capitalism toward socialism. Abolition cannot thrive within racial capitalism, as systems of punishment will continue to be invested in preserving profit and property and those who have the most of them.

The current political system is responsive only to disruption—and then it criminalizes and violently attempts to quell it. A true democracy is rooted in an ethic of justice, and justice requires deep listening, accountability, and action. To create a true democracy, we have to free ourselves from fear to imagine a new world that will be profoundly different.

Some steps can be taken now, such as the ones proposed by #8toAbolition: (1) defunding policing; (2) demilitarizing communities (which includes disarming police and private security); (3) removing police from schools; (4) freeing people from jails and prisons; (5) repealing laws that criminalize survival; (6) investing in community self-governance; (7) providing safe housing for everyone; and (8) investing in care and community resources, not cops.[48]

Thinking beyond the current punitive regime requires us to think through new ways of cultivating safety and accountability. In my vision of abolition, there are three central ways to approach safety:

Prevention: (1) Ensure that communities have their basic needs met and are not impoverished; (2) provide conflict resolution and de-escalation training; (3) help people learn how to resolve conflict without violence; (4) provide mental health and trauma support; (5) teach about bodily consent beginning in early childhood; and (6) provide tools and guidance to promote healthy relationships of all kinds.

Intervention: Interventions can involve specialized teams to deal with specific concerns to safety. They can include (1) creating community-based emergency response models to deal with conflict, violence, harm, and other situations in which people might require support; and (2) providing adequately trained (and compensated) noncarceral mental health workers, housing specialists, domestic violence intervenors, community violence intervenors, conflict resolution experts, civilian traffic safety managers, and other nonpunitive response teams.

Response: This involves developing approaches to deal with conflict, violence, and harm once it happens. Not only does the current model actively harm certain communities—particularly Black communities—but it also does not provide the safety it purports to. Most people who experience harm and violence do not report it to the police. Even more, when they do, they are exposed to traumatizing criminal-legal processes, in addition to the fact that rates for clearing open cases for many crimes are notoriously low. Restorative justice and transformative justice provide ways to respond to harm once it has occurred that center on accountability, repair, and changing culture and institutions to stop cycles of harm from recurring.

We can think of a building analogy to emphasize the ways in which policing is embedded in society and the depth of the work that must take place to end policing for good. Let's say you have a house and the foundation is unstable. There may be some places in the house where the structural damage is obvious. Some people may not notice, or they may perceive it differently. To create a space where people can thrive and feel free of harm, the house will have to be demolished. But that isn't a one-day job; it requires a plan, workers, resources, tools, and a blueprint for what will emerge once the house is leveled and the foundation is dug out.

The persistent policing of Black and marginalized communities is intimately shaped by structural racism and class inequality—centrally racial capitalism itself.[49] As Stuart Hall et al. discussed in the groundbreaking 1978 text *Policing the Crisis: Mugging, the State, and Law and Order*, policing and criminalization have largely grown as tools of social control to manage inequality and to preserve dominant political, economic, and ideological paradigms.

Those who have presented visions of abolition and reallocation have argued for the large-scale reduction and dismantling of punitive systems in favor of the creation of just, democratic, and noncoercive "life-affirming institutions," in the words of Ruth Wilson Gilmore. Specifically, recent calls for defunding have pushed for the shift of resources from policing to the resources that have been proven to increase safety in communities, including quality housing, dignifying employment, health care, and well-resourced schools, as well as alternative emergency and crisis response systems. Beyond this, organizers have called for a reimagining of the ways we address conflict, harm, and violence, centered on frameworks such as transformative justice, rather than the punitive approaches that have been fine-tuned in America's carceral state. These issues extend beyond the United States. Violence work in the form of militarism and policing together with nation-states that do not act in the interest of the public are widespread. In order to push back on these realities, we need international dialogue and solidarity with all people who experience illegitimate regimes of policing and military violence.

Anti-Black state violence and race-class subjugation extend far beyond the criminal-legal system. The violence of the welfare state, the criminalization of homelessness and mental illness, abandoned public housing, state-structured racialized poverty, and systematic school closings in addition to other forms of "organized violence" and "organized abandonment," as Ruth Wilson Gilmore called them,[50] contribute to the broader cascade of state-sanctioned violence that structures the lives of Black and other marginalized communities across the United States. As we look toward solutions, Gilmore's words are instructive: "Abolition requires that we change one thing, which is everything."[51]

What if our response to crisis wasn't about control but about care? How can we create conditions where safety is a shared responsibility? How can we design justice so that no community is routinely oppressed? Envisioning such a world isn't just a daydream; it's the first step toward building a society where violence and fear no longer dictate our lives.

GETTING INVOLVED

Resources and initiatives are available, and they need to be advanced and developed. But much of the work will require new visions and imagination — and sufficient resources. In addition to this more imaginative work, there are essential steps we can all take to combat the culture of policing and spread the message of abolition:

(1) **Divest from policing and punishment.** This includes defunding, deweaponization, demilitarization, and the dismantling of police units and departments, as well as surveillance, carceral tools, and incarceration — and investing in community resources and transformative systems of accountability. Centrally, successful campaigns require

organizing and strategy. To that end, people can join and form campaigns, and collectives and organizations can engage in political development and education around divest campaign strategies.

Guaranteed housing, health care, and employment, universal basic income, investments in schools, hospitals, parks and other community infrastructure, and investments in alternative emergency and crisis response systems are key in divesting from police and punishment. We can focus on developing equitable job transfer and retraining initiatives for police to areas of work where there are mechanisms of accountability and limited opportunities for abusive behavior. People who entered the police force in order to help their communities—or for social mobility—can undergo training to unlearn abusive behaviors ingrained through policing and can leave and take other forms of employment as a part of defund strategies, given that a large majority of police budgets goes toward personnel salaries.

(2) **Practice accountability and abolition in everyday life.** This includes forming copwatch collectives and nonpolice community safety systems. Are there any members of your community who have the skills (or are open to developing the skills) to be violence interrupters? Are there members who can disrupt cycles of domestic violence and support survivors? How can cycles of sexual assault be addressed, prevented, and intervened in? Are there ways to develop community-based safety plans in case someone within your network needs rapid intervention and support? We can also prioritize free school breakfasts and survival programs and form political development campaigns to shift people's understanding of the origins and functions of policing and the criminal punishment system.

As a society, we've internalized the idea that police keep us safe—even when we know it's not true. It's one of the starkest manifestations of hegemony in the twentieth century. Some people have eschewed the connection between police and safety, but many people who desire safety see police and the criminal-legal system as the only option—but that's because it's often the only option we're presented with. The criminal-legal system is also the only option that has been *invested* in. The criminal-legal system is based on vengeance and control, not safety and accountability.

Public safety is supposed to be a public good. If it's not working for the people, it should be dismantled and abolished so that new systems can emerge in its place. We have the right to demand something new. That is true for policing and so much more. Ultimately, what better way to make the case for a police-free world than to show a world in which it's possible?

CHAPTER 6

AN ABOLITIONIST FUTURE

Abolition is about presence, not absence. It's about building life-affirming institutions.

— Ruth Wilson Gilmore

ENVISION A SAFE AND JUST WORLD. WHAT DO YOU SEE?

To build a more safe and just world, we have to have the courage to reimagine every aspect of our society. Much of this is centered on transforming how we relate to resources and one another. Picture a place where every human being has access to essentials: food, water, education, health care, and housing. This isn't a utopia; it's a world in which the root causes of violence, namely poverty and precarity, are addressed head-on. We have to be willing to dream of that world together.

What better way to make the case for a police-free world than to show a world where it's possible? Let's dream of a police-free future at the turn of the twenty-second century.

It's 2105. There are no police. There haven't been for decades. We've learned about them in school and through reading. And really, we learned about what police were from our parents, who learned from their parents. We have been taught that in the United States they existed since slavery. At first they were called slave patrols; their role was to prevent slave rebellions and capture enslaved people who tried to escape. Hard to believe, right? And while policing evolved over the years and took up different forms, its violence toward Black people and other communities oppressed at the time ran rampant for centuries.

We learned that throughout the 1800s and 1900s, police basically did whatever they wanted to. Black communities resisted in sometimes subtle, sometimes loud ways. In the mid-1900s, uprisings mostly in direct response to police violence spread throughout the nation. In 1968, Dr. Martin Luther King Jr. called riots the language of the unheard. That language roared, and it continued to roar in the decades following, but each time it did, the government, as it was called, found ways to preserve and expand the power of police. That state of affairs continued and continued. There were moments of uprisings, other moments of sustained activism, and don't get me started on all the reforms. But the cycle continued.

Activism and unrest helped to create more breathing room at times, as many of our grandparents tell us. But in that breathing room, some people became comfortable. Other people thought the issues were a thing of the past. Until they weren't. And the cycle went on and on and on.

Then everything changed. Someone was killed by the police; people all across the country and world rose up—but it wasn't just against policing. It was sparked by the police, but it was about so much more. People had been connecting the dots between policing and the lack of important resources that help strengthen communities. The moment helped make many people understand that police were not only a tool to manage inequality, they were also siphoning up so many resources—along with what was the US military—that could be going to making people safer in a way that addressed causes, not just their consequences. Decades after that, the police killed another Black person, and that was the last person to be killed by police. Because those particular uprisings ushered in and paved the way to a fundamental shift in how society was organized. They changed the balance of who had power, and for the first time, the masses collectively governed resources and set priorities. That shift led to the establishment of more direct forms of democracy, in which decisions were made not by a distant elite but through inclusive, participatory processes that engaged every segment of the populace. After that period, often referred to as the Great Transition, for the first time our ancestors and elders finally realized what was often called by their contemporaries an "impossible dream," the complete abolition of police and prisons.

After the transition period, there were people who made sure that things didn't go back to the way they had been. They studied the past and made sure we created new systems and didn't just reconfigure the old. That happened all around the world, albeit in different ways, and communities engaged in processes in which they redesigned approaches to safety. All around the world, communities learned of Huey P. Newton's conception of revolutionary intercommunalism, in which people developed meaningful, interconnected, and just relationships to answer the world's most pressing concerns and challenges. They read books such as *Beyond Survival: Strategies and Stories from the Transformative Justice Movement* and *Healing Justice Lineages: Dreaming at the Crossroads of Liberation, Collective Care, and Safety.*

Today, in 2105, you'll notice that what's different is not just the lack of police; everything is different. The entire way we respond to and try to prevent conflict, violence, and harm is different. Police and prisons weren't replaced by single things but by a constellation of approaches that led to a more safe and just world.

The process to bring us to a point where the masses could redesign society in a way that prioritized people and not punishment or profit took a long time. And it wasn't clean or simple, but the approach to cultivating safety was thorough. Those organizing around safety concerns started by canvassing and hosting community meetings in which everyone was asked: What is safety to you? What are your main concerns about safety? They made sure not just to ask about interpersonal harm and violence. Things such as food security, housing, land, and employment all came up. Through a transformative lens of safety, we came to a much more holistic understanding of how to approach people's needs. So rather than having police stations, now we have community safety hubs. We have safety mobilizations and teams to deal with just about any problem you can think of. Fewer concerns arise as a result of the active preventive efforts, but when they do arise, they're managed peacefully and transformatively—and without the presence of violence work.

Now, don't get me wrong, it doesn't mean that things are perfect.

There's still a need for safety interventions and preventive approaches. But things in general are much less hectic. And the preventive measures do much of the work to create safety. They include things such as accessible life necessities, community-based safety strategies, and approaches to addressing harm. So much has changed since male domination and patriarchal violence no longer determine how we build institutions, how we are with one another, and how we build social bonds. People learn to share power with one another rather than constantly trying to dominate one another.

We all decide how to approach safety. In some places, grandmothers run the community safety hubs. In others, it's their children and children's children who are the stewards of safety work. People decide locally on safety hub initiatives and approaches, and neighboring communities and others that have similar dynamics help. We invite people to be accountable rather than relying on coercive control. If a situation gets out of hand, we have teams that are able to respond with the training and tools necessary to intervene, de-escalate, and try to achieve the best possible outcome and the least possible harm. We come up with plans and approaches to manage our local communities collectively and with autonomy. We don't have to wait around for housing repairs or decisions to come from above us. We meet and vote, but mostly we decide through consensus. The people govern in a way that is direct and democratic, and we no longer have government systems in the way they were before. And when problems and threats emerge, we address them together, always thinking about how we can deliver on safety and not depend on violence.

Firefighting and EMT cooperatives are as well resourced and strong as ever. And we have so many other emergency responders, such as mental health and psychological first aid responders, conflict resolution teams, crisis mobilization teams, safety approaches that center on children and families, traffic safety workers, and so many more. Punitive justice is a thing of the past; transformative justice seeks to get at the underlying causes of harm and violence rather than focusing on punishment. Everyone has designated pods to help manage their concerns, intervene in any potential issues, and to respond to them with the person who experienced harm in mind.

Name something that can happen to a person, and we can tell you the collectively decided on approaches that we apply nowadays. It all includes centering on the person who was harmed, trying to understand why it happened, and dedicating time and resources to preventing it from happening again—whether through public health approaches, community classes, accountability partners, or something else. We have healing centers, peace centers, and places to get immediate help and resources when someone is harmed. Through building new systems and approaches, we reduced the reliance on policing and prisons till they faded away. We've long moved beyond policing.

VISIONS OF A POSTCAPITALIST FUTURE

In this new world, this new reality we find ourselves in, every single person has a home to call their own and hunger is just a word in the history books; our streets echo with laughter and shared stories rather than sirens. This isn't a distant dream; it's a vision of a world that moved beyond policing by embracing social transformation. Before, our safety was thought to depend on the police. But we realized that true safety was interwoven with ensuring that everyone's needs were met. Why? Because many of the root causes of harm stem from the pangs of poverty and desperation.

Now grocery stores are like community pantries. You enter, pick what you need, and leave with a nod of gratitude. Imagine walking into a grocery store, not to calculate what you can afford but simply to get what you need. There are no police or security guards standing watch, no underlying tension, just a community's shared understanding that there's enough for all. Just outside, community gardens flourish, their fruits and vegetables available to anyone who passes by. Our elderly are well integrated into community life; they are much healthier and more social, and they have what they need to thrive. People in general live longer, fuller, more active, happier lives.

Our children? They grow up knowing that they belong, learning about consent, and understanding the spectrum of human identity without prejudices. Each child experiences the fullness of life, free of burdens shaped by poverty or avoidable traumas. Parenthood is a journey embarked upon not due to societal pressures but out of intrinsic human desire. The community, in its collective embrace, ensures that child care is universally accessible, free from the constraints of economic worries. Schools such as the Ella Baker Elementary School and the Steve Biko I Write What I Like Academy are beacons of creativity, fostering freethinkers who challenge norms, just as we did.

The pillars of capitalism that once towered above—where big corporations decided our worth and future—have crumbled. The landscape has changed. We work with passion, dignity, and a sense of responsibility to the commons, not out of desperation. Worker cooperatives thrive, fostering a sense of purpose and community. The chains of profiteering have broken, freeing us to truly value human connection over transactions. People are allowed the space to mourn, to spend time with their families and loved ones. Our relationships no longer bear the shadow of money hanging overhead. Interpersonal bonds have deepened, and people relate to one another authentically, without the taint of extractive motives. People can love whomever they want freely.

Health care, once monetized, is now universally guaranteed. Every clinic, every hospital, stands as a testament that health isn't a privilege but a right. Our relationship with medicine has been freed from the claws of profit, making for a healthier society. Pharmaceutical medicine is created by scientists and specialists through worker cooperatives and communes. Representatives and experts help steer certain decisions and efforts based on their focus areas—but pretty much everything is decided upon collectively. But there are no more megacorporations, and workers have direct control over their labor. It's pretty cool to see it in action. That's how everything works now. No one person owns everything. We all own what we produce and how we produce it. This ensures that workers are not exploited and unable to meet their basic needs. We also realized that when people have work they feel good about and proud of, they are less likely to engage in activities that would make other people, or themselves, unsafe.

Our earth breathes more easily. We are no longer burdened by the smog of industrial giants. We respect our land, tending to it not as owners but as stewards, ensuring a far more predictable coexistence. Land and homes are seen differently, too. We've realized that the earth doesn't belong to us; we belong to it. Sure, we have spaces we call our own, but the idea of land as a commodity, something to profit from, is a relic of the past. We looked to

Indigenous ways of stewarding the land for answers. The scale of climate disasters we've heard of? They've lessened drastically. Communities now work hand in hand, respecting the earth and ensuring that it will remain healthy for generations to come.

This transformative society wasn't built overnight. It took acknowledging that to move beyond policing, we needed to radically address the profound societal structures that bred injustice and violence. We saw that exploitation—whether by capitalism, racism, patriarchy, or environmental degradation—was a conduit for harm. When we addressed those systems at the root, we birthed a society that treasures every individual, understanding that when one thrives, we all do.

Key pillars of society—education, housing, utilities, work—are all managed by the very people they serve. Education is not only accessible but also diverse, tailored to the unique needs of every student. The concept of public housing has been revitalized, ensuring that every person has a roof over their head. Utilities and energy supplies, vital for everyday life, are community governed and collectively managed, ensuring fair access and efficient service.

This decentralized system prioritizes local decision making, fostering a culture of direct democracy and autonomy. As a result, interpersonal relationships have blossomed. With the shadow of financial instability and the pressure of capitalism no longer looming large, friendships, familial ties, and romantic relationships are no longer tainted by transactional undertones. Instead, they are forged and nurtured in an environment in which individuals have the resources and freedom to thrive. The bonds people form in this world are stronger, more genuine, and liberated from the burdens of the past capitalist structure.

Safety was never about policing; it's about community, understanding, and addressing root causes. It's about ensuring that the basics of life aren't a luxury but a right. And in this world, we've found our safety, not in the power of enforcers but in the hands of our neighbors, friends, and families. What we've built isn't just a world without policing; it's a society in which the need for such an institution has dissipated. By ensuring that everyone's needs are met, by stewarding the environment responsibly, and by allowing people to thrive, we've cultivated safety organically. This isn't just about eliminating police; it's about eliminating the conditions that made them seem necessary. We've learned, at last, that when exploitation ends, real safety begins.

Poverty is a thing of the past. This colossal task wasn't just about throwing money at the problem but about globally redistributing wealth and resources. Historically, our global economy thrived on creating disparities, extracting profit at the expense of human dignity. Corporate giants, predatory lenders, and financial conglomerates once held the strings, but no more. Community-driven cooperatives and shared ventures have replaced those entities. Debilitating debts? They're a relic of the past. Today's community financial collectives work harmoniously, valuing societal benefit over profit. In this new world, sharing isn't just an act; it's a way of life. From the food we eat to the dreams we chase, everything thrives on interconnectedness and mutual respect.

By dismantling entities that thrived on inequity, such as large financial institutions and predatory lenders, and bidding adieu to the likes of the World Bank and International Monetary Fund, communities found a new rhythm in cooperation. Our streets resonate with the warmth of communalism. Debt, once a crushing burden, was replaced by support provided by transparent community financial systems. This alone drastically reduced economic exploitation. We have universal income and guaranteed employment. Everyone contributes in ways that resonate with their passion and purpose. Gone are the days of toiling merely for survival. Today we seek purpose, and our society is all the richer for it. In this society, you're defined not by your job but by your passion. People regularly pivot in their careers, always seeking to make meaningful contributions. There's no looming fear of unemployment; if life calls for a change, our community embraces it. And because we prioritize community, no one is ever forced to uproot their lives merely for sustenance.

It's fascinating to see how humanity rediscovered itself in this liberated environment. The overarching fact is clear: when people control their labor, work becomes a vocation, not just an occupation. A lot of people had to go through processes where they thought about what they actually wanted to do with their labor—and that isn't always a single thing. It took a lot of time, and some people are still figuring it out. But people are much less miserable now that they themselves control their work. They are far more open to working because they see meaning in their work and don't feel exploited. Sometimes people change how they spend their days, and even when people don't know what to do and are idle for periods, their basic needs are still met and they find ways to contribute meaningfully to the community.

Employment is owned by the workers. If they can, most people work. But you won't be crushed if you don't. And people choose what they want to do based on what the community needs and what gives them the most meaning. Anywhere you go, people do the work that is meaningful for them, including, if they desire, community safety work. People are able to be. Just be. Regardless of their background, whom they love, their bodies, abilities, interests, or beliefs. Everyone has what they need. And as that changed, society naturally grew safer in so many ways. Everyone works where they feel that they can contribute the most. And people change careers whenever they like. It's easier since there are no bosses; the workers collectively run and operate different employment collectives. People don't have to move and leave their families and communities for work unless they decide to; never because they will be deprived of resources if they don't. People travel for experiences and feel a sense of global community and collectivity since we all are needed to make this world work.

While currency exists, it's just a mechanism for convenience, untethered from volatile market fluctuations or arbitrary standards. Luxurious excesses have lost their allure because well-being is universal. In the absence of capitalist pressures, desires have evolved. Do you dream of owning a boat? You can, but never at the cost of another's well-being.

Art, music, theater—creative pursuits blossomed as people discovered the freedom to express themselves without financial shackles. Art and culture are at the heart of our society. Centers such as the Whitney Houston Arts and Cultural Center, where people learn to play instruments and more, provide platforms for creativity, ensuring that talents aren't stifled due to financial constraints. The media landscape, too, has undergone a revolutionary shift. Once a tool for maintaining the status quo, it's now a vibrant platform that champions ethics, originality, and community narratives. Entertainment still thrives, with TV shows, sports, and games, but they're produced by fair, worker-controlled cooperatives. Moreover, our relationship with technology has transformed. Gone are the days of data mining and technology for profit; now technology is an ally of well-being. Innovative apps, for instance, empower communities, connecting members for collective safety and well-being.

This is a world in which we've moved beyond policing by transforming our societal fabric. In this future, we recognize that real safety and harmony stem from fulfilling human needs and fostering genuine community ties. It's a vision worth striving for, in which every individual thrives and contributes to the collective good.

The realization was profound yet simple: society required transformation. Angela Y. Davis said, "Radical simply means 'grasping things at the root.'" To transform safety, we had to grasp the issues at the root and carry out those transformations. Policing, historically rooted in property protection and societal order maintenance, became redundant in a community that prioritized collective well-being over individual gains. The journey was neither swift nor straightforward, but the results were unequivocal. A society without policing was not just feasible but, in many ways, far safer and more harmonious. The tides of change may have been challenging to navigate, but they led us to shores of unparalleled safety and justice.

We rely on people both within and outside our community. Political decisions and approaches to collective sharing are all navigated by intercommunal pods. We've managed to articulate a vision for the world that was structured by interconnectedness embedded in the local. People know their living conditions and coordinate and work with others to make sure, as much as possible, that all people have what they need.

There are no politicians in a traditional sense. Politicians used to make decisions about safety and justice that did not align with the needs of the masses. Now, we read texts like "Every Cook Can Govern," by C. L. R. James to deepen our understanding of direct democracy and guide how we approach decisions that impact us all. Although it can be challenging at times, our commitment to direct democracy ensures that our most important decisions reflect the collective will. We have community hubs and pods that we create based on the needs of our communities, and we make decisions collectively. It takes longer at times, but we don't have the issues of the past when people with power make decisions for all of us. We all vote and decide on things. We have community leaders, but there are mechanisms in place—namely the emphasis on direct, participatory democracy—that reduce the likelihood of anyone monopolizing and wielding too much power.

We have systems in place globally to make sure we are doing all we can to keep one another safe, discuss emerging needs, strengthen bonds, and strategize collectively around global priorities. We broke down borders and the myths and fallacies of nation-states. We remembered that for most of history nations did not exist, so we reorganized how we related to one another both politically and geographically. People had a sense of home and territory, of course. But we realized we were better off with collaboration around the world, rather than top-down political systems that don't serve the masses. Historically, war was engendered by the desire to seize control over natural resources and territory. But now, because most places relate to one another and humanity differently, we collaborate rather than hoard and fight.

Intercommunity pods steer our political and socioeconomic landscapes. This world, inspired by interconnectedness, revolves around local know-how. We've built a world in which resources are shared, ensuring that everyone's needs are met. While borders have dissolved, places retain their essence, devoid of political or nationalistic biases. The liberty to reside anywhere, paired with collective endeavors to provide for all, have revolutionized the very fabric of society.

Once things changed, we moved away from thinking of land as property with arbitrary boundaries. Places still have meaning, but not because of arbitrary countries or citizenship or politics. People live where they want, and collectively we try to make sure that everyone has what they need regardless of where they are. People travel to see the world and meet new people, not because they may starve or suffer if they don't. Visas aren't a thing. Some cities stayed similar in terms of layout and organization; others looked completely different after everything changed. But it's all democratically decided. And we're talking direct and participatory democracy. Not the stuff of the past.

HARVESTING LESSONS FROM A NEW WORLD

For years, the concept of crime was seen as a natural way of understanding harm and violence. But to the discerning eyes of abolitionists, it was clear that crime was not a natural state but rather a construct shaped by societal and political influences. To address this revelation, we embarked on a journey, initiating grassroots discussions on the true meaning of safety. Understandably, the interpretations varied, but a few universal truths emerged about the violence and harm that no one wanted in their communities.

However, instead of merely counting incidents or measuring crime rates, we dived deeper. We sought a more profound understanding: What does it mean for a person to *feel* safe? How can we ensure that safety is not just a number but an experienced reality? That led us to reimagine our approach from the ground up. Distributing the abundance of resources equitably became the backbone of our revamped strategy. The three pillars—prevention, intervention, and response—became the cornerstone of our new safety paradigm.

In this new world, theft became a rarity. After all, when everyone's needs are met, envy and resentment become obsolete. On the rare occasion that theft did occur, the community was equipped with agreed-upon strategies to address it, keeping in mind the broader objective: avoiding the pitfalls of the historical punitive measures that once dominated the US criminal-legal system.

Drugs, once stigmatized and criminalized, were seen in a new light. Drugs aren't criminalized. People can get help if they struggle with addiction, and other people don't judge those who use drugs. But people also abuse them less because times are different. And the factors that made people more likely to become addicted to drugs don't really exist anymore. Don't get me wrong, people still get high! But now it's primarily to enjoy and enrich their lives. People don't have as much that they want to escape or numb themselves to. And when they do, there are so many mental health resources that they get the help they need. People also are able to get the drugs they actually want and not derivatives or adulterated substances. There is also public education about how to use drugs responsibly, and test kits are widely available so people can make sure they know what they're using. Now if people want to use drugs responsibly, they can. Communities have guidelines and approaches to make sure that our relationship to drugs is as healthy and responsible as possible. Since drugs are not criminalized, people can use them more healthily, and if they decide to stop for whatever reason, they have the resources and support to help them do so.

Conflict still exists. But its nature has changed. Its intensity has subsided, replaced by understanding and communal resolutions. The specter of prisons no longer hangs over our heads; instead, accountability and rehabilitation play pivotal roles. Our transition wasn't instantaneous; it was lengthy. Yet the fruits of our efforts are evident in the world's newfound freedom. Everyone, irrespective of their health or abilities, receives the appropriate care. With healing spaces and trauma centers, our society has embraced a proactive approach to well-being.

For a world devoid of police, we didn't just eliminate law enforcement; we created a society in which it became obsolete. The existence of life-affirming institutions underpins this transformation. Daily life persists with its quirks, but the nature of problems has shifted, conflicts have mellowed, and alternative resolution methods thrive. In essence, the reconfiguration of our world was necessary to make policing obsolete. Many people who thought more rigidly across races began to see that the way things were did not really benefit most of them. Society was constructed to allow only a few to benefit fully from stability. So they were eager to envision radical changes in their own communities.

Problems still arise. Conflict still occurs. It's usually just not as intense; not as resentful; not as powerful. Harm happens less, on average, and when it does, it often isn't to the same degree. When it does, people who experience the harm have spaces where they can go through accountability and transformative justice processes with those who harmed them, and those who are responsible for the harm are far more open to understanding and being accountable for what they did without the idea of prison ruining their lives. There is accountability, and it's not always desirable, but it's necessary and understood. It's just. Traffic is handled much differently. And all the miscellaneous things police did, such as monitoring construction sites, are handled by safety coordinators. I'm not sure why police were even involved in that to begin with.

I'll tell you one story that I was told. Early in the transition, someone in the community was robbed. The community took a step back and asked: Why did this happen? The person who was robbed was immediately compensated for what he'd lost, and street outreach workers found out pretty quickly, given their ties, who had done it. The person who was robbed realized that he wasn't able to have a clear mind about what should happen to the person who had done it; responses should not be driven by individual feelings of anger and resentment in a particular moment. Rather than focusing on punishing the person, the man who had been robbed and the person who had robbed him went through a restorative process. The man who had been robbed was able to share his experience and the harm he had sustained as a result of the incident, and the other person apologized and accepted accountability for what he had done. It turned out that they had needed money to pay the rent in order not to be evicted, as that was before everyone had housing met as a basic need. He was an artist, too, and needed money to go to a studio to record. That doesn't excuse what he did, but by getting to the root the community was also able to make sure that the person responsible accepted accountability, and the reason why he had done it was addressed so he wouldn't continue doing it to other people. Through the process he was connected with support to get an income and help with his rent to make sure he wasn't evicted. That wouldn't happen today because recording is free at the Arts and Cultural Center, where there are DJs, audio engineers, and coaches. A lot of kids go there and collaborate. That was where I learned to play the drums. And everyone has a safe place to live in that they don't have to fear being evicted from.

The transition was slow and complex. But the world we have now is definitely more free.

Kids have places to go. People are not deprived. Anyone who is ill or experiences a disability has access to what they need so that they don't experience unnecessary suffering. Trauma treatment and healing spaces are big parts of our community. To be honest, there are fewer moments of harm and conflict, because of the life-affirming resources and systems that exist.

In order to have a world without police, we couldn't just take away the police. We needed to create a world that has no need for police. In other words, the presence of life-affirming institutions, rather than the mere absence of police and prisons, was what brought us to a new, different world. You wake up to your everyday life. People have problems. Siblings fight. Friends argue. But the problems are much different. Conflict is less intense. And there are other ways of handling those moments.

As you can see, the whole world had to change for police to no longer exist. We realized that we needed a hard reset of society. And it wasn't just about policing; once people realized that policing was largely about protecting property and maintaining social rules and expectations, we decided to change society altogether. And once society changed, so did the sense that we need police. It wasn't easy. It took struggle. And managing a society without police takes work. But in the end, we're safer for it.

———————

You can't create what you can't see. And you can't build what you don't believe is possible. Where this book ends is where I hope your journey of imagination and action will begin. I hope these pages will be a spark that ignites your dreams. Together we can surmount the boundaries of what once seemed impossible.

ACKNOWLEDGMENTS

In the journey of bringing *Beyond Policing* to life, my heart is filled with gratitude for those who have been pillars of support, wisdom, and inspiration.

Foremost, I extend a world of thanks to my family: my mother, Lorna Golding, and father, Philip McHarris, for their unwavering love and guidance. Immense appreciation also goes to my sisters, Tynesha McHarris and Tameika McHarris. They were not only supportive but instrumental in shaping the foundational political ideas that gave life to this book. My brothers, Philip A. McHarris and Josiah D. Johnson, have been steadfast sources of encouragement and support.

I am profoundly grateful to my friends Ben St. Gerard, Arissa Hall, Pedro A. Regalado, Stephane Andrade, Anthony Johns, and Luz Villar. Their insights and engaging conversations have greatly enriched this book. Abe Gruswitz and Rahman also read and provided helpful feedback on the book. Special thanks to Bedour Alagraa; the seed of this book was sown in our generative discussions.

My Legacy Lit team, including Krishan Trotman, Amina Iro, and Clarence Haynes, deserves heartfelt acknowledgment. Their dedication and expertise have been instrumental in bringing this project to fruition.

Deep gratitude is extended to my agent, Ethan Bassoff, for his faith in this work and unwavering support. A distinctive mention goes to Tamara K. Nopper for her exceptional editing support, which has significantly refined the essence of this book.

I am thankful to my graduate school colleagues and advisers at Yale in Sociology and African American Studies for their invaluable guidance and insight. Their support has been crucial in laying the groundwork for this work. Similarly, my colleagues in African American Studies at Princeton University and in the Frederick Douglass Institute and Department of Black Studies at the University of Rochester have greatly shaped my academic journey with their intellectual rigor and support.

Heartfelt thanks to Robin D. G. Kelley, Van Lathan Jr., Darnell Moore, Brea Baker, Charlene Carruthers, Maurice Mitchell, Alicia Garza, Alex Vitale, Tamika Mallory, Franchesca Ramsey, Ash-Lee Henderson, and Zellie Thomas for their generous contributions and enriching comments that have graced this book.

This book is not merely a reflection of my thoughts but a tapestry woven from the threads of others' support, wisdom, and encouragement. Writing *Beyond Policing* has been as transformative as it has been challenging. It would not have been possible without the collective strength and wisdom of all those mentioned here, and many others unmentioned, who have walked this path with me.

NOTES

INTRODUCTION

1. James Baldwin, "A Report from Occupied Territory," *Nation*, July 11, 1966, https://www .thenation.com/article/culture/report-occupied-territory/.
2. Tamara K. Nopper, "Abolition Is Not a Suburb," The New Enquiry, July 16, 2020, https:// thenewinquiry.com/abolition-is-not-a-suburb/.
3. Throughout this book, I deliberately use *criminal-legal system* instead of *criminal justice system* to confront the myth that justice is the foundational principle of the current system. This terminology choice stems from recognizing that the system is fundamentally built on unjust policing and carceral mechanisms that disproportionately impact marginalized communities. By designating it as the "criminal-legal system," I aim to underscore that its primary function is not the pursuit of justice, but the enforcement of law through criminalization and punitive measures. This terminology is an invitation to critically reevaluate and seek the transformation of how society addresses safety, harm, and accountability. It encourages us to pursue solutions that truly uphold justice for all, emphasizing restorative practices and community-based alternatives over punitive approaches.

CHAPTER 1

1. Keeanga-Yamahtta Taylor, *From #BlackLivesMatter to Black Liberation* (Chicago: Haymarket Books, 2016), 181.
2. Frederick Douglass, *Narrative of the Life of Frederick Douglass, an American Slave*. Boston : Anti-Slavery Office, 1845, 84–85.
3. I employ the term *public safety* with a specific intention. My use of *public safety* seeks to reclaim and redefine the term, aligning it closely with a perspective of community safety. This reimagined understanding of public safety emphasizes the role of communities as central to the creation and maintenance of safety, rather than relying on state mechanisms such as police, prisons, and the broader criminal-legal system. It is my aim to highlight and advocate for a shift toward community-based approaches that foster safety and accountability.
4. Kristian Williams, *Our Enemies in Blue: Police and Power in America* (Chico, CA: AK Press, 2015).
5. Cara Page and Erica Woodland, *Healing Justice Lineages: Dreaming at the Crossroads of Liberation, Collective Care, and Safety* (Berkeley, CA: North Atlantic Books, 2023).
6. Joe Soss and Vesla Weaver, "Police Are Our Government: Politics, Political Science, and the Policing of Race–Class Subjugated Communities," *Annual Review of Political Science* 20, no. 1 (2017): 565–91.

7. Sally E. Hadden, *Slave Patrols: Law and Violence in Virginia and the Carolinas* (Cambridge, MA: Harvard University Press, 2003); Alex S. Vitale, *The End of Policing* (New York: Verso, 2017).

8. Wilbur R. Miller, *Cops and Bobbies: Police Authority in New York and London, 1830–1870* (Columbus: Ohio State University Press, 1999).

9. Raymond W. Kelly, "The History of New York City Police Department." Accessed January 12, 2024, https://www.ojp.gov/pdffiles1/Digitization/145539NCJRS.pdf.

10. Raymond W. Kelly, *New York City Police* (Mt. Pleasant, SC: Arcadia Publishing, 2012).

11. Gary Potter, "The History of Policing in the United States, Part 1," EKU Online, June 25, 2013, https://ekuonline.eku.edu/blog/police-studies/the-history-of-policing-in-the-united-states-part-1/; Eric H. Monkkonen, "History of Urban Police," *Crime and Justice* 15 (1992): 547–80.

12. P. K. B. Reynolds, *The Vigiles of Imperial Rome* (London: Oxford University Press, 1926).

13. E. Echols, "The Roman City Police: Origin and Development," *Classical Journal* 53, no. 8 (1958): 377–85.

14. Micol Seigel, *Violence Work: State Power and the Limits of Police* (Durham: Duke University Press, 2018), 9–12.

15. Sally E. Hadden, *Slave Patrols: Law and Violence in Virginia and the Carolinas* (Cambridge, MA: Harvard University Press, 2003).

16. Elizabeth Hinton and DeAnza Cook, "The Mass Criminalization of Black Americans: A Historical Overview," *Annual Review of Criminology* 4 (2021): 261–86.

17. Ibid.

18. Betty L. Wilson, "Under the Brutal Watch: A Historical Examination of Slave Patrols in the United States and Brazil during the 18th and 19th Centuries," *Journal of Black Studies* 53, no. 1 (2022): 3–18; Sally Hadden, "Police and Slave Patrols," in *The Ethics of Policing: New Perspectives on Law Enforcement*, ed. Ben Jones and Eduardo Mendieta (New York: New York University Press, 2021), 205; Hadden, *Slave Patrols*.

19. Andy Alexis-Baker, "The Gospel or a Glock? Mennonites and the Police," *Conrad Grebel Review* 25, no. 2 (2007): 23.

20. C. W. A. David, "The Fugitive Slave Law of 1793 and Its Antecedents," *The Journal of Negro History* 9, no. 1 (1924): 18–25.

21. James W. Loewen, *Lies across America: What Our Historic Sites Get Wrong* (New York: Touchstone, 2000).

22. Richard J. M. Blackett, *The Captive's Quest for Freedom: Fugitive Slaves, the 1850 Fugitive Slave Law, and the Politics of Slavery* (Cambridge, UK: Cambridge University Press, 2018).

23. W. E. B. Du Bois, *The Souls of Black Folk* (New York: Oxford University Press, 2008), 120-21.

24. Celeste Winston, *How to Lose the Hounds: Maroon Geographies and a World beyond Policing* (Durham, NC: Duke University Press, 2023).

25. Richard Price, ed. *Maroon Societies: Rebel Slave Communities in the Americas* (Baltimore: JHU Press, 1996).

26. Katherine McKittrick, *Demonic Grounds: Black Women and the Cartographies of Struggle* (Minneapolis: University of Minnesota Press, 2006); Katherine McKittrick and Clyde Adrian Woods, eds., 2007 *Black Geographies and the Politics of Place* (Cambridge, MA: South End Press, 2007); Camilla Hawthorne and Jovan Scott Lewis, eds., *The Black Geographic: Praxis, Resistance, Futurity* (Durham, NC: Duke University Press, 2023).

27. Monica Muñoz Martinez, *The Injustice Never Leaves You: Anti-Mexican Violence in Texas* (Cambridge, MA: Harvard University Press, 2018); E. James Dixon, "Human Colonization of the Americas: Timing, Technology and Process," *Quaternary Science Reviews* 20, nos. 1–3 (2001): 277–99.

28. Allan Greer, "Commons and Enclosure in the Colonization of North America," *American Historical Review* 117, no. 2 (2012): 365–86.

29. Alex S. Vitale, *The End of Policing* (London: Verso Books, 2021).

30. Mike Cox, "A Brief History of the Texas Rangers." Texas Ranger Hall of Fame and Museum, accessed November 17, 2023, https://www.texasranger.org/texas-ranger-museum/history/brief-history/.

31. Kelly Lytle Hernández, *Migra!: A History of the U.S. Border Patrol* (Oakland: University of California Press, 2010).

32. Greer, "Commons and Enclosure in the Colonization of North America."

33. J. Pfaelzer, *Driven Out: The Forgotten War Against Chinese Americans* (New York: Random House, 2008); Judy Yung, Gordon H. Chang, and Him Mark Lai, eds., *Chinese American Voices: From the Gold Rush to the Present* (Oakland: University of California Press, 2006).

34. Michael Woo, "A Powerful Look at 'The Chinatown War,'" review of *The Chinatown War* by Scott Zesch, *Los Angeles Times*, September 2, 2012, https://www.latimes.com/entertainment/la-ca-scott-zesch-20120902-story.html.

35. Erika Lee, *At America's Gates: Chinese Immigration during the Exclusion Era, 1882–1943* (Chapel Hill: University of North Carolina Press, 2003); Philip P. Choy, *San Francisco Chinatown: A Guide to Its History and Architecture* (San Francisco: City Lights Publishers, 1995).

36. Him Mark Lai, Genny Lim, and Judy Yung, *Island: Poetry and History of Chinese Immigrants on Angel Island, 1910–1940* (Seattle: University of Washington Press, 1991).

37. Roger Daniels, *Asian America: Chinese and Japanese in the United States since 1850* (Seattle: University of Washington Press, 2005); Greg Robinson, *A Tragedy of Democracy: Japanese Confinement in North America* (New York: Columbia University Press, 2010).

38. Yuji Ichioka, *The Issei: The World of the First Generation Japanese Immigrants, 1885–1924* (New York: Free Press, 1988).

39. Yen Le Espiritu, *Home Bound: Filipino American Lives across Cultures, Communities, and Countries* (Oakland: University of California Press, 2003).

40. Robinson, *A Tragedy of Democracy*; Wendy Ng, *Japanese American Internment during World War II: A History and Reference Guide* (Westport, CT: Greenwood Press, 2002).

41. "The Hidden Toll of Fatal Police Violence on Some AAPI Communities," *PBS NewsHour*, May 31, 2023, https://www.pbs.org/newshour/show/the-hidden-toll-of-fatal-police-violence-on-some-aapi-communities.

42. Craig D. Uchida, "Development of the American Police: An Historical Overview," in *Critical Issues in Policing: Contemporary Readings*, ed. Roger G. Dunham and Geoffrey P. Alpert (Long Grove, IL: Waveland Press, 1993): 19–35.

43. Miller, *Cops and Bobbies*.

44. Ibid.

45. Marjorie Bley, "The Peel Web," A Web of English History, accessed August 17, 2023, http://www.historyhome.co.uk/peel/laworder/police.htm.

46. Wilbur R. Miller, "Police Authority in London and New York City 1830–1870," *Journal of Social History* 9, no. 2 (1975): 81–101.

47. Ibid.

48. Bley, "The Peel Web."

49. Georgina Sinclair, "The 'Irish' Policeman and the Empire: Influencing the Policing of the British Empire–Commonwealth," *Irish Historical Studies* 36, no. 142 (2008): 173–87.

50. Ibid.

51. "Sir Robert Peel's Nine Principles of Policing," *New York Times*, April 16, 2014, https://www.nytimes.com/2014/04/16/nyregion/sir-robert-peels-nine-principles-of-policing.html.

52. Mike Brogden, "The Emergence of the Police—the Colonial Dimension," *British Journal of Criminology* 27, no. 1 (1987): 4–14.

53. Miller, *Cops and Bobbies.*

54. William Lauriston Melville Lee, *A History of Police in England* (London: Methuen & Company, 1901), 243.

55. Miller, "Police Authority in London and New York City 1830–1870."

56. Potter, "The History of Policing in the United States."

57. James Lardner and Thomas Reppetto, *NYPD: A City and Its Police* (London: Macmillan, 2001).

58. Ibid.

59. Sidney L. Harring, *Policing a Class Society: The Experience of American Cities, 1865–1915* (New Brunswick, NJ: Rutgers University Press, 1983); Richard J. Lundman, *Police and Policing: An Introduction* (New York: Holt, Rinehart and Winston, 1980); Kevin Lynch, *Good City Form* (Cambridge, MA: MIT Press, 1984).

60. "About IACP," International Association of Chiefs of Police, accessed June 25, 2023, https://www.theiacp.org/about-iacp.

61. Upton Sinclair, *The Jungle* (New York: Doubleday, Page & Company, 1906), 303.

62. Daniel J. Czitrom, *New York Exposed: The Gilded Age Police Scandal That Launched the Progressive Era* (New York: Oxford University Press, 2016).

63. Ibid.; Samuel J. Thomas, "Holding the Tiger: Mugwump Cartoonists and Tammany Hall in Gilded Age New York," *New York History* 82, no. 2 (2001): 155–82.

64. National Commission on Law Observance and Enforcement, *Report on Lawlessness in Law Enforcement* (Washington, DC: U.S. Government Printing Office, 1931), 4.

65. James Baldwin, *No Name in the Street* (New York: Vintage, 2007), 161.

66. Robert M. Fogelson, *Big-City Police* (Cambridge, MA: Harvard University Press, 1977).

67. Lisa McGirr, *The War on Alcohol: Prohibition and the Rise of the American State*, illustrated ed. (New York: W. W. Norton & Company, 2015).

68. Naomi Murakawa, "Police Reform Works—for the Police," Level, October 21, 2020, https://level.medium.com/why-police-reform-is-actually-a-bailout-for-cops-ecf2dd7b8833.

69. Michael S. Hindus, *Prison and Plantation: Crime, Justice, and Authority in Massachusetts and South Carolina, 1767–1878* (Chapel Hill: University of North Carolina Press, 2017); Khalil Gibran Muhammad, *The Condemnation of Blackness: Race, Crime, and the Making of Modern Urban America* (Cambridge, MA: Harvard University Press, 2019).

70. Christopher Muller, "Freedom and Convict Leasing in the Postbellum South," *American Journal of Sociology* 124, no. 2 (2018): 367–405.

71. Edward Royce, *The Origins of Southern Sharecropping* (Philadelphia: Temple University Press, 2010).

72. Hinton and Cook, "The Mass Criminalization of Black Americans."

73. Muhammad, *The Condemnation of Blackness.*

74. Rashad Shabazz, *Spatializing Blackness: Architectures of Confinement and Black Masculinity in Chicago* (Champaign: University of Illinois Press, 2015).

75. W. E. B. Du Bois, *Black Reconstruction in America, 1860–1880*, (1935; reprint, New York: Free Press, 1992), 12.

76. Ida B. Wells-Barnett, *Mob Rule in New Orleans: Robert Charles and His Fight to Death* (Auckland, NZ: Floating Press, 2014), 20.

77. Hinton and Cook, "The Mass Criminalization of Black Americans."

78. Julia Longoria and Alvin Melathe, "Life, Liberty, and Drugs," *The Experiment* (podcast), June 17, 2021, https://www.theatlantic.com/podcasts/archive/2021/06/columbia-professor-drug-use-american-rights/619208/.

79. Carl L. Hart, "How the Myth of the 'Negro Cocaine Fiend' Helped Shape American Drug Policy," *Nation*, January 29, 2014, https://www.thenation.com/article/archive/how-myth -negro-cocaine-fiend-helped-shape-american-drug-policy/.

80. Ibid.

81. David F. Musto, *The American Disease: Origins of Narcotic Control*, 3rd ed. (New York: Oxford University Press, 1999), 7.

82. *Driving While Black: Race, Space and Mobility in America* (video), PBS, October 13, 2020, https://www.pbs.org/video/driving-while-black-race-space-and-mobility-in-america -achvfr/.

83. Frantz Fanon, *The Wretched of the Earth*, reprint edition (New York: Grove Press, 2005), 3.

84. "Puerto Rico and the Colonial Circuits of Policing," North American Congress on Latin America, accessed May 15, 2023, https://nacla.org/news/2017/09/27/puerto-rico -and-colonial-circuits-policing.

85. Julian Go, "The Imperial Origins of American Policing: Militarization and Imperial Feedback in the Early 20th Century," *American Journal of Sociology* 125, no. 5 (2020): 1193–254.

86. Vitale, *The End of Policing*, 40.

87. Alfred W. McCoy, *Policing America's Empire: The United States, the Philippines, and the Rise of the Surveillance State* (Madison: University of Wisconsin Press, 2009).

88. Ibid.

89. Vitale, *The End of Policing*.

90. Christopher J. Coyne and Abigail R. Hall, *Tyranny Comes Home: The Domestic Fate of U.S. Militarism* (Redwood City, CA: Stanford University Press, 2018), 145–46.

91. Matthew Guariglia, *Police and the Empire City: Race and the Origins of Modern Policing in New York*, (Durham, NC: Duke University Press, 2023).

92. Susan O. White, "A Perspective on Police Professionalization," *Law & Society Review* 7 (1972): 7, no. 1 (1972): 61–86.

93. Gary Potter and Philip Jenkins, *The City and the Syndicate: Organizing Crime in Philadelphia* (Boston: Ginn Press, 1985).

94. Victor Kappeler, Richard Sluder, and Geoff Alpert, *Forces of Deviance: Understanding the Dark Side of Policing*, 2nd ed. (Prospect Heights, IL: Waveland Press, 1998).

95. Fogelson, *Big-City Police*.

96. White, "A Perspective on Police Professionalization."

97. Vitale, *The End of Policing*, 50.

98. Seigel, Violence Work.

99. Christopher P. Wilson, *Cop Knowledge: Police Power and Cultural Narrative in Twentieth-Century America* (Chicago: University of Chicago Press, 2000).

100. Micol Seigel, "Objects of Police History," *Journal of American History* 102, no. 1 (2015): 152–61.

101. Elizabeth Hinton, *From the War on Poverty to the War on Crime: The Making of Mass Incarceration in America* (Cambridge, MA: Harvard University Press, 2016); Naomi Murakawa, *The First Civil Right: How Liberals Built Prison America* (Oxford, UK: Oxford University Press, 2014).

CHAPTER 2

1. "US Senate: Special Committee on Organized Crime in Interstate Commerce," Accessed April 11, 2024, https://www.senate.gov/about/powers-procedures/investigations/kefauver.htm.

2. Howard Newcomb Morse, "The Kefauver Investigation in Perspective," Dick. L. Rev. 55 (1950): 246.

3. Charisse Burden-Stelly, *Black Scare/Red Scare: Theorizing Capitalist Racism in the United States* (Chicago: University of Chicago Press, 2023).

4. Adom Getachew, *Worldmaking after Empire: The Rise and Fall of Self-Determination* (Princeton, NJ: Princeton University Press, 2019).

5. Kristian Williams, "The Other Side of the COIN: Counterinsurgency and Community Policing," *Interface* 3, no. 1 (2011): 81–117; Kristian Williams, *Our Enemies in Blue: Police and Power in America* (Chico, CA: AK Press, 2015).

6. Charles E. Cobb Jr., *This Nonviolent Stuff'll Get You Killed: How Guns Made the Civil Rights Movement Possible* (Durham, NC: Duke University Press, 2015), 7.

7. Clark McPhail, David Schweingruber, and John McCarthy, "Policing Protest in the United States: 1960–1995," in *Policing Protest: The Control of Mass Demonstrations in Western Democracies*, vol. 6 of *Social Movements, Protest, and Contention*, ed. Donatella della Porta and Herbert Reiter (Minneapolis: University of Minnesota Press, 1998), 49–69.

8. Stuart Schrader, *Badges without Borders: How Global Counterinsurgency Transformed American Policing* (Oakland: University of California Press, 2019).

9. Frank Kusch, *Battleground Chicago: The Police and the 1968 Democratic National Convention* (Chicago: University of Chicago Press, 2008).

10. Vesla M. Weaver, "Frontlash: Race and the Development of Punitive Crime Policy," *Studies in American Political Development* 21, no. 2 (2007): 230–65.

11. Elizabeth Hinton, *From the War on Poverty to the War on Crime: The Making of Mass Incarceration in America* (Cambridge, MA: Harvard University Press, 2016).

12. Paul G. Chevigny, "Politics and Law in the Control of Local Surveillance," *Cornell Law Review* 69 (1983): 735.

13. Hinton, *From the War on Poverty to the War on Crime.*

14. Radley Balko, *Rise of the Warrior Cop: The Militarization of America's Police Forces* (New York: PublicAffairs, 2013).

15. Jerry Flores, *Caught Up: Girls, Surveillance, and Wraparound Incarceration*, vol. 2 (Oakland: University of California Press, 2016).

16. Ibid.

17. Michael C. Campbell and Heather Schoenfeld, "The Transformation of America's Penal Order: A Historicized Political Sociology of Punishment," *American Journal of Sociology* 118, no. 5 (March 2013): 1375–423.

18. Mike Maciag, "Skyrocketing Court Fines Are Major Revenue Generator for Ferguson," Governing, August 21, 2014, https://www.governing.com/archive/gov-ferguson-missouri -court-fines-budget.html.

19. Elizabeth Hinton, *America on Fire: The Untold History of Police Violence and Black Rebellion since the 1960s* (New York: Liveright Publishing, 2021).

20. Joshua Bloom and Waldo E. Martin Jr., *Black against Empire: The History and Politics of the Black Panther Party* (Oakland: University of California Press, 2016).

21. Charles Houston Harris and Louis R. Sadler, *The Texas Rangers and the Mexican Revolution: The Bloodiest Decade, 1910–1920* (Albuquerque: University of New Mexico Press, 2007).

22. Ron Porambo, *No Cause for Indictment: An Autopsy of Newark* (New York: Holt, Rinehart and Winston, 1971).

23. Don Gorton, "What Really Happened at the Stonewall Inn?," *Gay & Lesbian Review Worldwide* 11, no. 6 (2004): 37–39.

24. *Law Enforcement Assistance Act of 1965: Hearings before a Subcommittee of the Senate Committee on the Judiciary*, 89th Congress, 1st session (1965), https://www.ojp.gov/ncjrs/virtual-library /abstracts/law-enforcement-assistance-act-1965-hearings-subcommittee-senate.

25. Hinton, *From the War on Poverty to the War on Crime.*

26. Naomi Murakawa, *The First Civil Right: How Liberals Built Prison America* (New York: Oxford University Press, 2014).

27. Otto Kerner, *The Kerner Report: The 1968 Report of the National Advisory Commission on Civil Disorders* (New York: Pantheon Books, 1988).

28. Ward Churchill and Jim Vander Wall, *The COINTELPRO Papers: Documents from the FBI's Secret Wars Against Dissent in the United States* (Boston: South End Press, 1990).

29. Athan G. Theoharis, "FBI Surveillance during the Cold War Years: A Constitutional Crisis," *Public Historian* 3, no. 1 (1981): 4–14.

30. Jeffrey Haas, *The Assassination of Fred Hampton: How the FBI and the Chicago Police Murdered a Black Panther* (Chicago: Chicago Review Press, 2011).

31. Ibid.

32. Ward Churchill and Jim Vander Wall, *Agents of Repression: The FBI's Secret Wars against the Black Panther Party and the American Indian Movement*, corr. ed. (Boston, MA: South End Press, 1990).

33. Ibid.

34. Orisanmi Burton, "Targeting Revolutionaries: The Birth of the Carceral Warfare Project, 1970–78," *Radical History Review* 2023, no. 146 (2023): 11–31.

35. Hinton, *America on Fire*.

36. Dr. Martin Luther King Jr., Speech at Stanford University: The Other America (April 14, 1967). For a recording of this speech, see "Martin Luther King, Jr. visits Stanford (1967)," Stanford University Libraries. (September 23, 2016), https://www.youtube.com/watch?v=cYK9xGALPrU.

37. Bocar A. Ba, Roman Rivera, and Alexander Whitefield. *Market Response to Racial Uprisings*. No. w31606. National Bureau of Economic Research, 2023.

38. Jerome H. Skolnick, "Racial Profiling—Then and Now," *Criminology & Public Policy* 6, no. 1 (2007): 65.

39. Bloom and Martin, *Black against Empire*.

40. Black Panther Party Alumni Legacy Network, "Black Panther Party Community Survival Programs," accessed March 8, 2024, https://bppaln.org/programs.

41. "The Black Panther Party: Challenging Police and Promoting Social Change," National Museum of African American History & Culture, accessed June 29, 2023, https://nmaahc.si.edu/explore/stories/black-panther-party-challenging-police-and-promoting-social-change.

42. Cynthia Deitle Leonardatos, "California's Attempts to Disarm the Black Panthers," *San Diego Law Review* 36, no. 4 (1999): 947.

43. Ibid.

44. Matthew Fleischer, "50 Years Ago, SWAT Raided the L.A. Black Panthers. It's Been Targeting Black Communities Ever Since," *Los Angeles Times*, December 8, 2019, https://www.latimes.com/opinion/story/2019-12-08/50-years-swat-black-panthers-militarized-policinglos-angeles.

45. Katrina Feldkamp and S. Rebecca Neusteter, "The Little Known, Racist History of the 911 Emergency Call System," *In These Times*, January 26, 2021, https://inthesetimes.com/article/911-emergency-service-racist-history-civil-rights.

46. Ibid.

47. Ibid.

48. Ibid.

49. Ibid.

50. Ibid.

51. Ibid.

52. Donald Janson, "Dial-911 Plan Calls Forth Opposition in Big Cities," *The New York Times*, March 31, 1970, sec. Archives, https://www.nytimes.com/1970/03/31/archives /dial911-plan-calls-forth-opposition-in-big-cities-dial911-plan.html.

53. Ibid.

54. David Burnham, "Success of 911 Puts Strain on Police Here," *The New York Times*, November 29, 1969.

55. Ibid.

56. Ibid.

57. Hinton, *From the War on Poverty to the War on Crime.*

58. Michelle Alexander, *The New Jim Crow: Mass Incarceration in the Age of Colorblindness* (New York: New Press, 2010).

59. Weaver, "Frontlash."

60. Jamila Hodge and Nazish Dholakia, "Fifty Years Ago Today, President Nixon Declared the War on Drugs," Vera Institute of Justice, June 17, 2021, https://www.vera.org/news /fifty-years-ago-today-president-nixon-declared-the-war-on-drugs.

61. David T. Courtwright, "The Opium Debate and Chinese Exclusion Laws in the Nineteenth Century American West (Review)," *Bulletin of the History of Medicine* 82, no. 2 (2008): 469–70.

62. Isaac Campos, "Mexicans and the Origins of Marijuana Prohibition in the United States: A Reassessment," *Social History of Alcohol and Drugs* 32, no. 1 (2018): 6–37.

63. Tom LoBianco, "Report: Aide Says Nixon's War on Drugs Targeted Blacks, Hippies," CNN, March 23, 2016, https://www.cnn.com/2016/03/23/politics/john-ehrlichman-richard -nixon-drug-war-blacks-hippie/index.html.

64. Michelle Alexander, *The New Jim Crow: Mass Incarceration in the Age of Colorblindness* (New York: New Press, 2010).

65. Robert W. Fairlie, "Drug Dealing and Legitimate Self-Employment," *Journal of Labor Economics* 20, no. 3 (2002): 538–67.

66. Donald Janson, "A Jury in Camden to Investigate Police," *The New York Times*, June 6, 1974, https://www.nytimes.com/1974/06/06/archives/a-jury-in-camden-to-investigate-police .html.

67. George L. Kelling and Mark H. Moore, "The Evolving Strategy of Policing," *Perspectives on Policing* no. 4 (1988).

68. John L. Worrall and Tomislav V. Kovandzic, "Cops Grants and Crimes Revisited," *Criminology* 45, no. 1 (February 2007): 159–90.

69. Hubert Williams and Patrick V. Murphy, *The Evolving Strategy of Police: A Minority View Perspectives on Policing* no. 13 (1990).

70. Tamara Gene Myers, *Youth Squad: Policing Children in the Twentieth Century* (Montreal: McGill-Queen's University Press, 2019).

71. Ibid.

72. Mariame Kaba and Andrea J. Ritchie, *No More Police: A Case for Abolition* (New York: New Press, 2022).

73. Valerian J. Derlega, James R. K. Heinen, and Nancy K. Eberhardt, "Officer Friendly: Changing Children's Attitudes about the Police," *Journal of Community Psychology* 7, no. 3 (1979): 220–27.

74. Rebecca Onion, "Playing Good Cop," Slate, August 27, 2020, https://slate.com/human -interest/2020/08/officer-friendly-police-copaganda-history.html.

75. Ibid.

76. Donovan X. Ramsey, *When Crack Was King: A People's History of a Misunderstood Era* (New York: One World, 2023).

77. Doris Marie Provine, "Race and Inequality in the War on Drugs," *Annual Review of Law and Social Science* 7, no. 1 (2011): 41–60.

78. Orisanmi Burton, *Tip of the Spear: Black Radicalism, Prison Repression, and the Long Attica Revolt* (Oakland: University of California Press, 2023).

79. Vesla M. Weaver, "The Missed Opportunity of Robert Woodson," The Marshall Project, February 25, 2015, https://www.themarshallproject.org/2015/02/25/the-missed-opportunity -of-robert-woodson.

80. Angela Y. Davis and Dylan Rodriguez, "The Challenge of Prison Abolition: A Conversation," *Social Justice* 27, no. 3 (2000): 212–18; Angela Y. Davis, *Are Prisons Obsolete?* (New York: Seven Stories Press, 2011).

81. LaShawn Harris, "Beyond the Shooting: Eleanor Gray Bumpurs, Identity Erasure, and Family Activism against Police Violence," *Souls* 20, no. 1 (January 2, 2018): 86–109.

82. Jon Hurwitz and Mark Peffley, "Playing the Race Card in the Post–Willie Horton Era: The Impact of Racialized Code Words on Support for Punitive Crime Policy," *Public Opinion Quarterly* 69, no. 1 (2005): 99–112.

83. Elizabeth E. Joh, "Police Surveillance Machines: A Short History," The Law and Political Economy Project, June 13, 2018, https://lpeproject.org/blog/police-surveillance -machines-a-short-history/; Stephen William Smith, "Policing Hoover's Ghost: The Privilege for Law Enforcement Techniques," *American Criminal Law Review* 54 (2017): 233.

84. Neil Websdale, *Policing the Poor: From Slave Plantation to Public Housing* (Lebanon, NH: Northeastern University Press, 2001).

85. Ibid.

86. Khalil Gibran Muhammad, *The Condemnation of Blackness: Race, Crime, and the Making of Modern Urban America* (Cambridge, MA: Harvard University Press, 2019); Rashad Shabazz, *Spatializing Blackness: Architectures of Confinement and Black Masculinity in Chicago* (Champaign: University of Illinois Press, 2015).

87. Alan Feuer, "Fatal Police Shooting in Bronx Echoes One from 32 Years Ago," *New York Times*, October 20, 2016, https://www.nytimes.com/2016/10/20/nyregion/fatal-police -shooting-in-bronx-echoes-one-from-32-years-ago.html.

88. Williams and Murphy, *The Evolving Strategy of Police*.

89. James Q. Wilson and George L. Kelling, "Broken Windows," *Atlantic Monthly* 249, no. 3 (1982): 29–38.

90. Bench Ansfield, "The Broken Windows of the Bronx: Putting the Theory in Its Place," *American Quarterly* 72, no. 1 (2020): 103–27.

91. Clifford R. Shaw and Henry D. McKay, *Juvenile Delinquency and Urban Areas: A Study of Rates of Delinquents in Relation to Differential Characteristics of Local Communities in American Cities*, Behavior Research Fund Monographs (Chicago: University of Chicago Press, 1942).

92. George L. Kelling and Catherine M. Coles, *Fixing Broken Windows: Restoring Order and Reducing Crime in Our Communities* (New York: Simon & Schuster, 1997).

93. Victor M. Rios, Greg Prieto, and Jonathan M. Ibarra, "Mano Suave–Mano Dura: Legitimacy Policing and Latino Stop-and-Frisk." *American Sociological Review* 85, no. 1 (2020): 58–75.

94. Office of Policy Planning and Research, United States Department of Labor, *The Negro Family: The Case for National Action* (Washington, DC: U.S. Government Printing Office, March 1965).

95. Robert J. Sampson, *Great American City: Chicago and the Enduring Neighborhood Effect* (Chicago: University of Chicago Press, 2012).

96. Sampson, Robert J. "Disparity and Diversity in the Contemporary City: Social (Dis) Order Revisited." *The British Journal of Sociology* 60, no. 1 (March 2009): 1–38.

97. Alex S. Vitale, *City of Disorder: How the Quality of Life Campaign Transformed New York Politics* (New York: NYU Press).

98. Worrall and Kovandzic, "Cops Grants and Crime Revisited."

99. Kelling and Moore, "The Evolving Strategy of Policing."

100. Pedro A. Regalado, "The Washington Heights Uprising of 1992: Dominican Belonging and Urban Policing in New York City," *Journal of Urban History* 45, no. 5 (2019): 961–86.

101. Kelling and Moore, "The Evolving Strategy of Policing."

102. Ibid.

103. Peter Hanink, "Don't Trust the Police: Stop Question Frisk, COMPSTAT, and the High Cost of Statistical Over-reliance in the NYPD," *Journal of the Institute of Justice and International Studies* 13 (2013): 99.

104. Murakawa, *The First Civil Right*; Worrall and Kovandzic, "Cops Grants and Crime Revisited."

105. Aaron Stagoff-Belfort, "Biden Plans to 'Reinvigorate' a Community Policing Office That Has a Dark History," Slate, February 24, 2021, https://slate.com/news-and-politics /2021/02/biden-cops-office-funding-police-history.html.

106. About the COPS Office | COPS Office, accessed March 5, 2024, https://cops.usdoj.gov /aboutcops.

107. Andrew Kaczynski, "Biden in 1993 Speech Pushing Crime Bill Warned of 'Predators on Our Streets' Who Were 'beyond the Pale,'" CNN, March 7, 2019, https://www.cnn .com/2019/03/07/politics/biden-1993-speech-predators/index.html.

108. Catherine Kim, "A 1994 Law Joe Biden Wrote Put These 4 Men on Death Row," Vox, July 26, 2019, https://www.vox.com/2019/7/26/8931612/joe-biden-death-penalty-tough-on-crime.

109. Robert Vargas and Philip McHarris, "Race and State in City Police Spending Growth: 1980 to 2010," *Sociology of Race and Ethnicity* 3, no. 1 (2017): 96–112.

110. Paula M. Ditton and Doris James Wilson, "Truth in Sentencing in State Prisons," Bureau of Justice Statistics, Office of Justice Programs, U.S. Department of Justice, January 1999.

111. Sheryl Gay Stolberg and Astead W. Herndon, "'Lock the S.O.B.s Up': Joe Biden and the Era of Mass Incarceration," *New York Times*, June 25, 2019, https://www.nytimes .com/2019/06/25/us/joe-biden-crime-laws.html.

112. Kim, "A 1994 Law Joe Biden Wrote Put These 4 Men on Death Row."

113. Michael C. Campbell and Heather Schoenfeld, "The Transformation of America's Penal Order: A Historicized Political Sociology of Punishment," *American Journal of Sociology* 118, no. 5 (March 2013): 1375–423.

114. William J. Sabol et al., *The Influences of Truth-in-Sentencing Reforms on Changes in States' Sentencing Practices and Prison Populations*, Urban Institute, April 2002, https: //www.urban.org/sites/default/files/publication/60401/410470-The-Influences-of-Truth -in-Sentencing-Reforms-on-Changes-in-States-Sentencing-Practices-and-Prison -Populations.PDF.

115. Ibid.

116. Ibid.

117. Derecka Purnell and Marbre Stahly-Butts, "The Police Can't Solve the Problem. They Are the Problem," *New York Times*, September 26, 2019, https://www.nytimes .com/2019/09/26/opinion/the-police-cant-solve-the-problem-they-are-the-problem.html.

118. Stagoff-Belfort, "Biden Plans to 'Reinvigorate' a Community Policing Office That Has a Dark History."

119. Peter Baker, "Bush Made Willie Horton an Issue in 1988, and the Racial Scars Are Still Fresh," *New York Times*, December 4, 2018, https://www.nytimes.com/2018/12/03/us/politics/bush-willie-horton.html.

120. Michael Leo Owens, Akira Drake Rodriguez, and Robert A. Brown, "'Let's Get Ready to Crumble': Black Municipal Leadership and Public Housing Transformation in the United States," *Urban Affairs Review* 57, no. 2 (2021): 342–72.

121. Websdale, *Policing the Poor.*

122. Jay Holder et al., "Concentrated Incarceration and the Public-Housing-to-Prison Pipeline in New York City Neighborhoods," *Proceedings of the National Academy of Sciences* 119, no. 36 (September 6, 2022): e2123201119.

123. Mike Davis, "Hell Factories in the Field: A Prison-Industrial Complex," *Nation*, February 20, 1995, 229–34.

124. "Rest in Power, Mike Davis!," Critical Resistance, October 31, 2022, https://criticalresistance.org/updates/rest-in-power-mike-davis/.

125. "Surveillance Under the Patriot Act," American Civil Liberties Union, accessed August 17, 2023, https://www.aclu.org/issues/national-security/privacy-and-surveillance/surveillance-under-patriot-act.

126. "21st Century Policing: The Rise and Reach of Surveillance Technology," Community Resource Hub for Safety and Accountability, https://communityresourcehub.org/resources/21st-century-policing-surveillance-technology/.

127. Ibid.

128. Sarah Brayne, *Predict and Surveil: Data, Discretion, and the Future of Policing* (New York: Oxford University Press, 2020).

129. Sarah Brayne, "Big Data Surveillance: The Case of Policing," *American Sociological Review* 82, no. 5 (2017): 977–1008; Elizabeth E. Joh, "Policing by Numbers: Big Data and the Fourth Amendment," *Washington Law Review* 89 (2014): 35.

130. Brayne, *Predict and Surveil.*

131. Jeffrey Lane, "The Digital Street: An Ethnographic Study of Networked Street Life in Harlem," *American Behavioral Scientist* 60, no. 1 (2016): 43–58.

132. Elizabeth E. Joh, "The New Surveillance Discretion: Automated Suspicion, Big Data, and Policing," *Harvard Law & Policy Review* 10 (2016): 15.

133. Joh, "Policing by Numbers," 35.

134. Josmar Trujillo and Alex S. Vitale, "Gang Takedowns in the de Blasio Era: The Dangers of 'Precision Policing,'" The Policing and Social Justice Project at Brooklyn College, 2019, https://static1.squarespace.com/static/5de981188ae1bf14a94410f5/t/5df14904887d561d6cc9455e/1576093963895/2019+New+York+City+Gang+Policing+Report+-+FINAL%29.pdf.

135. Forrest Stuart, *Ballad of the Bullet: Gangs, Drill Music, and the Power of Online Infamy* (Princeton, NJ: Princeton University Press, 2020).

136. Marion Orr, *Black Social Capital: The Politics of School Reform in Baltimore, 1986–1999* (Lawrence: University Press of Kansas, 2000).

137. Philip Bump, "Over the Past 60 Years, More Spending on Police Hasn't Necessarily Meant Less Crime," *Washington Post*, June 7, 2020, https://www.washingtonpost.com/politics/2020/06/07/over-past-60-years-more-spending-police-hasnt-necessarily-meant-less-crime/#.

138. Amanda Geller et al., "Aggressive Policing and the Mental Health of Young Urban Men," *American Journal of Public Health* 104, no. 12 (2014): 2321–27; Christopher M. Sullivan and Zachary P. O'Keeffe, "Evidence That Curtailing Proactive Policing Can Reduce Major Crime," *Nature Human Behaviour* 1, no. 10 (October 2017): 730–37; Joscha Legewie and

Jeffrey Fagan, "Aggressive Policing and the Educational Performance of Minority Youth," *American Sociological Review* 84, no. 2 (2019): 220–47.

139. "Government Current Expenditures: State and Local: Public Order and Safety: Police," Federal Reserve Bank of St. Louis, https://fred.stlouisfed.org/series/G160851A027NBEA.

140. Mary Harris, "Why the Coronavirus Is Hitting Black Americans Hardest," Slate, April 8, 2020, https://slate.com/technology/2020/04/coronavirus-covid19-black-americans-im pact.html; Shruti Magesh et al., "Disparities in COVID-19 Outcomes by Race, Ethnicity, and Socioeconomic Status: a Systematic Review and Meta-Analysis," JAMA network open 4, no. 11 (2021): e2134147-e2134147.

141. Joshua Kaplan and Benjamin Hardy, "Early Data Shows Black People Are Being Dispro-portionally Arrested for Social Distancing Violations," ProPublica, May 8, 2020, https:// www.propublica.org/article/in-some-of-ohios-most-populous-areas-black-people-were-at -least-4-times-as-likely-to-be-charged-with-stay-at-home-violations-as-whites.

142. Kurtis Lee, "No Running Water. No Electricity. On Navajo Nation, Coronavirus Cre-ates Worry and Confusion as Cases Surge," *Los Angeles Times*, March 29, 2020, https: //www.latimes.com/world-nation/story/2020-03-29/no-running-water-no-electricity -in-navajo-nation-coronavirus-creates-worry-and-confusion-as-cases-surge.

143. Alice Speri, "NYPD's Aggressive Policing Risks Spreading the Coronavirus," The Inter-cept, April 3, 2020, https://theintercept.com/2020/04/03/nypd-social-distancing-arrests -coronavirus/.

144. Chas Danner, "Philly Police Drag Man from Bus for Not Wearing a Face Mask," *New York*, April 10, 2020, https://nymag.com/intelligencer/2020/04/philly-police-drag-man -from-bus-for-not-wearing-a-face-mask.html.

145. Johnny Diaz, "Police Handcuff Black Doctor Who Tests Homeless for Coronavirus," *New York Times*, April 14, 2020, https://www.nytimes.com/2020/04/14/us/armen-henderson -arrested-homeless-coronavirus-testing.html.

146. P. R. Lockhart, "Why Police Violence Needs to Be Treated as a Public Health Issue," Vox, August 14, 2019, https://www.vox.com/identities/2019/8/14/20803872/police-violence -mortality-public-health-black-men-rutgers.

147. Kristian Williams, *Our Enemies in Blue: Police and Power in America* (Chico, CA: AK Press, 2015).

148. "Addressing Law Enforcement Violence as a Public Health Issue," American Public Health Association, November 13, 2018, https://www.apha.org/policies-and-advocacy /public-health-policy-statements/policy-database/2019/01/29/law-enforcement -violence.

149. Nicholas Rondinone, "Dozens Gather for Virtual Rally Calling for Justice for Jose Soto, Killed by SWAT Police Officers in Manchester," *Hartford Courant*, April 22, 2020, https://www.courant.com/2020/04/22/dozens-gather-for-virtual-rally-calling-for-just ice-for-jose-soto-killed-by-swat-police-officers-in-manchester/.

150. Edde Glaude, "Those Who Survive This Pandemic Will Have to Learn to Live with Grief," *Washington Post*, April 6, 2020, https://www.washingtonpost.com/opinions/2020 /04/06/pandemic-will-pass-our-grief-will-endure/.

151. Max Fisher and Emma Bubola, "As Coronavirus Deepens Inequality, Inequality Wors-ens Its Spread," *New York Times*, March 15, 2020, https://www.nytimes.com/2020/03/15 /world/europe/coronavirus-inequality.html.

152. Robyn Maynard and Andrea J. Ritchie, "Black Communities Need Support, Not a Coronavirus Police State," Vice, April 9, 2020, https://www.vice.com/en/article/z3bdmx /black-people-coronavirus-police-state.

153. Deborah Barfield Berry, "Black People Dying from Coronavirus at Much Higher Rates in Cities across the USA," *USA Today*, April 7, 2020, https://www.usatoday .com/story/news/nation/2020/04/07/who-dying-coronavirus-more-black-people -die-major-cities/2961323001/.

154. Jim Zarroli and Avie Schneider, "Deluge Continues: 26 Million Jobs Lost In Just 5 Weeks," NPR, April 23, 2020, https://www.npr.org/sections/coronavirus -live-updates/2020/04/23/841876464/26-million-jobs-lost-in-just-5-weeks.

155. Jamiles Lartey, "How Is the Justice System Responding to the Coronavirus? It Depends on Where You Live," The Marshall Project, March 28, 2020, https://www.themarshallproject .org/2020/03/28/how-is-the-justice-system-responding-to-the-coronavirus-it-depends -on-where-you-live.

156. Ruth Wilson Gilmore, *Golden Gulag: Prisons, Surplus, Crisis, and Opposition in Globalizing California* (Berkeley and Los Angeles: University of California Press, 2007).

157. Dean Spade, *Mutual Aid: Building Solidarity during This Crisis (and the Next)* (London: Verso Books, 2020).

INTERLUDE II

1. Star-Ledger Staff, "Killed in Apparent Drug-Related Shooting, Yale Alumnus Remembered for Leadership," NJ.com, May 24, 2001, https://www.nj.com/news/2011/05 /killed_in_apparent_drug-relate.html.

2. "Oregon's Measure 110: What Really Happened," Drug Policy Alliance, February 28, 2024, accessed April 24, 2024, https://drugpolicy.org/resource/oregons-measure-110 -what-really-happened/#.

CHAPTER 3

1. James Baldwin, *No Name in the Street* (New York: Vintage Books, 2007), 160.

2. "The J. Cole Episode," *Combat Jack Show*, YouTube, April 20, 2018, https://www.youtube .com/watch?v=2JrUxTy2Vh8.

3. S. N. Tapp and E. J. Davis, "Contacts between Police and the Public, 2020," 2020, https:// bjs.ojp.gov/sites/g/files/xyckuh236/files/media/document/cbpp20.pdf.

4. "The Stanford Open Policing Project," Stanford University, accessed August 16, 2023, https://openpolicing.stanford.edu/.

5. Susannah N. Tapp and Elizabeth J. Davis, "Contacts Between Police and the Public, 2020," Bureau of Justice Statistics, Office of Justice Programs, U.S. Department of Justice, November 2022, https://bjs.ojp.gov/sites/g/files/xyckuh236/files/media/document /cbpp20.pdf.

6. Mapping Police Violence, accessed March 11, 2024, https://mappingpoliceviolence.org.

7. Bocar A. Ba, Roman Rivera, and Alexander Whitefield. *Market Response to Racial Uprisings*. No. w31606. National Bureau of Economic Research, 2023.

8. Connor Brooks, "Federal Law Enforcement Officers, 2020—Statistical Tables," Bureau of Justice Statistics, Office of Justice Programs, U.S. Department of Justice, September 2022, rev. September 29, 2023, https://www.ojp.gov/library/publications/federal -law-enforcement-officers-2020-statistical-tables.

9. Andrea M. Gardner and Kevin M. Scott, "Census of State and Local Law Enforcement Agencies, 2018—Statistical Tables," Bureau of Justice Statistics, Office of Justice Programs, U.S. Department of Justice, October 2022, https://bjs.ojp.gov/sites/g/files /xyckuh236/files/media/document/csllea18st.pdf.

10. "Defund Sheriffs: A Toolkit for Organizers," Defund Sheriffs, https://drive.google.com/uc?export=download&id=1M0DMClac610DELo1E_LY5Eb-sGkAm9j5.

11. Mireya Navarro and Joseph Goldstein, "Policing the Projects of New York City, at a Hefty Price," *New York Times*, December 27, 2013, https://www.nytimes.com/2013/12/27/nyregion/policing-the-projects-of-new-york-city-at-a-hefty-price.html.

12. Jeff Asher and Ben Horwitz, "How Do the Police Actually Spend Their Time?," *New York Times*, June 19, 2020, https://www.nytimes.com/2020/06/19/upshot/unrest-police-time-violent-crime.html.

13. E. Pierson et al., "A Large-Scale Analysis of Racial Disparities in Police Stops across the United States," *Nature Human Behaviour*, Vol. 4, 2020.

14. Tapp and Davis, "Contacts between Police and the Public, 2020," https:// bjs.ojp.gov/sites/g/files/xyckuh236/files/media/document/cbpp20.pdf.

15. "Native Lives Matter: The Overlooked Police Brutality against Native Americans," Lakota People's Law Project, November 21, 2017, https://lakotalaw.org/news/2017-11-21/native-lives-matter-the-overlooked-police-brutality-against-native-americans.

16. Alyasah Ali Sewell et al., "Illness Spillovers of Lethal Police Violence: The Significance of Gendered Marginalization," *Ethnic and Racial Studies* 44, no. 7 (2021): 1089–114.

17. Alyasah Ali Sewell, Kevin A. Jefferson, and Hedwig Lee, "Living under Surveillance: Gender, Psychological Distress, and Stop-Question-and-Frisk Policing in New York City," *Social Science & Medicine* 159, no. 4 (2016): 1–13.

18. Doris A. Fuller et al., "Overlooked in the Undercounted: The Role of Mental Illness in Fatal Law Enforcement Encounters," Treatment Advocacy Center, December 2015, https://www.treatmentadvocacycenter.org/storage/documents/overlooked-in-the-undercounted.pdf.

19. Joscha Legewie and Jeffrey Fagan, "Aggressive Policing and the Educational Performance of Minority Youth," *American Sociological Review* 84, no. 2 (2019): 220–47.

20. Monique W. Morris, *Pushout: The Criminalization of Black Girls in Schools* (New York: New Press, 2016).

21. Sarah Brayne, "Surveillance and System Avoidance: Criminal Justice Contact and Institutional Attachment," *American Sociological Review* 79, no. 3 (2014): 367–91.

22. Philip V. McHarris, "The Spillover Effects of Police Violence," *Social Psychological Review*, Autumn 2020, 22, no. 2: 11–14.

23. James Forman Jr., *Locking Up Our Own: Crime and Punishment in Black America* (New York: Farrar, Straus and Giroux, 2017).

24. *Whren v. United States*, 517 U.S. 806 (1996).

25. "Pretextual Police Stops Are Unreasonable and Drive Racial Profiling," ACLU Massachusetts, September 26, 2017, https://www.aclum.org/en/press-releases/pretextual-police-stops-are-unreasonable-and-drive-racial-profiling.

26. Joseph Goldstein, "Officers Said They Smelled Pot. The Judge Called Them Liars," *New York Times*, September 12, 2019, https://www.nytimes.com/2019/09/12/nyregion/police-searches-smelling-marijuana.html.

27. Wendi C. Thomas, "There Is Reason for Black Women to Fear Traffic Stops," Andscape, August 23, 2016, https://andscape.com/features/there-is-reason-for-black-women-to-fear-traffic-stops/.

28. Daniel L. Rotenberg, "An Essay on Consent(less) Police Searches," *Washington University Law Quarterly* 69, no. 1 (1991): 176–91.

29. Julie Dressner and Edwin Martinez, "The Scars of Stop-and-Frisk" (video), *New York Times*, June 13, 2012, https://www.nytimes.com/video/opinion/100000001601732/the-scars-of-stop-and-frisk.html.

30. Matthew Segal, "Beyond #BlackLivesMatter: Police Reform Must Be Bolstered by Legal Action," *Guardian*, July 27, 2016, https://www.theguardian.com/commentisfree/2016 /jul/27/beyond-black-lives-matter-police-reform-legal-action.

31. "*Floyd, et al. v. City of New York, et al.*," Center for Constitutional Rights, accessed August 18, 2023, https://ccrjustice.org/node/1765.

32. Jason Hanna, "Judge Rules NYC's Stop-and-Frisk Policy Unconstitutional; City Vows Appeal," CNN, August 12, 2013, https://www.cnn.com/2013/08/12/justice/new-york -stop-frisk/index.html.

33. Corey Kilgannon, "N.Y.P.D. Anti-Crime Units Still Stopping People Illegally, Report Shows," *The New York* Times, June 5, 2023, sec. New York, https://www.nytimes.com/2023 /06/05/nyregion/nypd-anti-crime-units-training-tactics.html.

34. Ibid.

35. "Some States Move to Curb 'Pretext' Traffic Stops," The Crime Report, September 4, 2020, https://thecrimereport.org/2020/09/04/some-states-move-to-curb-pretext-traffic-stops/.

36. Ned Oliver, "Virginia Lawmakers Pass Bill Limiting Pretextual Traffic Stops, Barring Searches Based on Smell of Marijuana," *Virginia Mercury*, October 2, 2020, https://www .virginiamercury.com/2020/10/02/virginia-lawmakers-pass-bill-banning-pretextual-traffic -stops-and-searches-based-on-the-smell-of-marijuana/.

37. Ray Gronberg, "Durham Adopts Written-Consent Policy for Searches," Southern Coalition for Social Justice, September 16, 2014, https://southerncoalition.org/durham-adopts -written-consent-policy-for-searches/.

38. Radley Balko, "How Municipalities in St. Louis County, Mo., Profit from Poverty," *Washington Post*, October 26, 2021, https://www.washingtonpost.com/news/the-watch/wp/2014 /09/03/how-st-louis-county-missouri-profits-from-poverty/.

39. Anthony A. Braga, David Weisburd, and Brandon Turchan, "Focused Deterrence Strategies and Crime Control," *Criminology & Public Policy* 17, no. 1 (2018): 205–50.

40. Christopher M. Sullivan and Zachary P. O'Keeffe, "Evidence That Curtailing Proactive Policing Can Reduce Major Crime," *Nature Human Behaviour* 1, no. 10 (2017): 730–37.

41. Jon Seidel, "New Lawsuit Aims to Halt Chicago's Use of ShotSpotter," *Chicago Sun-Times*, July 21, 2022, https://chicago.suntimes.com/news/2022/7/21/23273332/shotspotter-lawsuit -chicago-police-toledo-shooting-michael-williams-arrest-charges-dropped.

42. Khalil Gibran Muhammad, *The Condemnation of Blackness: Race, Crime, and the Making of Modern Urban America* (Cambridge, MA: Harvard University Press, 2019); Rashad Shabazz, *Spatializing Blackness: Architectures of Confinement and Black Masculinity in Chicago* (Champaign: University of Illinois Press, 2015).

43. Elijah Anderson, *Code of the Street: Decency, Violence, and the Moral Life of the Inner City* (New York: W.W. Norton & Company, Inc.).

44. Ethan Brown, *Snitch: Informants, Cooperators, and the Corruption of Justice*, (Philadelphia, PA: Public Affairs Press) 2007.

45. Braga, Weisburd, and Turchan, "Focused Deterrence Strategies and Crime Control."

46. Braga, Weisburd, and Turchan, "Focused Deterrence Strategies and Crime Control."

47. Marie Skubak Tillyer, Robin S. Engel, and Brian Lovins, "Beyond Boston: Applying Theory to Understand and Address Sustainability Issues in Focused Deterrence Initiatives for Violence Reduction," *Crime & Delinquency* 58, no. 6 (2012): 973–97.

48. Robin S. Engel, Marie Skubak Tillyer, and Nicholas Corsaro, "Reducing Gang Violence Using Focused Deterrence: Evaluating the Cincinnati Initiative to Reduce Violence (CIRV)," *Justice Quarterly* 30, no. 3 (2013): 403–39.

49. Braga, Weisburd, and Turchan, "Focused Deterrence Strategies and Crime Control."

50. Ibid.

51. David DeBolt, "2021 Is Oakland's Deadliest Year since 2006," The Oaklandside, December 23, 2021, https://oaklandside.org/2021/12/23/2021-oakland-deadliest-year-since-2006 -homicides-shootings-gun-violence/.

52. Ibid.

53. Samantha Michaels, "Whose Streets?," *Mother Jones*, September–October 2020, https: //www.motherjones.com/crime-justice/2020/07/oakland-ceasefire-shootings-murder -rate-social-services-life-coach-boston-miracle-thomas-abt-david-kennedy-cat-brooks/.

54. Tillyer, Engel, and Lovins, "Beyond Boston."

55. Anthony A. Braga, David M. Hureau, and Andrew V. Papachristos, "Deterring Gang-Involved Gun Violence: Measuring the Impact of Boston's Operation Ceasefire on Street Gang Behavior," *Journal of Quantitative Criminology* 30, no. 1 (March 1, 2014): 113–39; Anthony A. Braga et al., "Problem-Oriented Policing, Deterrence, and Youth Violence: An Evaluation of Boston's Operation Ceasefire," *Journal of Research in Crime and Delinquency* 38, no. 3 (2001): 195–225.

56. Nikki Jones, *The Chosen Ones: Black Men and the Politics of Redemption* (Oakland: University of California Press, 2018).

57. The House of Umoja, accessed August 5, 2023, https://www.houseofumoja.net/.

58. "From West Africa to West Philadelphia," The House of Umoja, accessed August 5, 2023, https://www.houseofumoja.net/aboutus.html.

59. Vesla M. Weaver, "The Missed Opportunity of Robert Woodson," The Marshall Project, February 25, 2015, https://www.themarshallproject.org/2015/02/25/the-missed-opportunity-of -robert-woodson. See also *Restructuring the Law Enforcement Assistance Administration: Hearings before the Subcommittee on Crime of the Committee on the Judiciary*, House of Representatives, 89th Congress, 1–2 (1978), https://catalog.hathitrust.org/Record/011341579.

60. Weaver, "The Missed Opportunity of Robert Woodson."

61. Baynard Woods and Brandon Soderberg, "Credible Messengers: Baltimore's Violence Interrupters Confront Shootings, the Coronavirus, and Corrupt Cops," The Intercept, July 26, 2020, https://theintercept.com/2020/07/26/baltimore-safe-streets-public-health -gun-violence-police/.

62. John Schuppe, "Newark, N.J., Wants to Be a Model for Police Reform. But Black People Are Still Stopped More Often," NBC News, July 18, 2020, https://www.nbcnews.com /news/us-news/newark-n-j-wants-be-model-police-reform-black-people-n1234190.

63. Stuart Schrader, *Badges without Borders: How Global Counterinsurgency Transformed American Policing* (Oakland: University of California Press, 2019).

64. Mapping Police Violence, accessed March 11, 2024, https://mappingpoliceviolence.org.

65. Amelia Thomson-DeVeaux, Nathaniel Rakich, and Likhitha Butchireddygari, "Why It's So Rare for Police Officers to Face Legal Consequences," FiveThirtyEight, June 4, 2020, https://fivethirtyeight.com/features/why-its-still-so-rare-for-police-officers-to-face-legal -consequences-for-misconduct/.

66. Joanna Schwartz, *Shielded: How the Police Became Untouchable* (New York: Viking, 2023).

67. *Pierson v. Ray*, 386 U.S. 547 (1967).

68. "Qualified Immunity," Legal Information Institute, Cornell Law School, accessed August 16, 2023, https://www.law.cornell.edu/wex/qualified_immunity.

69. Joanna C. Schwartz, "How Qualified Immunity Fails," *Yale Law Journal* 127, no. 1 (2017–2018): 1–245.

70. Ibid.

71. Margaret Carlson, "Supreme Court: No Lives Matter If a Cop Feels Threatened," The Daily Beast, April 5, 2018, https://www.thedailybeast.com/supreme-court-no-lives-matter-if-a-cop-feels-threatened.

72. Mapping Police Violence, accessed November 20, 2023, https://mappingpoliceviolence.org/.

73. Melissa Chan, "A Cop Shot and Killed Their Mom, and These Men Want to Know Why He Still Hasn't Faced Trial," Time, July 18, 2019, https://time.com/5628206/police-shooting-trial-knowlton-garner/.

74. Osagie K. Obasogie and Anna Zaret, "Plainly Incompetent: How Qualified Immunity Became an Exculpatory Doctrine of Police Excessive Force," University of Pennsylvania Law Review 170, no. 2 (2022): 407–85.

75. J. Justin Wilson, "Police Stole $225k in Cash and Coins, and the Courts Said 'Okay,'" Institute for Justice, March 18, 2020, https://ij.org/press-release/police-stole-225k-in-cash-and-coins-and-the-courts-said-okay/.

76. Tim Cushing, "Appeals Court Says No Rights Were Violated When a Cop Shot at a 'Non-Threatening' Dog but Hit a Kid Instead," Techdirt, July 24, 2019, https://www.techdirt.com/2019/07/24/appeals-court-says-no-rights-were-violated-when-cop-shot-non-threatening-dog-hit-kid-instead/.

77. John Kramer, "George Floyd and Beyond: How 'Qualified Immunity' Enables Bad Policing," Institute for Justice, February 14, 2020, https://ij.org/press-release/beyond-george-floyd-how-qualified-immunity-enables-bad-policing/.

78. Kimbriell Kelly, Wesley Lowery, and Steven Rich, "Fired/Rehired: Police Chiefs Are Often Forced to Put Officers Fired for Misconduct Back on the Streets," Washington Post, August 3, 2017, https://www.washingtonpost.com/graphics/2017/investigations/police-fired-rehired/.

79. Jennifer Smith Richards, Geoffrey Hing, and Jason Meisner, "Over 125K Complaints against More than 25K Chicago Cops," Chicago Tribune, October 14, 2016, https://www.chicagotribune.com/investigations/ct-chicago-police-complaints-met-20161013-story.html.

80. Shane Shifflett et al., "Police Abuse Complaints by Black Chicagoans Dismissed Nearly 99 Percent of the Time," Huffington Post, December 7, 2015, https://data.huffingtonpost.com/2015/12/chicago-officer-misconduct-allegations.

81. Ibid.

82. John Kelly and Mark Nichols, "We Found 85,000 Cops Who've Been Investigated for Misconduct. Now You Can Read Their Records," USA Today, April 24, 2019, https://www.usatoday.com/in-depth/news/investigations/2019/04/24/usa-today-revealing-misconduct-records-police-cops/3223984002/.

83. Mara H. Gottfried and Sarah Horner, "How Often Do Arbitrators Reinstate Fired Cops? Just under Half the Time," Twin Cities, June 23, 2019, https://www.twincities.com/2019/06/23/how-often-do-arbitrators-reinstate-fired-cops-just-under-half-the-time/.

84. Astead W. Herndon, "How a Pledge to Dismantle the Minneapolis Police Collapsed," New York Times, September 26, 2020, https://www.nytimes.com/2020/09/26/us/politics/minneapolis-defund-police.html.

85. D. Packman (2010), The Cato Institute's National Police Misconduct Reporting Project. Retrieved from https://www.leg.state.nv.us/Session/77th2013/Exhibits/Assembly/JUD/AJUD338L.pdf; Andrea J. Ritchie, Invisible No More: Police Violence against Black Women and Women of Color (Boston: Beacon Press, 2017); Andrea J. Ritchie 2021, "Shrouded in Silence, Police Sexual Violence: What We Know & What We Can Do About It," New York City, https://www. interruptingcriminalization.com/publications.

86. Alex Roslin, Police Wife: The Secret Epidemic of Police Domestic Violence, 2nd ed. (Knowlton, QC: Sugar Hill Books, 2017); L. B. Johnson, On the Front Lines: Police Stress and

Family Well-Being. Hearing before the Select Committee on Children, Youth, and Families, House of Representatives, 102nd Congress, 1st Session, May 20, 1991 (Washington, DC: US Government Printing Office), 3248; Peter H. Neidig, Harold E. Russell, and Albert F. Seng, "Interspousal Aggression in Law Enforcement Families: A Preliminary Investigation," *Police Studies* 15, no. 1 (1992): 30–38; "Police Family Violence Fact Sheet," National Center for Women & Policing, https://olis.oregonlegislature.gov/liz/2017R1/Downloads/CommitteeMeetingDocument/132808.

87. John Feltgen, "Domestic Violence: When the Abuser Is a Police Officer," *Police Chief* 63 (1996): 42–47; Conor Friedersdorf, "Police Have a Much Bigger Domestic-Abuse Problem than the NFL Does," *Atlantic*, September 19, 2014, https://www.theatlantic.com/national/archive/2014/09/police-officers-who-hit-their-wives-or-girlfriends/380329/.

88. "Reducing Jail and Prison Population," Vera Institute of Justice, accessed March 11, 2024, https://www.vera.org/ending-mass-incarceration/reducing-incarceration/reducing-jail-and-prison-population#:~:text=In%20fact%2C%20if%20incarceration%20could,11%20million%20times%20each%20year.

89. Alex S. Vitale, *The End of Policing* (London: Verso Books, 2021).

90. Ryan W. Miller, "Shake-up at Atlanta Police Department Latest in Law Enforcement Firings Following Protests," *USA Today*, June 8, 2020, https://www.usatoday.com/story/news/nation/2020/06/08/george-floyd-protests-have-sparked-some-police-firings-charges/5318019002/.

91. Antonio Gramsci, *Prison Notebooks*, vol. 2 (New York: Columbia University Press, 2011).

92. Stuart Hall et al., *Policing the Crisis: Mugging, the State and Law and Order* (London: Bloomsbury Publishing, 2017).

93. Keeanga-Yamahtta Taylor, *From #BlackLivesMatter to Black Liberation* (Chicago: Haymarket Books, 2016).

94. Forrest Stuart, *Down, Out, and Under Arrest: Policing and Everyday Life in Skid Row* (Chicago: University of Chicago Press, 2016), 15.

95. projectlets, "There's a way out of the cycle. It's called abolition. 🔥 ID: a black circle with several points—brutality and murder, outrage/protest, police reform, police budgets increase to pay for reforms. there is a green arrow pointing outside of the circle that says 'abolition' #BlackLivesMatter #BlackDisabledLivesMatter #BurnItDown #AbolishThe Police," Instagram, August 27, 2020, https://www.instagram.com/p/CEZXbcKDzgQ/.

96. Philip V. McHarris and Thenjiwe McHarris, "No More Money for the Police," *New York Times*, May 30, 2020, https://www.nytimes.com/2020/05/30/opinion/george-floyd-police-funding.html.

97. Kimberlé W. Crenshaw et al., "Say Her Name: Resisting Police Brutality Against Black Women," Columbia Law School, 2015, https://scholarship.law.columbia.edu/faculty_scholarship/3226.

98. Andrea J. Ritchie, *Invisible No More: Police Violence against Black Women and Women of Color* (Boston: Beacon Press, 2017).

99. Jay Dow, "Newark to Slash Police Budget, Ban Racism on the Job for City Employees," WPIX, June 10, 2020, https://pix11.com/news/local-news/new-jersey/newark-to-slash-police-budget-ban-racism-on-the-job-for-city-employees/.

100. https://www.economist.com/by-invitation/2020/07/06/ras-baraka-on-reforms-to-bring-communities-and-police-closer-together.

101. S. P. Sullivan, "How Should N.J. Reform Police? Lawmakers Eye Host of Changes amid Protests over Killings," NJ.com, July 21, 2020, https://www.nj.com/politics/2020/07/how-should-nj-reform-police-lawmakers-eye-host-of-changes-amid-protests-over-killings.html.

102. https://www.nytimes.com/2020/08/10/nyregion/defund-police-nyc-council.html.

103. https://www.cbsnews.com/newyork/news/newark-community-street-team-newark
-police-crime/; Ras Baraka, "Newark's Mayor: Non-Law Enforcement People Helped
Us Reduce Crime | Opinion." Nj, April 4, 2023, sec. Opinion, https://www.nj.com
/opinion/2023/04/newarks-mayor-our-ecosystem-of-non-law-enforcement-people
-helped-us-reduce-crime-opinion.html.; City of Newark. "Mayor Baraka Hosts National
League Of Cities To Address Ways To Reinvent Public Safety," accessed March 8, 2024,
https://www.newarknj.gov/news/mayor-baraka-hosts-national-league-of-cities-to-address
-ways-to-reinvent-public-safety.

104. The White House, "Fact Sheet: President Biden Issues Call for State and Local Leaders to
Dedicate More American Rescue Plan Funding to Make Our Communities Safer—And
Deploy These Dollars Quickly," The White House, May 13, 2022, https://www.white
house.gov/briefing-room/statements-releases/2022/05/13/fact-sheet-president-biden
-issues-call-for-state-and-local-leaders-to-dedicate-more-american-rescue-plan-fund
ing-to-make-our-communities-safer-and-deploy-these-dollars-quickly/.

105. Anastasia Valeeva, Weihua Li, and Susie Cagle, "Rifles, Tasers, and Jails: How Cities and States Spent Billions of COVID-19 Relief," The Marshall Project, September 7,
2022, https://www.themarshallproject.org/2022/09/07/how-federal-covid-relief-flows-to
-the-criminal-justice-system.

106. Jessica Hatrick and Olivia González, "Watchmen, Copaganda, and Abolition Futurities
in US Television," Lateral11, no. 2 (2022).

107. M. Kaba and A. J. Ritchie, No More Police: A Case for Abolition (New York: The New
Press, 2022).

108. Brendan McQuade, "The Camden Police Department Is Not a Model for Policing in
the Post–George Floyd Era," The Appeal, June 12, 2020, https://theappeal.org/camden
-police-george-floyd/.

109. James Baldwin, "The View from Here," speech, National Press Club, December 10, 1986.
James Baldwin, National Press Club Luncheon Speakers: James Baldwin (Recorded
Sound Research Center, Library of Congress), 1986, https://www.loc.gov/rr/record
/pressclub/baldwin.html.

110. Carl L. Hart, Drug Use for Grown-ups: Chasing Liberty in the Land of Fear (London: Pen-
guin, 2022).

111. Naomi Murakawa, "Toothless: The Methamphetamine 'Epidemic,' 'Meth Mouth,' and
the Racial Construction of Drug Scares," Du Bois Review: Social Science Research on Race
8, no. 1 (2011): 219–28.

112. Dan Werb et al., "Effect of Drug Law Enforcement on Drug Market Violence: A Systematic Review," International Journal of Drug Policy 22, no. 2 (2011): 87–94.

113. Audrey McGlinchy, "Abbott Signs into Law Bill Penalizing Texas Cities That Cut Police
Funding," KUT 90.5, May 28, 2021, https://www.kut.org/crime-justice/2021-05-28
/bill-penalizing-texas-cities-that-cut-funding-for-police-heads-to-governors-desk.

114. Richard Rosenfeld, "Crime Is Up. But It's Not Because People Are Criticizing the Police,"
Washington Post, September 13, 2020, https://www.washingtonpost.com/outlook/2020/09
/14/crime-increase-pandemic-protests/.

115. Ibid.

116. Christopher Briot. "Obama Criticizes Defund the Police Messaging: 'You Lost a Big
Audience the Minute You Say It'—CBS News," December 2, 2020, https://www.cbsnews
.com/news/obama-defund-the-police-slogan/.

117. David Wilson, Inventing Black-on-Black Violence: Discourse, Space, and Representation
(Syracuse, NY: Syracuse University Press, 2005).

118. James Baldwin, No Name in the Street (New York: Vintage Books, 2007), 158–59.

119. D. R. Lynam et al., "Project DARE: No Effects at 10-Year Follow-Up." *Journal of Consulting and Clinical Psychology* 67, no. 4 (1999): 590–93.

120. Rosalind S. Chou and Joe R. Feagin, *Myth of the Model Minority: Asian Americans Facing Racism* (New York: Routledge, 2015).

121. President's Task Force on 21st Century Policing, *Final Report of the President's Task Force on 21st Century Policing* (Washington, DC: Office of Community Oriented Policing Services, 2015), https://cops.usdoj.gov/pdf/taskforce/taskforce_finalreport.pdf.

122. K.C. Basile et al., (2022), The National Intimate Partner and Sexual Violence Survey: 2016/2017 Report on Sexual Violence (Atlanta, GA: National Center for Injury Prevention and Control, Centers for Disease Control and Prevention).

123. R.W. Leemis et al., (2022), The National Intimate Partner and Sexual Violence Survey: 2016/2017 Report on Intimate Partner Violence (Atlanta, GA: National Center for Injury Prevention and Control, Centers for Disease Control and Prevention).

124. Angela Y. Davis et al., *Abolition. Feminism. Now.*, vol. 2 (Chicago: Haymarket Books, 2022).

125. Janet L. Lauritsen and Karen Heimer, "Gender Gap in Violent Victimization, 1973–2004," *Journal of Quantitative Criminology* 24, no. 2 (2008): 125–47.

126. Ramona R. Rantala, "Sexual Victimization Reported by Adult Correctional Authorities, 2012–15," Bureau of Justice Statistics, Office of Justice Programs, U.S. Department of Justice, July 2018, https://bjs.ojp.gov/content/pub/pdf/svraca1215.pdf.

127. Todd R. Clear, *Imprisoning Communities: How Mass Incarceration Makes Disadvantaged Neighborhoods Worse* (New York: Oxford University Press, 2019).

128. Critical Resistance and Incite!, "Critical resistance-incite! statement on gender violence and the prison-industrial complex," *Social Justice* (2003), 141–150.

129. Oakland Power Projects, accessed August 28, 2023, https://oaklandpowerprojects.org.

130. Ashley Southall, "Police Face Backlash over Virus Rules. Enter 'Violence Interrupters,'" *New York Times*, May 22, 2020, https://www.nytimes.com/2020/05/22/nyregion/Coronavirus-social-distancing-violence-interrupters.html.

131. Bay Area Transformative Justice Collective, https://batjc.wordpress.com/.

132. "Evaluation of Baltimore's Safe Streets Program," Robert Wood Johnson Foundation, January 11, 2012, https://publichealth.jhu.edu/sites/default/files/2023-10/estimating-the-effects-of-safe-streets-baltimore-on-gun-violence-july-2023.pdf.

133. Patrick Sharkey, Gerard Torrats-Espinosa, and Delaram Takyar, "Community and the Crime Decline: The Causal Effect of Local Nonprofits on Violent Crime," *American Sociological Review* 82, no. 6 (2017): 1214–40.

134. Sara B. Heller, "Summer Jobs Reduce Violence among Disadvantaged Youth," *Science* 346, no. 6214 (2014): 1219–23.

135. Sara B. Heller et al., "Thinking, Fast and Slow? Some Field Experiments to Reduce Crime and Dropout in Chicago," *Quarterly Journal of Economics* 132, no. 1 (2017): 1–54.

136. Charles C. Branas et al., "A Difference-in-Differences Analysis of Health, Safety, and Greening Vacant Urban Space," *American Journal of Epidemiology* 174, no. 11 (2011): 1296–306.

137. Julianne Cuba, "Campaign to Remove NYPD from Traffic Enforcement Gains Steam," Streetsblog NYC, June 25, 2020, https://nyc.streetsblog.org/2020/06/25/campaign-to-remove-nypd-from-traffic-enforcement-gains-steam#.

138. #8toAbolition, accessed July 24, 2023, https://www.8toabolition.com.

139. Cherrell Brown and Philip V. McHarris, "#8cantwait Is Based on Faulty Data Science," Medium, June 14, 2020, https://medium.com/@8cantwait.faulty/8cantwait-is-based-on-faulty-data-science-a4e0b85fae40.

140. TransformHarm.org, accessed August 16, 2023, https://transformharm.org/.

141. "Invest-Divest," Movement for Black Lives, 2024, https://m4bl.org/policy-platforms/invest-divest/.

142. Ibid.

143. Greg Bluestein, "Kemp Unveils $69M School Safety Plan, New Gang Crackdown," *Atlanta Journal-Constitution*, January 6, 2019, https://www.ajc.com/blog/politics/kemp-unveils-school-safety-and-gang-crackdown-plans/NcBlwSjIulEv7cFNQughKK/.

144. Catherine Lizette Gonzalez, "REPORT: The Urgent Need to Dismantle School Policing in Communities of Color," Colorlines, September 13, 2018, https://colorlines.com/article/report-urgent-need-dismantle-school-policing-communities-color/.

145. "We Came to Learn: A Call to Action for Police-Free Schools," Advancement Project, https://advancementproject.org/wp-content/uploads/WCTLweb/index.html#page=1.

146. David Washburn, "Many California Schools Have Police but No Counselors, ACLU Report Finds," EdSource, March 10, 2019, https://edsource.org/2019/many-california-schools-have-police-but-no-counselors-aclu-report-finds/609643.

147. Barry Friedman, "We Spend $100 Billion on Policing. We Have No Idea What Works," *Washington Post*, October 6, 2021, https://www.washingtonpost.com/posteverything/wp/2017/03/10/we-spend-100-billion-on-policing-we-have-no-idea-what-works/.

148. The Breathe Act, https://breatheact.org/.

149. Participatory Budgeting Project, accessed August 18, 2023, https://www.participatorybudgeting.org/.

150. Thomas L. Friedman "Opinion | A Warning from the Garden." *The New York Times*, January 19, 2007, sec. Opinion, https://www.nytimes.com/2007/01/19/opinion/19friedman.html.

151. Robert D. Bullard, *Dumping in Dixie: Race, Class, and Environmental Quality*, 3rd ed. (New York: Routledge, 2000).

152. "A Brief History of the Atlanta City Prison Farm," Atlanta Community Press Collective, August 14, 2021, https://atlpresscollective.com/2021/08/14/history-of-the-atlanta-city-prison-farm/.

153. J. D. Capelouto, Anjali Huynh, and Wilborn Nobles. "17 Hours of Comments Continue to Play before Tonight's Vote on Atlanta Police Training Center." *The Atlanta Journal-Constitution*, September 8, 2021, https://www.ajc.com/news/atlanta-news/17-hours-of-public-comment-pour-in-ahead-of-police-training-center-vote/RDE6OHCQRRCZXPQFHFS776CX2I/.

154. Aja Arnold, "Why Atlantans Are Pushing to Stop 'Cop City,'" The Appeal, December 8, 2021, https://theappeal.org/atlanta-cop-city-police-training-facility/.

155. Joyce Sohyun Lee and Sarah Cahlan, "Atlanta Police Release Body-Camera Video from Raid after Fatal Shooting of Activist," *Washington Post*, March 7, 2023, https://www.washingtonpost.com/nation/2023/02/09/atlanta-police-body-cam-footage-shooting/.

156. "Autopsy Report Says 'Cop City' Protester Had Hands Raised When Killed," *PBS NewsHour*, March 13, 2023, https://www.pbs.org/newshour/nation/autopsy-report-says-cop-city-protester-had-hands-raised-when-killed.

157. Benji Hart, "The #StopCopCity Movement Didn't Lose," In These Times, July 24, 2023, https://inthesetimes.com/article/atlanta-stop-cop-city.

158. Prem Thakker, "Atlanta Officials Unveil Onerous Verification Requirements for Cop City Referendum," The Intercept, August 21, 2023, https://theintercept.com/2023/08/21/atlanta-cop-city-referendum-signatures/.

159. Jocelyn James, "The Fate of Atlanta's Cop City Could Be in the Hands of Voters," *Teen Vogue*, August 25, 2023, https://www.teenvogue.com/story/cop-city-referendum-atlanta.

160. Benji Hart, "No Cop City Anywhere." *In These Times*, February 22, 2023, https://inthese times.com/article/cop-city-atlanta-police-violence-no-cop-academy-chicago-climate.

161. Jon Blistein. "Atlanta 'Cop City' Protesters Are Now Being Hit with RICO Charges." *Rolling Stone* (blog), September 5, 2023. https://www.rollingstone.com/politics/politics -news/cop-city-protesters-rico-act-violation-charges-georgia-1234818278/.

162. Amy, Jeff, and Kate Brumback. "Atlanta Police Arrest 3 Organizers behind Bail Fund Supporting Protests against 'Cop City.'" *PBS NewsHour*, May 31, 2023, sec. Politics. https://www.pbs.org/newshour/politics/atlanta-police-arrest-3-organizers-behind-bail -fund-supporting-protests-against-cop-city.

163. Ryan Young, Kevin Conlon, and Holly Yan. "61 'Cop City' Protesters Indicted on RICO Charges. Opponents Question the Timeline and Motivation." CNN, September 6, 2023. https://www.cnn.com/2023/09/06/us/cop-city-protesters-indicted-rico/index.html.

164. Frederick Douglass, *Two Speeches by Frederick Douglass* (Rochester, NY: C. P. Dewey, 1857), 22.

INTERLUDE III

1. Emma Whitford, "With Crime at Record Lows, Should NYC Have Fewer Cops?," Gothamist, November 5, 2019, https://gothamist.com/news/crime-record-lows-should -nyc-have-fewer-cops.

2. National Initiative for Building Community Trust and Justice, accessed August 18, 2023, https://trustandjustice.org.

3. Mapping Police Violence, accessed September 30, 2020, https://mappingpoliceviolence .org.

4. John L. Worrall and Jihong Zhao, "The Role of the COPS Office in Community Polic- ing," *Policing: An International Journal of Police Strategies & Management* 26, no. 1 (2003): 64–87.

5. Brittany N. Fox-Williams, "The Rules of (Dis)engagement: Black Youth and Their Strate- gies for Navigating Police Contact," *Sociological Forum* 34, no. 1 (2019): 115–37.

6. "Neighborhood Policing," New York Police Department, May 3, 2021, https://www.nyc .gov/site/nypd/bureaus/patrol/neighborhood-coordination-officers.page.

7. Harold Stolper, "When the Police Ignore the Law: Racialized Policing at Turnstile," Community Service Society, October 22, 2018, https://www.cssny.org/news/entry /when-the-police-ignore-the-law.

8. Christopher M. Sullivan and Zachary P. O'Keeffe, "Evidence That Curtailing Proactive Policing Can Reduce Major Crime," *Nature Human Behaviour* 1, no. 10 (October 2017): 730–37, https://doi.org/10.1038/s41562-017-0211-5.

9. Kings Against Violence Initiative, accessed August 18, 2023, https://kavibrooklyn.org/.

10. No Cop Academy, https://nocopacademy.com/.

11. "Black Queer Feminist Curriculum Toolkit," 2020, https://drive.google.com/file/d /1e9clSyQdl4H1KGdFRlzQuSqIZFwcWqBy/view?usp=embed_facebook.

12. LiberateMKE, accessed August 18, 2023, https://www.liberatemke.com.

13. Zaina Alsous, "'Starve the Beast': No New Cops," Scalawag, November 4, 2019, https: //scalawagmagazine.org/2019/11/close-jails-atlanta-durham-nashville/.

CHAPTER 4

1. Cara Page and Erica Woodland, *Healing Justice Lineages: Dreaming at the Crossroads of Liberation, Collective Care, and Safety* (Berkeley, CA: North Atlantic Books, 2023); Leah

Lakshmi Piepzna-Samarasinha and Ejeris Dixon, eds., *Beyond Survival: Strategies and Stories from the Transformative Justice Movement* (Chico, CA: AK Press, 2020).

2. "About DJDS," November 17, 2022, https://designingjustice.org/about/.

3. Ruth Wilson Gilmore, *Abolition Geography: Essays towards Liberation* (London: Verso Books, 2022).

4. Dominique Moran, *Carceral Geography: Spaces and Practices of Incarceration* (London: Routledge, 2016); Dominique Moran, Jennifer Turner, and Anna K. Schliehe, "Conceptualizing the Carceral in Carceral Geography," *Progress in Human Geography* 42, no. 5 (2018): 666–86.

5. Michel Foucault, "Discipline and Punish," in *Social Theory Re-wired*, ed. Wesley Longhofer and Daniel Winchester (New York: Routledge, 2023), 291–99.

6. Anne H. Berry et al., eds., *The Black Experience in Design: Identity, Expression & Reflection* (New York: Simon & Schuster, 2022); Gilmore, *Abolition Geography*.

7. Mariame Kaba, "To Live and Die in 'Chiraq,'" in *The End of Chiraq: A Literary Mixtape* 9, 10 (Javon Johnson and Kevin Coval eds., 2018).

8. Patrick Sharkey, *Uneasy Peace: The Great Crime Decline, the Renewal of City Life, and the Next War on Violence* (New York: W. W. Norton & Company, 2018).

9. Daniel W. Webster, Carla G. Tilchin, and Mitchell L. Doucette, "Estimating the Effects of Safe Streets Baltimore on Gun Violence 2007–2022," Center for Gun Violence Solutions, Johns Hopkins Bloomberg School of Public Health, March 2023, https://publichealth.jhu.edu/sites/default/files/2023-10/estimating-the-effects-of-safe-streets-baltimore-on-gun-violence-july-2023.pdf.

10. Juana Summers, "In Baltimore's Streets, Interrupters Face Danger to Stop a Cycle of Violence," NPR, February 13, 2022, https://www.npr.org/2022/02/06/1078634134/baltimores-safe-streets-has-been-good-for-the-community-but-can-be-dangerous-wor.

11. Chip Brownlee, "Violence Interruption Programs Are Receiving Millions. This Initiative Wants to Make Sure They're Prepared," The Trace, June 12, 2023, https://www.thetrace.org/2023/06/gun-violence-chicago-chico-tillmon/.

12. Deena Zaru, "Another Violence Interrupter Killed in Baltimore as Community Reels from Gun Violence," ABC News, January 4, 2022, https://abcnews.go.com/US/violence-interrupter-killed-baltimore-community-reels-gun-violence/story?id=82430617.

13. J. Brian Charles, "The Human Toll of Keeping Baltimore Safe," The Trace, March 3, 2022, https://www.thetrace.org/2022/03/baltimore-safe-streets-shootings-gun-violence-mayor-scott/.

14. The Health Alliance for Violence Intervention, accessed August 16, 2023, https://www.thehavi.org.

15. Karenna Warden, "Hospital-Based Intervention Programs Reduce Violence and Save Money," Center for American Progress, August 4, 2022, https://www.americanprogress.org/article/hospital-based-intervention-programs-reduce-violence-and-save-money/.

16. Giffords Law Center, "Healing Communities in Crisis: Life Saving Solutions to the Urban Gun Violence Epidemic," 2016, https://giffords.org/wp-content/uploads/2019/01/Healing-Communities-in-Crisis.pdf.

17. Ibid.

18. Ibid.

19. Ibid.

20. "Stick Talk," Stick Talk, accessed March 11, 2024, www.sticktalk.org/.

21. Cristian Farias, "How Do We Prevent Gun Violence without Police? Look to Abolitionists," Truthout, July 13, 2023, https://truthout.org/articles/how-do-we-prevent-gun-violence-without-police-look-to-abolitionists/.

22. Mia Mingus, "Pods and Pod Mapping Worksheet," Bay Area Transformative Justice Collective, June 2016, https://batjc.wordpress.com/resources/pods-and-pod-mapping-worksheet/.

23. L., Collier (2014, October 1) Incarceration nation, *Monitor on Psychology*, 45(9), https://www.apa.org/monitor/2014/10/incarceration.

24. Ayobami Laniyonu and Phillip Atiba Goff, "Measuring Disparities in Police Use of Force and Injury among Persons with Serious Mental Illness," *BMC Psychiatry* 21, no. 1 (October 12, 2021): 500, https://doi.org/10.1186/s12888-021-03510-w.

25. Sarah DeGue, Katherine A. Fowler, and Cynthia Calkins, "Deaths Due to Use of Lethal Force by Law Enforcement: Findings from the National Violent Death Reporting System, 17 U.S. States, 2009–2012," *American Journal of Preventive Medicine* 51, no. 5 (November 1, 2016): S173–87, https://doi.org/10.1016/j.amepre.2016.08.027.

26. Roge Karma, "4 Ideas to Replace Traditional Police Officers," Vox, June 24, 2020, https://www.vox.com/2020/6/24/21296881/unbundle-defund-the-police-george-floyd-rayshard-brooks-violence-european-policing.

27. White Bird Clinic, accessed July 23, 2023, https://whitebirdclinic.org/.

28. Ashley Abramson, "Building Mental Health into Emergency Responses," *Monitor on Psychology* 52, no. 5 (2021): 30.

29. Christie Thompson, "This City Stopped Sending Police to Every 911 Call," The Marshall Project, July 24, 2020, https://www.themarshallproject.org/2020/07/24/crisisresponders.

30. Rob Waters, "Enlisting Mental Health Workers, Not Cops, in Mobile Crisis Response," *Health Affairs* 40, no. 6 (June 1, 2021): 864–69.

31. Ibid.

32. Ibid.

33. Amam Z. Saleh et al., "Deaths of People with Mental Illness during Interactions with Law Enforcement," *International Journal of Law and Psychiatry* 58 (2018): 110–16; Ayana Jordan, Aza Stephen Allsop, and Pamela Y. Collins, "Decriminalising Being Black with Mental Illness," *Lancet Psychiatry* 8, no. 1 (2021): 8–9.

34. "Defund OPD," Critical Resistance, August 2, 2021, https://criticalresistance.org/projects/defund-opd/.

35. "M.H. First," Anti Police-Terror Project, accessed January 6, 2024, https://www.antipoliceterrorproject.org/mh-first-oakland.

36. Emily Nonko, "A Volunteer-Run Program Could Be Model for Mental Health Response without Police Intervention," Next City, October 1, 2020, https://nextcity.org/urbanist-news/volunteer-run-program-model-mental-health-response-police-intervention.

37. Ibid.

38. Healing and Justice Center, Instagram, accessed December 2, 2023, https://www.instagram.com/healingandjusticecenter/.

39. "Healing and Justice Center 2022 Annual Report," Healing and Justice Center, accessed December 2, 2023, https://drive.google.com/file/d/1uVOeWBbE0rpRKkULkoNY2dGN-qv3dVf2/view?usp=sharing&usp=embed_facebook.

40. David Leonhardt, "Vehicle Crashes, Surging," *New York Times*, February 15, 2022, https://www.nytimes.com/2022/02/15/briefing/vehicle-crashes-deaths-pandemic.html.

41. "Investing in Evidence-Based Alternatives to Policing: Non-Police Responses to Traffic Safety," Vera Institute of Justice, August 2021, https://www.vera.org/downloads/publications/alternatives-to-policing-traffic-enforcement-fact-sheet.pdf.

42. Emilie Raguso, "Plans Firm Up to Remove Police from Traffic Stops, but It's a Long Road Ahead," Berkeleyside, May 25, 2021, https://www.berkeleyside.org/2021/05/25/berkeley-department-of-transportation-civilian-traffic-enforcement.

43. Letter from Councilmembers Rigel Robinson, Lori Droste, Ben Bartlett, and Mayor Jesse Arreguin to Honorable Mayor and Members of the City Council re BerkDOT: Reimagining Transportation for a Racially Just Future, City of Berkeley, July 14, 2020, https://berkeleyca.gov/sites/default/files/documents/2020-07-14%20Item%2018e%20BerkDOT%20Reimagining%20Transportation.pdf.

44. Brett Simpson, "Why Cars Don't Deserve the Right of Way," *Atlantic*, October 15, 2021, https://www.theatlantic.com/ideas/archive/2021/10/end-police-violence-get-rid-traffic-cop/620378/

45. Raguso, "Plans Firm Up to Remove Police from Traffic Stops."

46. Julianne Cuba, "Vision Zero Cities: Removing Police from Traffic Enforcement Is Crucial—and Hard!," Streetsblog NYC, October 21, 2020, https://nyc.streetsblog.org/2020/10/21/vision-zero-cities-removing-police-from-traffic-enforcement-and-self-enforced-streets.

47. Ariana MacNeill, "Cambridge Is Considering Shifting 'Routine Traffic Enforcement' Away from Police. Here's What to Know," Boston.com, July 30, 2020, https://www.boston.com/news/local-news/2020/07/30/cambridge-routine-traffic-enforcement-proposal/.

48. Seth Rowe, "St. Louis Park Police Department's Role Debated," *Sun Sailor*, August 4, 2020, https://www.hometownsource.com/sun_sailor/st-louis-park-police-department-s-role-debated/article_d4d99f0c-d6a1-11ea-a089-e7bb8ea1ff9c.html.

49. Deena Winter, "Brooklyn Center Mayor Proposes New Public Safety Agency, Ban on Arrests during Traffic Stops," *Minnesota Reformer*, May 8, 2021, https://minnesotareformer.com/2021/05/08/brooklyn-center-mayor-proposes-new-public-safety-agency-ban-on-arrests-during-traffic-stops/.

50. Meg O'Connor, "A Florida Lawmaker Introduced Legislation to Remove Traffic Enforcement from Police," The Appeal, March 5, 2021, https://theappeal.org/florida-bill-traffic-enforcement-without-police/.

51. Adam Tuss, "Montgomery Co. Exploring Whether to Reassign Traffic Stops Away from Police," NBC4 Washington, September 9, 2020, https://www.nbcwashington.com/news/local/montgomery-co-exploring-whether-to-reassign-traffic-stops-away-from-police/2414272/.

52. Erika D. Smith, "How California Could Become the Model for Getting Cops Out of Traffic Stops," *Los Angeles Times*, February 18, 2023, https://www.latimes.com/california/story/2023-02-18/california-police-pretextual-traffic-stop-bill-erika-column.

53. Mike McIntire and Michael H. Keller, "The Demand for Money Behind Many Police Traffic Stops," *New York Times*, October 31, 2021, https://www.nytimes.com/2021/10/31/us/police-ticket-quotas-money-funding.html.

54. David Eads and Melissa Sanchez, "The Ticket Trap: Where Chicago Issues Parking Tickets and Who Pays for Them," ProPublica, May 30, 2018, https://projects.propublica.org/chicago-tickets/.

55. Karin Edvardsson Björnberg, Sven Ove Hansson, Matts Åke Belin, and Claes Tingvall, *The Vision Zero Handbook: Theory, Technology and Management for a Zero Casualty Policy*, Springer Nature, 2022, https://urn.kb.se/resolve?urn=urn:nbn:se:kth:diva-333044.

56. Philip V. McHarris, "Research Memo: Alternatives to Policing," Community Resource Hub for Safety and Accountability, https://communityresourcehub.org/wp-content/uploads/2020/10/CRH_Alternative_Memo_Final.pdf.

57. Bradley R. Haywood, "Ending Race-Based Pretextual Stops: Strategies for Eliminating America's Most Egregious Police Practice," *Richmond Public Interest Law Review* 26, no. 1 (2023): 47–83.

58. Max Carter-Oberstone, "America's Traffic Laws Give Police Way Too Much Power," *Time*, May 11, 2022, https://time.com/6175852/pretextual-traffic-stops/.

59. US Department of Health and Human Services, Administration for Children and Families, Administration on Children, Youth and Families, Children's Bureau (2024), *Child Maltreatment 2022*, available from https://www.acf.hhs.gov/cb/data-research/child-maltreatment.

60. US Department of Health and Human Services, Administration for Children and Families, Administration on Children, Youth and Families, Children's Bureau (2024), *The AFCARS Report #30*, https://www.acf.hhs.gov/cb.

61. Hyunil Kim et al., "Lifetime Prevalence of Investigating Child Maltreatment among US Children," *American Journal of Public Health* 107, no. 2 (2017): 274–80.

62. Dorothy Roberts, "Abolish Family Policing, Too." *Dissent Magazine*, 2021, https://www.dissentmagazine.org/article/abolish-family-policing-too/.

63. Dorothy Roberts, *Torn Apart: How the Child Welfare System Destroys Black Families—and How Abolition Can Build a Safer World* (New York: Basic Books, 2022).

64. Network to Advance Abolitionist Social Work, accessed November 27, 2023, https://www.naasw.com.

65. "A National Homes Guarantee: Briefing Book," People's Action, September 5, 2019, https://homesguarantee.com/wp-content/uploads/Homes-Guarantee-_-Briefing-Book.pdf.

66. "Ankinyi Wirranjiki Night Patrol," Julalikari Council Aboriginal Corporation, accessed July 23, 2023, https://julalikari.org.au/project/night-patrol/.

67. "About Us," Nyoongar Outreach Services, accessed July 23, 2023, http://www.nyoongaroutreach.com.au/about-us.

68. Sharon Gray et al., *Community Safety Workers: An Exploratory Study of Some Emerging Crime Prevention Occupations* (Montreal: International Centre for the Prevention of Crime, 2006), https://cipc-icpc.org/wp-content/uploads/2019/08/Community_Safety_Workers._An_exploratory_Study_of_Some_Emerging_Crime_Prevention_Occupations2_ANG.pdf.

69. Patrick Sharkey, *Uneasy Peace: The Great Crime Decline, the Renewal of City Life, and the Next War on Violence*, first edition (New York: W. W. Norton & Company, 2018, 177–78).

70. Ibid.

71. Ibid.

72. Tamar Manasseh, "We Are Reclaiming Chicago One Corner at a Time," *New York Times*, October 22, 2017, https://www.nytimes.com/2017/10/22/opinion/chicago-gangs-crime-mothers.html.

73. "Safe Passage Program," Chicago Public Schools, accessed July 25, 2023, https://www.cps.edu/services-and-supports/student-safety-and-security/safe-passage-program/.

INTERLUDE IV

1. A'mani Howard and Kaleb Autman, "Why Did Chicago Activists Shut Down an International Police Conference?," Truthout, October 31, 2015, https://truthout.org/articles/why-did-chicago-activists-shut-down-an-international-police-conference/.

2. Ibid.

CHAPTER 5

1. sujatha baliga, "A Different Path for Seeking Justice for Sexual Assault," Vox, October 10, 2018, https://www.vox.com/first-person/2018/10/10/17953016/what-is-restorative-justice-definition-questions-circle; Paul Tullis, "Can Forgiveness Play a Role in Criminal Justice?," *New York Times Magazine*, January 4, 2013, https://www.nytimes.com/2013/01/06/magazine/can-forgiveness-play-a-role-in-criminal-justice.html.

2. sujatha baliga, Sia Henry, and Georgia Valentine, "Restorative Community Conferencing: A Study of Community Works West's Restorative Justice Youth Diversion Program in Alameda County," Impact Justice, 2023, https://impactjustice.org/wp-content/uploads/CWW_RJreport.pdf, 1. Note that this initiative is facilitated by the criminal-legal system, and as a result, criminal-legal language and framing of "crime" are used. As mentioned, the ultimate goal is to facilitate these processes outside the criminal-legal system.

3. baliga, "A Different Path for Seeking Justice for Sexual Assault."

4. "Restorative Justice Project," Impact Justice, accessed November 26, 2023, https://impactjustice.org/innovation/restorative-justice/.

5. Maarten Kunst, Lieke Popelier, and Ellen Varekamp, "Victim Satisfaction with the Criminal Justice System and Emotional Recovery: A Systematic and Critical Review of the Literature," *Trauma, Violence & Abuse* 16, no. 3 (2015): 336–58.

6. "Thinking about How to Abolish Prisons with Mariame Kaba," NBC News, April 10, 2019, https://www.nbcnews.com/think/opinion/thinking-about-how-abolish-prisons-mariame-kaba-podcast-transcript-ncna992721.

7. "The Burge Case," Chicago Torture Justice Memorials, accessed July 25, 2023, https://chicagotorture.org/reparations/history/.

8. Logan Jaffe, "The Nation's First Reparations Package to Survivors of Police Torture Included a Public Memorial. Survivors Are Still Waiting," ProPublica, July 3, 2020, https://www.propublica.org/article/the-nations-first-reparations-package-to-survivors-of-police-torture-included-a-public-memorial-survivors-are-still-waiting.

9. Mia Mingus, "Transformative Justice: A Brief Description," Leaving Evidence, January 10, 2019, https://leavingevidence.wordpress.com/2019/01/09/transformative-justice-a-brief-description/.

10. Don't Call the Police, accessed July 24, 2023, https://dontcallthepolice.com/.

11. "What We Do," Ahimsa Collective, accessed July 24, 2023, https://www.ahimsacollective.net/what-we-do.

12. "A Look at Feminist Forms of Justice That Don't Involve the Police," TransformHarm.org, accessed July 24, 2023, https://transformharm.org/tj_resource/a-look-at-feminist-forms-of-justice-that-dont-involve-the-police/.

13. Sam Levin and Alex Kane, "ADL Leaders Debated Ending Police Delegations to Israel, Memo Reveals," *Guardian*, March 17, 2022, https://www.theguardian.com/us-news/2022/mar/17/adl-police-delegations-israel.

14. Jeffery C. Mays, "400-Pound N.Y.P.D. Robot Gets Tryout in Times Square Subway Station," *New York Times*, September 22, 2023, https://www.nytimes.com/2023/09/22/nyregion/police-robot-times-square-nyc.html.

15. Mizue Aizeki, Matt Mahmoudi, and Coline Schupfer, *Resisting Borders and Technologies of Violence*, (Chicago: Haymarket Books, 2024); Gracie Mae Bradley and Luke De Noronha, *Against Borders: The Case for Abolition* (London; New York: Verso, 2022).

16. *The Feminist on Cellblock Y*, CNN, April 18, 2018, https://www.cnn.com/videos/us/2018/04/18/the-feminist-on-cellblock-y-doc-orig.cnn.

17. "Our Program: In Prisons," Success Stories Program, accessed December 3, 2023, https://www.successstoriesprogram.org/in-prisons.

18. "Outside of Prisons," Success Stories, accessed December 3, 2023, https://www.successstoriesprogram.org/outside-of-prisons.

19. "NYC Transformative Justice Hub," Project NIA, accessed July 24, 2023, https://project-nia.org/nyc-transformative-justice-hub.

20. Descriptions of programs drawn from https://project-nia.org/past-projects.

21. TransformHarm.org, https://transformharm.org.

22. Mariame Kaba and Andrea J. Ritchie, *No More Police: A Case for Abolition* (New York: New Press, 2022).

23. "MPD150 Sunsetting Reflections and Resources," MPD150, September 22, 2022, http://www.mpd150.com/sunset/.

24. Philip V. McHarris, "Increases in Police Funding Will Not Make Black People Safe, It Is Time City Leaders Listened," Black Youth Project, January 29, 2020, https://blackyouthproject.com/increases-in-police-funding-will-not-make-black-people-safe-its-time-city-leaders-listened/.

25. Mary Retta, "MPD150, Reclaim the Block, and the Black Visions Collective Have Been Fighting to Abolish Minneapolis Police for Years," *Teen Vogue*, June 12, 2020, https://www.teenvogue.com/story/mpd150-reclaim-the-block-black-visions-collective-abolish-minneapolis-police-organizing.

26. Jenna Wortham, "How a New Wave of Black Activists Changed the Conversation." *New York Times Magazine*, August 25, 2020, https://www.nytimes.com/2020/08/25/magazine/black-visions-collective.html.

27. Astead W. Herndon, "How a Pledge to Dismantle the Minneapolis Police Collapsed," *New York Times*, September 26, 2020, https://www.nytimes.com/2020/09/26/us/politics/minneapolis-defund-police.html.

28. Jenny Gross and John Eligon, "Minneapolis City Council Votes to Remove $8 Million From Police Budget," *The New York Times*, December 10, 2020, sec. U.S. https://www.nytimes.com/2020/12/10/us/minneapolis-police-funding.html.

29. Ibid.

30. "About Us," 4FRONT, accessed December 3, 2023, https://www.4frontproject.org/about.

31. "Our Work," 4FRONT, accessed December 3, 2023, https://www.4frontproject.org/our-work.

32. David Harvey, *A Brief History of Neoliberalism* (Oxford, UK: Oxford University Press, 2007).

33. Ruth Wilson Gilmore, "Making Abolition Geography in California's Central Valley." *The Funambulist* 21 (December 20, 2018), https://thefunambulist.net/magazine/21-space-activism/interview-making-abolition-geography-california-central-valley-ruth-wilson-gilmore.

34. Tamara K. Nopper, "Abolition Is Not a Suburb," The New Inquiry, July 16, 2020, https://thenewinquiry.com/abolition-is-not-a-suburb/.

35. "Our Mission," Mothers/Men against Senseless Killings, accessed August 16, 2023, https://www.ontheblock.org/about.

36. One Million Experiments, https://millionexperiments.com/.

37. Sandra Bogar and Kirsten M. Beyer, "Green Space, Violence, and Crime: A Systematic Review," *Trauma, Violence, & Abuse* 17, no. 2 (2016): 160–71.

38. Maria Cramer, "What Happened When a Brooklyn Neighborhood Policed Itself for Five Days," *New York Times*, June 4, 2023, https://www.nytimes.com/2023/06/04/nyregion/brooklyn-brownsville-no-police.html. This case included police collaboration. As a point of reference, community-based safety initiatives should strive to be free of police collaboration and involvement to avoid influence and a range of issues that emerge when community-based safety initiatives are fused with police agencies' involvement.

39. National Campaign for Police Free Schools, https://policefreeschools.org/.

40. Edwin Rios, "How Black Oaklanders Finally Expelled the School Police," *Mother Jones*, November–December 2020, https://www.motherjones.com/crime-justice/2020/10/how-black-oaklanders-finally-expelled-the-school-police/.

41. Davarian L. Baldwin, "Why We Should Abolish the Campus Police," *Chronicle of Higher Education*, May 19, 2021, https://www.chronicle.com/article/why-we-should-abolish-campus-police.

42. "FAQs," Cops off Campus Coalition, https://copsoffcampuscoalition.com/faq/; https://www.policefreecampus.org/our-vision.

43. *The Demand Is Still #DefundPolice*, Interrupting Criminalization, 2020, https://www.interruptingcriminalization.com/defundpolice-update.

44. Huey P. Newton, "Intercommunalism," *Viewpoint Magazine*, June 11, 2018, https://viewpointmag.com/2018/06/11/intercommunalism-1974/.

45. Jeff Asher and Ben Horwitz, "How Do the Police Actually Spend Their Time?," *New York Times*, June 19, 2020, https://www.nytimes.com/2020/06/19/upshot/unrest-police-time-violent-crime.html.

46. "Emerging Findings," Vera Institute of Justice, accessed August 11, 2021, https://www.vera.org/publications/arrest-trends-every-three-seconds-landing/arrest-trends-every-three-seconds/findings.

47. Micol Seigel, *Violence Work: State Power and the Limits of Police* (Durham, NC: Duke University Press, 2018).

48. #8toAbolition, accessed July 24, 2023, https://www.8toabolition.com.

49. Robin D. G. Kelley, "What Did Cedric Robinson Mean by Racial Capitalism?" *Boston Review*, January 12, 2017, https://www.bostonreview.net/articles/robin-d-g-kelley-introduction-race-capitalism-justice/.

50. Ruth Wilson Gilmore, "Organized Abandonment and Organized Violence: Devolution and the Police," Critical Race and Ethnic Studies lecture, UC Santa Cruz, November 9, 2015.

51. Ruth Wilson Gilmore and Léopold Lambert, "Making Abolition Geography in California's Central Valley," *The Funambulist*, no. 21, December 20, 2018, https://thefunambulist.net/magazine/21-space-activism/interview-making-abolition-geography-california-central-valley-ruth-wilson-gilmore.